D0853521

Life at Death

LIFE AT DEATH

A Scientific Investigation of the Near-Death Experience

KENNETH RING, PH. D.

New York 1982

Previously published in 1980 by Coward, McCann & Geoghegan in New York and simultaneously in Canada by Academic Press Canada, Ltd.

Acknowledgment is made to the following for permission to quote copyrighted material:
Mind/Brain Bulletin for the selection from *Re-Vision:* "A New Perspective on Realit·· " by Marilyn Ferguson. *Re-Vision,* 1978, Volume 1, Numbers 3/4.
Confucian Press, Inc., for the selection from *At the Hour of Death* by Karlis Osis and Erlendur Haraldsson.
Doubleday & Company, Inc., for the excerpt from *The Astral Journey* by Herbert B. Greenhouse. Copyright © 1974 by Herbert B. Greenhouse.
Institute of Psychophysical Research for selections from *Out-of-the-Body Experiences* by Celia Green, Institute of Psychophysical Research, Oxford.
The Julian Press, Inc., for selections from *The Center of the Cyclone* by John C. Lilly, M.D. Copyright 1972 by John C. Lilly, M.D.
Lyle Stuart, Inc., for selections from *Out of the Body Experiences* by Robert Crookall.
Mockingbird Books, Inc., for selections from *Life After Life* and *Reflections on Life After Life* by Raymond A. Moody, Jr., M.D.
Pantheon Books, a Division of Random House, Inc., for selections from *Memories, Dreams, Reflections* by C. G. Jung, translated by Richard and Clara Winston, recorded and edited by Aniela Jaffe. Copyright © 1961, 1962, 1963 by Random House, Inc.
G. P. Putnam's Sons for selections from *Psychic Explorations* by Edgar Mitchell. Copyright © 1974 by Edgar D. Mitchell & Associates, Inc.
J. P. Tarcher, Inc., Los Angeles, California, for a selection from *The Probability of the Impossible* by Dr. Thelma Moss. Copyright © 1974, published by New American Library.
The Theosophical Publishing House, Wheaton, Illinois, for selections from *The Transition Called Death* by Charles Hampton, 1979 Quest Edition.
Ziff-Davis Publishing Company for selections from *Psychology Today:* "Holographic Memory," by Daniel Goleman, February 1979. Copyright © 1979 Ziff-Davis Publishing Company.

Library of Congress Cataloging in Publication Data

Ring, Kenneth.
Life at death.

Reprint. Originally published : New York : Coward, McCann & Geoghegan, c1980.
Bibliography: p.
Includes index.
1. Death—Psychological aspects. 2. Death, Apparent.
I. Title.
[BF789.D4R56 1982] 155.9'37 82-5427
ISBN 0-688-01253-1 (pbk.) AACR2

Printed in the United States of America

3 4 5 6 7 8 9 10

To Susan Palmer and Theresa Carilli,
who did the real work
to make this project possible.

Contents

Appendixes

Acknowledgments

For their support—of various kinds—of the research reported in this book I am indebted to many individuals and a number of institutions.

First of all, I wish to thank the University of Connecticut Research Foundation for its financial support throughout the two years this research was conducted. I am particularly grateful to Dr. Hugh Clark, Acting Vice-President of the Graduate School, who responded promptly and positively to every request I made in connection with this project: for an extension of time in which to complete it; for supplementary funds for additional personnel and analyses; and for travel funds in order to attend several conferences where my work was to be presented.

Second, my deep appreciation goes to the physicians and administrators of the various hospitals involved in our study for their help in enabling my research staff and me to obtain the names of potentially interviewable patients and former patients. It was through their assistance and the cooperation of their hospital staffs that this book was possible, and my debt to them is immense. So many hospital personnel provided help to us that it would be impossible to acknowledge them all, but I need to make special mention of these individuals: at Hartford Hospital, Dr. Cornelis Boelhouwer, Dr. Arthur Wolfe, Dorothy Riley, and Sue Thompson; at St. Francis Hospital, Francis J. Greaney, Dr. Robert M. Jeresaty, Martha Johnson, and Ann Gibbons; at Mount Sinai Hospital, Dr. Jacob J. Haksteen and Dr. Alfred Aronson; at Elmcrest Psychiatric Institute, Julie Minear.

Third, to the members of my own research staff who helped me to collect the data for this study no words of thanks are sufficient. Theresa Carilli and Susan Palmer undertook the mammoth job of arranging for the interviews and rating the tapes afterward, and the dedication of this book to them speaks for their indispensable role. I also owe a profound debt to Charlene Alling for conducting most of the interviews I was not able to arrange to do myself, as well as for securing for us a small sample of near-death survivors from Maine; she also helped in the laborious task of rating tapes. Deborah Stack-O'Sullivan and Jane Van Dusen each contributed significantly to the research by carrying out several interviews and by rating some tapes, and to them, in addition, my warmest thanks. Finally, to my friend and colleague Joyce Duffy, my appreciation for referring to us several near-death survivors who would not otherwise have come to our attention.

Fourth, there are many people who took the time to discuss the ideas in this book with me and to encourage me in various ways throughout the period I was working on it. For their contributions here I wish to thank: John Audette, Boyce Batey, the late Itzhak (Ben) Bentov, Dr.

Don McLaughlin, Nancy Miller, Dr. Karlis Osis, Bob and Thelma Peck, Dr. Michael Sabom, and Alexandra Teguis. I owe a special debt here to two exceptional men: to John White, whose expert editorial hand on this manuscript improved it immeasurably and whose general guidance was instrumental in the publishing of this work; and to Dr. Raymond A. Moody, Jr., who was kind enough to write the introduction to this book and to have otherwise laid the foundation for the research I have reported here. To Sherry Slate, who patiently typed and retyped all drafts of this manuscript, a thousand thanks for her labors. Finally, I am indebted to Patricia B. Soliman, my editor, not only for her professional work on the manuscript, but, even more, for her understanding of what I intended to convey through this book and for giving me the editorial freedom to attempt it.

Fifth, no list of acknowledgments could omit the members of my family, whose support, understanding, and love made the writing of this book truly a joyful experience. To my daughter, Kathryn, I owe the suggestion for the title I would have liked to use for this book (*The Death Experience*), but finally had to reject on the grounds that it was misleading. And to Norma, hugger to the world and helpmate to me, I give my thanks for her criticisms designed to keep my writing honest and restrained and for her willingness to put up with my obstinacy when I chose to disregard her strictures.

Finally, to all those whose story I try to tell in these pages—our near-death survivors themselves—I offer this book as an expression of my gratitude to them for being willing to share their experiences with me and, by so doing, teaching me more than they ever knew. And to three in particular—Helen, Virginia, and Iris—my teachers and my friends, much love.

Storrs, Connecticut
May 1979

Moving, yet holding still,
seeing yourself entering a new way.
Your essence feels the questioning
doubt. Must I? Where is this? Why?
It enfolds you, becomes you,
cradles you.
You look and you behold
yourself moving—yet holding
still, through time, into eternity,
into the source.
Dark, yet light, moving,
yet holding still, oblivion or
eternity.
Softly—silence—clear sound,
brilliant awareness—all these and
then—the deep abiding sadness
that comes—when you must stay.
How do you live with the
knowledge of what isn't yet to be?
By the remembrance of that
timelessness beyond—and the reassurance
that you will return to the light,
the source and the way.

Fran Sherwood
A near-death survivor

Introduction

When, much to my surprise, my book, *Life After Life,* began to attract attention not only all over the United States but also throughout much of the world, I must confess that I was extremely uncomfortable. One of my concerns was that some of the sensational claims that were made for my work by other persons might have the effect of frightening off legitimate investigators from an area that I continue to believe has profound significance for clinical medicine and human psychology. Hence, it was profoundly gratifying (and also a great relief!) to me when, within a year or so of the publication of *Life After Life,* I learned of several studies that were underway to attempt systematically to confirm or to disconfirm the very preliminary observations made in that work. In consequence, at the present time, Dr. Kenneth Ring, author of this volume, Dr. Michael Sabom, a cardiologist, and other physicians who are yet publicly to announce their findings, have, in independent studies, verified that in a surprisingly large percentage of patients who undergo a close call with death there occurs a transcendent, clear, and spiritually life-changing experience, which, overall, is remarkably similar from individual to individual.

One thing must be emphasized about the work done by Dr. Ring, Dr. Sabom, and others, however. Their studies are at a much higher level of systematization than is the one reported in *Life After Life.* Therefore, when Dr. Ring honored me by asking me to write the introduction to his book, I expressed to him my own amusement at the idea, for it seems to me that his work is more sophisticated than my own. (Besides, at my age, I refuse to be regarded as the grandfather of research into near-death experiences!)

There are only three things I might add here. First, it is very important that many different points of view about near-death experiences be publicly aired and discussed. For, with the growing use of modern techniques of resuscitation, I suspect that near-death experiences are here to stay, and we need to be able to discuss them with patients who have them, to reassure them that they are not alone. We must keep an open mind about what these experiences mean. The finding of a common pattern of experiences occurring at or near death is unusual enough in itself; we can only guess at its significance.

Second, let us hope that the attempt everyone who learns about near-death experiences makes to "explain" them does not cause us to forget that they have a great *clinical* significance, too. Regardless of what one thinks of their explanation, the fact remains that doctors simply must deal sympathetically with patients who have them. Near-death experiences happen most often, after all, in *hospitals,* during the course of medical treatment.

Finally, it might be helpful for me to introduce Dr. Ring briefly to his readers. He is a warm, refreshing, careful, and thoughtful human being, and, in addition, has a fantastic sense of humor. His readers can be assured that, as incredible as what he reports may sound, it is not the work of a person who has any interest in sensationalizing what he has found. Indeed, these same observations have now been made by a number of qualified independent investigators. If I may take the liberty of speaking for all of us, I am sure that we all agree in one thing: The facts about near-death experiences are in themselves fantastic enough. Any exaggerations on our part could only succeed in making the case for their importance *less* plausible than it in fact is.

Dr. Raymond Moody
July 1979

Preface

Beginning in May 1977, I spent thirteen months tracking down and interviewing scores of people who had come close to death. I do not mean people who "merely" risk their lives by engaging in a hazardous occupation or avocation. Rather, I was interested to find people who had *actually* nearly died. In some cases, my research subjects had suffered "clinical" death, that is, they had lost all vital signs, such as heartbeat and respiration. In most cases, however, the men and women I talked to had found themselves on the brink of medical death but had not, biologically speaking, quite slipped over.

My aim in conducting these interviews was to find out what people experience when they are on the verge of apparent imminent death. What they told me is, in a word, fascinating—as I think the material presented here will amply demonstrate—and for two quite distinct reasons. One has to do with the intrinsic content of these experiences themselves: No one who reads of them can come away without having been profoundly stirred—emotionally, intellectually and spiritually—by the features they contain. The other is, if anything, even more significant: Most near-death experiences seem to unfold according to a *single pattern,* almost as though the prospect of death serves to release a stored, *common* "program" of feelings, perceptions, and experiences.

What to make of this common set of elements associated with the onset of death is the central challenge of this book. Whether this experience—what I have called the core near-death experience—can be interpreted in naturalistic terms is the overriding *scientific* issue raised by the findings presented here. The *meaning* of the core experience, which obviously depends on its interpretation, is the major *metaphysical* question which must ultimately be addressed. Toward the end of the book, therefore, I will give my own views on these matters.

Because this study was undertaken in a scientific spirit of inquiry and was conducted using scientific procedures, I have made a deliberate effort to present my material as objectively as possible, letting my interviewees do most of the talking. In my descriptions of various aspects of the core experience, I have tried not to filter the data through the lenses of my own biases, and where I felt it appropriate to express a personal opinion or interpretation, I have always tried to label it as such. I am certain that I have not altogether succeeded in these efforts at impartiality, but it has at least been my ideal. Although my reasons for approaching my material in this manner may be obvious, I should perhaps be a little more explicit concerning my aims in writing *Life at Death.*

My interest from the start has been to examine near-death experiences from a scientific point of view. We already have a plethora of anecdotal books on the topic and, while they have done much to stimulate interest in near-death experiences, they have failed to answer many basic questions about these phenomena, as I will make clear in a moment. To make real headway in our understanding of near-death phenomena, we need, I believe, more scientific research.[1] If members of the scientific and medical community are to take these experiences seriously, they need sound research on which to base their evaluations. Accordingly, this book has been written with such professionals—as well as the public—in mind. That is why I have laced my chapters not only with illustrative quotations but with graphs and statistical tables as well. Readers not interested in these fine points may certainly skim this material, but professionals may wish to linger here. In writing *Life at Death*, I have consistently tried to strike a balance between the needs of the general reader and those of the interested professional. My hope is that I have written a book about near-death experiences that meets the criteria of scientific inquiry without sacrificing its appeal for anyone who is simply intrigued by these phenomena.

When I discuss my research publicly, however, audiences are rarely content to allow me to maintain my role of the "impartial scientist" or a "mere teller of other people's tales." They want to know such things as how I got into this unusual line of research, or whether I had had a near-death experience myself, or how *I* was affected by interviewing so many near-death survivors. I imagine some readers may also come to wonder about these questions and, since they will not be dealt with directly in the book itself, perhaps I had best try to answer them candidly here.

Concerning my reasons for embarking on this work, I am aware that both professional and personal motives had an influence on me. As a psychologist interested in altered states of consciousness, I have been familiar with near-death experiences for some years. My curiosity was further kindled by reading Raymond Moody's book *Life After Life*, shortly after it was published in 1975. I found that although I didn't really question the basic model Moody describes—it fit too well with other findings with which I was already familiar—I was left with many questions after finishing the book. How frequent were these experiences? Did it make any difference *how* one (almost) died? For example, do suicide attempts, which bring one close to death, engender the typical near-death experience? What role, if any, does prior religiousness play in shaping these experiences? Can the changes that allegedly follow from these experiences be systematically and quantitatively documented?

I doubt, however, that these "academic" questions in themselves would have been sufficient for me to undertake the research reported here. Were it not for certain personal considerations that were present in my life at the time of reading *Life After Life*, I would probably have only speculated on what the answers to these questions might be.

Although I myself have never had a near-death experience, I had for some time been highly intrigued by reports of their existence. This interest was to remain latent, however, until, for a variety of personal reasons, I entered a time of sorrow and inward emptiness in my life. I remember feeling spiritually adrift, as if I had somehow lost my way. Suddenly, I found that I simply did not know what to *do*. Concealing my barrenness and distress, I took myself that summer to a nearby convalescent home and offered my services as a "volunteer." I was, I guess, secretly hoping that some old, wise person, contemplating his own imminent death, would give me some clue as to what I might do to escape the pervasive feeling of "spiritual death" which was continuing to paralyze me. Instead, I spent most of my time playing cards with people in desperate physical straits and saw suffering all around. And our conversations were mostly about how adroitly someone had played a hand of bridge or when the refreshment cart would arrive. Philosophical reflections on life were not the vogue.

It was while I was vainly seeking "the answer" at the convalescent home that I "happened" to read Moody's book.

During the thirteen months of interviewing near-death survivors, I received my answer. These were mostly ordinary people, who described, in a consistent way, an extraordinary patterning of experiences that occurs at the point of death. The effect, combined with a certain quality of luminous serenity which many near-death survivors display, made me feel that I myself was undergoing an extended spiritual awakening. In any event, as my interviews continued, I found that I was no longer oppressed by the spiritual deadness that had, ironically, provided the initial impetus to my research. In fact, my feeling was becoming just the opposite.

Although my experience in conducting this study must of course remain private and nontransferrable, it is my personal hope that many readers, on finishing it, will find that they, too, have been moved and inspired by having had the opportunity to listen to the accounts of those who have returned from the brink of death to tell the rest of us what it is like to die.

ONE

The Near-Death Experience

During the 1970s, a wave of interest in the near-death experience swept over the public and professionals alike. The ground swell for this development was created by two remarkable physicians, first by the distinguished psychiatrist Elisabeth Kübler-Ross, who has become, over the last decade, this country's most renowned, if controversial, thanatologist. Celebrated for years for her pioneering work with dying patients, Kübler-Ross now claims to have spoken to more than one thousand men, women and children about their near-death experiences, and on this basis she declares that she "knows for a fact there is life after death." Although she has not published her findings in any systematic way, Kübler-Ross has been very energetic in disseminating the results of her investigations through her many public lectures, workshops, and interviews. As a direct result of her industry, eminence, and charisma, she has almost single-handedly brought about a high degree of public and professional awareness of near-death phenomena and their implications. Undoubtedly the climate of awareness generated by Kübler-Ross's work enabled an engaging small book on near-death experiences, written by another physician, to achieve bestseller status within a short time in this country, leading to its translation into at least twenty languages and enormous popularity abroad. *Life After Life* by Dr. Raymond A. Moody described the results of more than eleven years of inquiry into near-death experiences and was based on a sample of about 150 cases. Moody's findings largely dovetailed with those of Kübler-Ross, a fact acknowledged by her in a generous foreword she contributed to Moody's book. In a subsequent publication, *Reflections on Life After Life,* Moody indicates that he, like Kübler-Ross, has come to conclude that his data are indicative of a life after death.

The fact that these mutually supporting sets of findings were reported by two highly credible physicians, one eminent to begin with and the other compellingly persuasive in print, lent a certain "scientific aura" to these accounts, which previously had been, in the eyes of many, merely the kind of unauthenticated testimony that appears regularly in such periodicals as *The National Enquirer* and *Reader's Digest.*

Nevertheless, the impression of scientific validity is not really justified—and for two quite distinct reasons.

First of all, neither Kübler-Ross's nor Moody's data have yet been presented in a form that renders them susceptible to scientific analysis and evaluation. As I remarked earlier, although Kübler-Ross has spoken extensively about her findings, she has nowhere published them, and thus what the public record consists of are her summary descriptions and illustrative case histories—hardly a solid base for a scientific judgment of her material. As for Moody's published work, he is at pains to be explicit that his investigation should not be regarded as a scientific study. The case history material he presents appears to be highly selective, his "sampling procedures" were essentially haphazard, and his data were not subjected to any statistical analysis. Thus, though the findings they described were highly suggestive, and even credible to many who learned of them (including me), they cannot, by any rigorous standard of evaluation, be considered *in themselves* as constituting *scientific* evidence even for the experience of dying, much less the question of what Moody calls "life after life."

The second reason is this: The wave of interest in near-death phenomena, occasioned by the publicity given the work of Kübler-Ross and Moody, has obscured the fact that the scientific study of such phenomena dates back nearly a century.

Historically, the pioneers of what was then called "psychical research"—today, parapsychology—were among the first to tackle "the problem of survival," as it tends to be called in this field. Although by the 1930s, the evidential value of much of this work came to be questioned by parapsychologists themselves,[1] the contributions of such early researchers as Edmund Gurney, F.W.H. Myers, and Sir William Barrett need to be acknowledged as paving the way for more sophisticated parapsychological investigations.

Perhaps the best known of such modern studies have been conducted by Karlis Osis and Erlendur Haraldsson. These parapsychologists, building on a methodology first used more than half a century ago by Barrett, have examined both the phenomenological features of and mood changes associated with deathbed visions, as reported by physicians, nurses, and, occasionally, directly by the survivors. Osis and Haraldsson have undertaken these studies in both the United States and India, and have found impressive cross-cultural similarities in those experiential aspects of dying that their research is designed to examine. Despite severe problems in representative sampling and other methodological flaws, their results, presented in detailed statistical fashion, show a remarkable internal consistency and closely resemble those reported by Kübler-Ross and Moody.

The early psychical researchers were not the only investigators who made pioneering studies of near-death phenomena. Professor Albert Heim was a Swiss geologist fond of mountain climbing, who more than once nearly lost his life in mountain climbing accidents. Because of these experiences, he spent the last twenty-five years of his life systematically gathering accounts from others involved in a variety of life-threatening accidents. This material was originally published in the last century and, as with other studies to follow, disclosed a clear similarity among reported near-death experiences triggered by accidents.

Heim's work lay forgotten until interest in it was revived in the early 1970s by the psychiatrist Russell Noyes, Jr. and a colleague, Ray Kletti, who published a translation of it.[2] Noyes and Kletti have gone on to conduct some important descriptive and statistical studies in the Heimian tradition, which have supported and extended the data in Heim's original collection.[3] Their work, which emphasizes the experience of (apparently) impending accidental death, also reveals many of the transcendent features described by Kübler-Ross, Moody, and others, but it is worth observing that Noyes and Kletti use a very different explanatory framework from most investigators' in interpreting their findings. Specifically, they propose "depersonalization" as a response to the stress of (apparent) imminent death. Depersonalization is seen as an ego-defensive reaction to protect the individual against the unbearable prospect of his death. The result is a pervasive feeling of detachment and transcendence, which cushions the expected impact of the near-death crisis. This psychodynamic explanation of near-death phenomena provides a clear contrast with the Kübler-Ross–Moody "survival" view.

The original work of Heim and of his "methodological descendents," Noyes and Kletti, have in turn influenced other professional investigators interested in near-death phenomena. For example, Stanislav Grof, a Czech psychoanalyst and one of the foremost authorities on the effects of LSD on human consciousness, and Joan Halifax, an American anthropologist who is a student of visionary experience, have recently co-authored a volume, *The Human Encounter with Death,* in which they are concerned to compare the prototypic near-death experience (to be delineated shortly) with the psychedelically-induced experience. In making the case for the similarity between these differently engendered experiences, they draw heavily on the work of Heim and Noyes and Kletti and seem to adopt the latter's interpretative outlook.

These brief allusions to the work of other researchers[4] should be sufficient to show that while the spotlight of attention in recent years may have been focused on Kübler-Ross and Moody, other investigators with solid credentials have also been enlarging our knowledge of death-related experiences.

Despite these recent studies, however, it is evident that we are still very much in need of well-designed and thorough investigations of near-death experiences. When examined critically, the existing studies all suffer from such methodological failings as unsatisfactory sampling procedures, inadequate quantification of variables, and lack of proper comparison groups. These shortcomings, when coupled with the unscientific status of the Kübler-Ross and Moody studies, dictate that more rigorous research programs be undertaken in an effort to shore up the methodological weaknesses of already published research. The implications of near-death experiences are far too momentous to be allowed to rest on such an inadequate foundation.

Accordingly, early in 1977, I set out to conduct my own scientific investigation of near-death phenomena. Beginning in May 1977, my research staff and I interviewed more than one hundred people who had come close to death. In some cases, these were men and women who appeared to undergo "clinical" death, where there is no heartbeat or respiration; in most cases, however, the individuals we talked with had "merely" edged toward the brink of death but did not, so far as we could determine, actually "die." In this book, I will present the results of our research. With the exception of a study carried out concurrently and independently by a Florida cardiologist, Dr. Michael Sabom, I believe that our investigation represents the most systematic and exhaustive scientific study of near-death experiences thus far reported. As the next chapter will make clear, however, this study, too, is not without its methodological problems. Nevertheless, I believe that even the most critical reader, on assessing the evidence to be presented in the chapters to come, will be persuaded that we now have sufficient scientific grounds for asserting that there is a consistent and remarkable experiential pattern that often unfolds when an individual is seemingly about to die. I will call this reliable near-death pattern the *core experience.*

Now, to lay the groundwork for this study, it is necessary to return to Moody's account from *Life After Life* of the core experience. We need to know, *specifically,* of what elements it consists.

In presenting his account, Moody stresses that it is idealized and represents a composite experience, not an actual one. He observes that different people in his sample approximated this composite, but no one reported every feature he describes. Let me first quote Moody's idealized version of the core experience. Following it, I will list the major elements that Moody has abstracted from it.

> A man is dying and, as he reaches the point of greatest physical distress, he hears himself pronounced dead by his doctor. He begins to hear an uncomfortable noise, a loud ringing or buzzing, and at the same time feels himself moving very rapidly through a long tunnel. After this, he suddenly finds himself outside his own

physical body, but still in the same immediate physical environment, and sees his own body from a distance, as though he is a spectator. He watches the resuscitation attempt from this vantage point and is in a state of emotional upheaval.

After a while, he collects himself and becomes more accustomed to his odd condition. He notices that he still has a "body," but one of a very different nature and with very different powers from the physical body he has left behind. Soon other things begin to happen. Others come to meet him and help him. He glimpses the spirits of relatives and friends who have already died, and a loving, warm spirit of a kind he has never encountered before—a being of light—appears before him. This being asks him a question, nonverbally, to make him evaluate his life and helps him along by showing him a panoramic, instantaneous playback of the major events of his life. At some point, he finds himself approaching some sort of a barrier or border, apparently representing the limit between earthly life and the next life. Yet, he finds that he must go back to the earth, that the time for his death has not yet come. At this point he resists, for by now he is taken up with his experiences in the afterlife and does not want to return. He is overwhelmed by intense feelings of joy, love, and peace. Despite his attitude, though, he somehow reunites with his physical body and lives.

Later he tries to tell others, but he has trouble doing so. In the first place, he can find no human words to describe these unearthly episodes. He also finds that others scoff, so he stops telling other people. Still, the experience affects his life profoundly, especially his views about death and its relationship to life.[5]

The components of this experience that Moody designates as its recurrent motifs do not all occur in any actual instance, nor do they appear in an invariant sequence.[6] They are:

1. Ineffability
2. Hearing the news (of one's own death)
3. Feelings of peace and quiet
4. The noise
5. The dark tunnel
6. Out of the body
7. Meeting others
8. The being of light
9. The review

10. The border
11. Coming back

If we use Moody's account and componential analysis as a provisional basis for grasping the core experience, we are obviously left with a number of intriguing research questions—questions this book will attempt to answer.

I will begin with the fundamental one: How common is this experience in near-death episodes? Moody's publication gives the reader only the positive instances—only the "hits," as it were. But it would seem to be important to determine how frequently this experience occurs and whether this figure varies substantially with the population studied or with the condition associated with apparent imminent death. If, for example, the core experience is reported only 10% of the time, the interpretation of the effect is likely to be very different than if the figure is 50% or 90%. Indeed, if the overall figure turns out to be quite low, it could certainly be argued that Moody's book and Kübler-Ross's pronouncements may have deceived many people by implying that a transcendent experience of dying is the rule, whereas it might be the exception.

In *Reflections on Life After Life*, Moody reports that he has talked with many people who remember nothing in connection with a near-death episode, but he refuses, for cogent reasons, to speculate on how large this category of nonrecallers (or nonexperiencers) might be. Moody leaves the impression that any diligent and sympathetic investigator will find abundant evidence in support of the core experience he describes, but his discussion leaves the issue unresolved. In this book, I will undertake to provide at least a crude estimate of this important parameter.

A corollary question raised but not answered by Moody's research (or anyone else's for that matter) is whether the core experience, however common, is independent of the condition that brings it about. In other words, we may ask: Does it make a difference how one (almost) dies? For example, is the experience of nearly dying after a serious automobile accident different in certain characteristic ways from a near-death experience triggered by a heart attack? And what of suicide? There are certain dark hints in the literature, including Moody's books, that nearly dying as a result of a suicide attempt is *unlikely* to provide a transcendent near-death experience. Yet though such *opinions* are common, reliable empirical data on this point are remarkably rare and what data do exist tend to contradict this opinion.[7] The question of what is experienced during a serious suicide attempt is obviously one of both urgent theoretical and practical significance. If the experience tends *not* to be transcendent or is unpleasant, this will not only sharply reduce the limits of the core experience but should act as a deterrent to people who might be tempted to take their own lives after hearing about (and misconstruing) the findings of Kübler-Ross, Moody, and others.

A second purpose of this book, therefore, is to compare the experiences associated with three different modes of near-death onset: illness, accident, and suicide attempt.

A third issue left unexamined by Moody's work is the relationship between religiousness and the core experience. A frequent objection to the apparent religious quality of many near-death experiences is based on the assumption that the death crisis tends merely to trigger visual images based on a person's religious belief system. According to this argument, since most people are at least nominally religious and are known from various national polls to subscribe to some idea of life after death, it is to be expected that when death approaches, religious and otherworldly imagery will be found to predominate. In short, believing is seeing.

If this interpretation is correct, we ought to anticipate a positive correlation between religiousness, on the one hand, and the likelihood or the depth of a core experience, on the other. In short, religious individuals would be expected to have more or deeper core experiences.

The other view, for which some fragmentary support exists in the literature, holds that religiousness *per se* is not a determinant of core experiences but may affect their interpretation. Such a finding would tend to undercut the glib assumption that core experiences are fantasied or hallucinatory wish-fulfillments. We shall, accordingly, also explore what, if any, relationship exists between religiousness and near-death experiences.

Finally, a fourth focus of my investigation will be the subsequent life changes experienced by near-death survivors. Most existing studies have either stated or implied (as does Moody) that profound personal changes tend to occur following a near-death episode. For the most part, however, these changes have been illustrated only by selected cases, making it difficult to determine how representative they are. We have had many anecdotes (which have their place, of course) but little systematic reportage concerning these aftereffects. Another problem with interpreting what little data we do have is distinguishing the effects that can be attributed to the circumstance of nearly dying from those that are dependent on having a *core experience* at the time of one's near-death crisis. *Life at Death* will examine these matters in systematic and quantitative detail.

In sum, my objective in making this investigation has been to scientifically gather evidence bearing on the following unresolved issues of near-death research: first, the incidence of the core experience; second, the invariance of the core experience; third, prior religiousness as it relates to the core experience; and, finally, the nature of changes following near-death episodes.

Two

The Connecticut Study

To carry out our investigation, arrangements were made with several large hospitals in central Connecticut and with a few smaller hospitals elsewhere in Connecticut and, finally, with one hospital in Maine, to secure the names of patients or former patients who met the criteria for inclusion. These criteria were: (1) the survivor had to have come close to death or been resuscitated from clinical death, as a result of a serious illness, accident, or suicide attempt; (2) the survivor had to be sufficiently recovered from his near-death incident to be able to discuss it coherently; (3) the survivor had to speak English well enough for an interview to be conducted in that language; and (4) the survivor had to be at least eighteen years old.

In the larger hospitals, we were able to use various contacts, including physicians, nurses, clergymen, and administrative personnel, in key locations (for example, cardiology, internal medicine, the emergency room, the chaplain's office, and so on) to serve as sources of referral. In smaller hospitals, usually a single contact was used. Members of my research staff would call our contacts on a regular basis to obtain the names of potential subjects. Once a name had been suggested, that individual's physician would be called and, if necessary, the purpose of our study would be explained and permission sought to interview the candidate. If the physician consented, the next step would be to get in touch with the candidate—who, in the meantime, may have been approached by a hospital staff member—and explain our interest in talking to him. If the candidate agreed to be interviewed, he was asked to sign an informal consent sheet and a time was set for the interview. If a candidate was no longer hospitalized or under the direct care of a physician, the person was called directly and the consent form was omitted.

Several months into our investigation, I realized that our hospital referrals were not likely to lead to a sufficient number of cases in our accident and suicide attempt categories to permit meaningful statistical comparisons to be made. At that point, we tried to increase our sample sizes in these categories by writing letters to many psychiatrists and by advertising in local newspapers. The letters and advertisements were always phrased in terms of our interest in speaking to persons who had come close to death as a result of either accident or suicide attempt. No mention was ever made of any special interest in near-death experiences *per se*, nor was any remuneration offered or given to individuals for their participation.

As word of our work spread, we found that we were also the recipients of word-of-mouth referrals. Several people referred themselves as a result of this kind of publicity, while others referred friends who had come close to death. Since we were still in need of respondents in certain categories, these persons were also interviewed.

As a result of these different recruitment procedures, it is necessary to present a breakdown of interviewees by source of referral. This information is given in Table 1.

Table 1

Number of Referrals by Source

Source	*Number*
Hospital	54
Physician	5
Nonmedical	16
Self	6
Advertisement	21
Total	102

Interview Schedule

Our method of data collection involved the use of a structured interview schedule. The interview itself was composed of five distinct information-gathering segments:

1. Demographic information
2. A free narrative of the near-death episode
3. A series of probing questions designed to determine the presence or absence of the various components of the core experience as described by Moody
4. Aftereffects
5. Pre- and post-incident comparison of religious beliefs and attitudes

(A copy of the entire interview schedule can be found in Appendix I.)

Prior to the interview, each respondent was assured of both anonymity and confidentiality. Since the interview was to be tape-recorded, appropriate justification was given for this procedure. In order not to bias the respondent's comments, most questions about the study and its underlying purposes were deferred until the end, at which time all were answered. Before the interviewer left, he gave each respondent a card indicating where he could be reached. All those interested were also promised a report of our findings.[1]

Most of the interviews took between one-half and one hour to complete; a few required more or less time, but never longer than one and a half hours. Most of the interviews were conducted in the respondent's home. Some took place in hospitals, where usually a private room was available, and a few were held in my office or home. Of the 102 interviews obtained, I conducted 74. An additional 20, including all 10 Maine interviews, were the responsibility of a graduate student working closely with me;[2] the remainder were done by several graduate students affiliated with the project. All interviews were carried out between May 1977 and May 1978.

Respondents

A total of 102 persons recounting 104 near-death incidents were interviewed. Of these, 52 nearly died as a result of a serious illness; 26 from a serious accident; and 24 as a result of a suicide attempt. Some basic demographic information on all of the respondents is presented in Table 2.

Table 2

Demographic Data on Interviewees

Total interviewed	102
Sex	
Male	45
Female	57
Race	
White	97
Black	5
Marital status	
Married	47
Single	32
Divorced/separated	16
Widowed	7

Religious denomination	
Catholic	37
Protestant	34
None	21
Other	3
Agnostic/atheist	7
Education	
College graduate	11
Some college/college student	34
High school graduate	39
Some high school	10
Grade school only	8
Age range	18–84
Mean age at interview	43.01
Mean age of near-death incident	37.81

Although, for the most part, frequency data are given in Table 2, the frequencies are nearly equal to percentages, since the total number of interviewees was 102. For legal reasons, no one under eighteen was interviewed in this study. A perusal of Table 2 shows that, with the exception of youngsters and race, our sample of near-death survivors represents a considerable range of demographic diversity. Before turning to issues related to the selectiveness of our sample, the last entries listed in Table 2 call for some comment.

In this study, we made an attempt to interview respondents as soon after their near-death incident as was medically and ethically feasible. Our intention was to minimize both the tendency to embellish and the danger of forgetting. Despite our efforts, only slightly more than one-third of our respondents could be interviewed within a year of their incident. The average time gap between incident and interview, as can be seen from Table 2, is slightly more than five years, but this figure is misleading because a few people had their episode more than twenty years previously.[3] Table 3 presents these data in more precise detail.

Table 3

Interview-Incident Interval Data*

I-I Interval	*No. of Respondents*
<1 year	37
1–2 years	23
2–5 years	17
5–10 years	11
>10 years	16

*For purposes of this breakdown, all 104 near-death incidents were included.

Thus, about 60% of our respondents were interviewed within two years of their near-death episode; the proportion of respondents having had their episode in the distant past was quite small.

As can be inferred from what has already been said, the 102 persons who were interviewed for our study were drawn from a larger group, of which many members were either unable or unwilling to participate for a variety of reasons. These sampling problems are discussed in detail in Appendix II for the benefit of the interested professional reader, but they can be briefly summarized here in nontechnical language.

We found that participation in our study was strongly affected by the condition that had brought an individual close to death. Accident victims, while difficult to locate, were almost always willing to consent to an interview when contacted. On the other hand, only about half of the illness victims—who were by far the most numerous of near-death survivors—eventually took part in our investigation. Suicide attempters had, as expected, the lowest rate of participation, with only one of every five such individuals agreeing to be interviewed.

Moreover, there were differences between these categories in *source* of referral. Illness victims, for example, were generally referred to us by medical sources, whereas suicide attempters were recruited mainly by advertisements. Accident victims came to our attention by a variety of means, with slightly less than half being referred by medical personnel.

How much of a difference these differences in availability and source of referral *actually* make is not possible to state precisely. From my own examination of the data, I would hazard a guess that these differences are more likely to affect our estimate of the incidence of the near-death experience within each of these categories than they are to distort the kind of experience that is described. As will be seen, however, our findings regarding the incidence of these near-death experiences *are* comparable to what other researchers have recently reported, despite these differences. In any case, these sampling factors should be borne in mind when interpreting our data, and the reader will be reminded of them in appropriate contexts.

Measuring the Near-Death Experience

In *Reflections on Life After Life,* Moody, in discussing what I have called the core experience, predicts that "any investigator who enters into this type of study sympathetically and diligently will find that there is ample case material."

In our investigation, Moody's prediction was completely upheld. Our evidence on this question is in total accord with the findings earlier reported by him and other near-death researchers.

Altogether, forty-nine of our cases, or 48% of our entire sample, recounted experiences that conform in an obvious way, at least in part, to the core experience pattern as delineated by Moody.

Nevertheless, in interpreting this data the reader should bear in mind all the qualifications concerning the estimate of the incidence of the core experience that were raised in the preceding section.

Moreover, it is important at this point to specify our criteria for deciding who did and who did not have a Moody-type experience.

On the basis mainly of Moody's analysis of the principal features of the core experience, as modified slightly by the form of our interview questions, I constructed a near-death experience index, which is essentially a weighted measure of the depth of the experience. The ten components of this index, together with their respective weights, are presented in Table 4. Although the weighting factors are slightly arbitrary, they were arrived at before the formal analysis of the data was undertaken.

Table 4

Components and Weights for the Core Experience Index

Component	*Weight*
Subjective sense of being dead	1
Feeling of peace, painlessness, pleasantness, etc. (core affective cluster)	2*
Sense of bodily separation	2*
Sense of entering a dark region	2*

Encountering a presence/hearing a voice	3
Taking stock of one's life	3
Seeing, or being enveloped in, light	2
Seeing beautiful colors	1
Entering into the light	4
Encountering visible "spirits"	3

*Individuals could be assigned a score of either 1 or 2 on these components, if present. The rules for scoring were as follows: (1) for the affective cluster, assign 2 if the feelings were very strong, otherwise 1; (2) for the sense of bodily separation, assign 2 if a clear out-of-body experience was described, otherwise 1; (3) for entering into a dark region, assign 2 if perception was accompanied by a sense of movement, otherwise 1. A given score would then be multiplied by the appropriate *weight* for that component, resulting in a weighted score of *either* 2 or 4 for that component. All nonasterisked components were scored either present (1) or absent (0).

It can be determined that scores on this weighted index, abbreviated WCEI (for weighted core experience index), can range from a theoretical low of 0, indicating the absence of any kind of Moody-type experience, to 29, representing the deepest Moody-type experience. Thus the higher the index, the deeper, or richer, the experience. In fact, WCEI scores varied from 0 to 24.

How were these scores obtained?

Each interview was tape-recorded and each tape was rated by three people associated with the research, including myself, using a detailed rating schedule (see Appendix III). Determining the presence or absence or the strength of a given component for a given individual required taking into account three sets of ratings. Only if at least two of the three judges agreed on the presence of a given characteristic was it scored. Thus, if anything, the WCEI may err on the conservative side.

In using the WCEI for the purpose of classification, certain arbitrary but, in my judgement, reasonable cutoff points were assigned. If a person's score was less than 6, he was adjudged not to have had "enough" of an experience to qualify as a "core experiencer." This undoubtedly eliminates some people who might have been counted as positive instances by Moody (indeed, it was my impression that this index failed to include some interviewees who probably *did* experience some aspects of the Moody pattern), but again it seems better to err on the side of underinclusion than the reverse. Respondents scoring between 6 and 9 on the WCEI will be designated *moderate experiencers* and those with scores in excess of 10 will be referred to as *deep experiencers.*

In terms of this tripartite classification scheme, 27 persons (26%) were deep experiencers, 22 (22%) were moderate experiencers, while the remainder, 53 (52%) were nonexperiencers. This division is of course based on the entire sample and ignores the factor of *how* a person came close to death, a matter we shall consider later.

If we take into account the source of referral, we find that 39% of those who were referred by medical sources were found to have had a core experience, whereas for those who were referred either by nonmedical sources or were self-referred the corresponding figure is 58%. The difference here, though suggestive, is not statistically significant.[4] Since it seems likely that the 58% figure may be *more* inflated than the first, we may regard the figure of 39% as probably being closer to an accurate incidence estimate for a population of (relatively!) unselected near-death cases (in a ratio of approximately 2:1:1 for illness-accident- and suicide-attempt victims, respectively). Of course, because even these (59) cases were not selected randomly, this last assertion is not really warranted on statistical grounds. Nevertheless, used as a ballpark figure, it is not likely to be too misleading, especially in the light of Sabom and Kreutziger's own revised estimate of 43% (see Chapter Ten).

Incidentally, there were virtually no sex differences in either frequency or depth of the core experience. The percentages are as follows:

	Men	*Women*
Deep experiencers	27	26
Moderate experiencers	20	23
Nonexperiencers	53	51

Before examining the different facets of the core experience more closely in an effort to be quantitatively precise where Moody is vague, it will be relevant to provide some illustrative protocols for the different degrees of depth I have distinguished. Indeed, throughout this book I shall attempt to blend the statistical treatment of the data with the descriptive, in order to provide a comprehensive overview of the core experience.

I will begin with an account of a fairly minimal experience (at least in terms of our index). The man in question had been suffering from a malarialike disease and while hospitalized had the following experience:

> At that time, I was in a coma. I could hear everything that went on and I could see everything that went on, but I could not move, I could not talk. To all appearances, I was dead. I even heard the doctor tell the nurse to let me alone, that I was as good as

> dead. . . . I could hear, I could hear very well. To me, it seemed as though I was standing alongside of myself and seeing everything that was going on. *(Could you actually see your physical body?)* Yes. I was strapped to the bed. I had no pain whatsoever at this time. Like I say, it almost seemed as though I was standing in the room watching the doctors come and look at me and the nurse come in and look at me, and I could hear them talking, and, as a matter of fact, the doctor was even playing grab-ass with the nurse. This is true, so help me. *(51)*[5]

This respondent received the lowest possible core experience score on the WCEI, 6. Four points were awarded for his description of his out-of-body state and an additional 2 were assigned for his description of his feelings at the time, amplified somewhat in another segment of his interview not quoted here.

The next case, that of a woman with a fairly deep experience, was occasioned by the onset of a very rapid loss of blood pressure while giving birth to her second child. She recounted her experience in these words:

> All of a sudden, everything went absolutely black. I was not aware of any kind of time. What it was like, I was up in the left-hand corner of the room, looking down at what was going on. *(Could you see clearly?)* I could see very clearly, yeh, yeh. I recognized it as being me. I had absolutely no fear whatsoever. That is one thing that is *very* definite, that there was no fear. It was as if I was supposed to be watching it. It was part of what you were supposed to do. . . . I was aware that I felt good and felt increasingly more at peace very rapidly. . . . I would have been perfectly content to stay there forever and ever. I mean, I had no desire to do anything but stay right there. . . . I became aware of not a voice, but of thoughts that began to come very rapidly, to stop it. To say, "No, O.K., fine, you've had a taste of what this is all about, but you can't stay here. This isn't allowed. You've got to go back, you've got too much to do. You've got to go back, the child is in danger, there is something wrong with him. It is a boy" and the name Peter—now, we had thought about other names, in fact at that point it was going to be Harold—this was a name that came. [About her son's physical condition, she was told] that it was going to be a heart problem. Which did come out later after I came back and I was in labor when the doctor said to me, "We've got to hurry this thing up because this little thing is starting to do strange things." I told him that I knew there was a problem, that it was a heart problem, and I assured him that he was going to be all right,

> that he was going to have the problem, but he wasn't going to die. *(25)*

In this case, the woman scored 13 on our index—4 points for both the core affective cluster and her out-of-body experience, 2 points for entering a dark region, and 3 points for encountering a "presence" (later in the interview she asserts that these thoughts were not her own). I might mention in passing, that according to my interviewee, her son did have a heart problem, which cleared up spontaneously to the surprise of her physician. The presence also informed the mother that her son would be an unusual child, gifted with rare talents, and that her relationship with him would be especially close and different from that with her other children (she now has three). She has since informed me that all these things have come about, but I have not had time to investigate this myself. Even if independently confirmed, these developments are susceptible to a variety of interpretations. This "hint" of paranormal knowledge occuring at the time of a near-death experience, however, is by no means limited to this case in my collection, and has been reported by other investigators.

For an example of a very rich experience, I have selected the case of a woman in her mid-thirties, who, at the time of her near-death incident, was undergoing surgery for a chronic intestinal disorder. Her WCEI score of 18 was exceeded by only two others in our sample, though nine others achieved scores of 15 or higher, so it is presented strictly as illustrative of the deepest experiences I encountered, not as typical of core experiences.[6]

> [She remembers hearing someone say that they were going to do a "cut down" on her and then] I remember being *above* the bed—I was not *in* the bed anymore—looking down on *me* lying in the bed and I remember saying to myself, "I don't want you to do a cut down on me." . . . I know [from what she was told afterward] that the doctors worked on me for many hours. And I remember being first above my body and then I remember being in, like a valley. And this valley reminded me of what I think of as the valley of the shadow of death. I also remember it being a very *pretty* valley. Very pleasant. And I felt very *calm* at that point. I met a person in this valley. And this person—I realized it later on—was my [deceased] grandfather, who I had never met. [She then describes how she was able to identify him after talking to her grandmother about it.] I remember my grandfather saying to me, "Helen, don't give up. You're still needed. I'm not ready for you yet." It was that kind of a thing. And then I remember *music. (Can you describe it for me?)* It was kind of like church music, in a sense. Spiritual music. *(Was*

there singing? Were there musical instruments that you could identify?) No. No . . . it had . . . somehow a *sad* quality about it. A very awesome quality to it. *(7)*

In this instance, the WCEI score of 18 was the result of the following component values: one point was assigned for her subjective sense of being dead, 4 points for both the affective cluster and her out-of-body experience, 2 points for taking stock of her life, and 3 points for her encounter with the (apparent) spirit of her deceased grandfather. (Some of these values were also based on interview material not quoted in the foregoing excerpt.)

Sometime after my interview with her, she sent me a poem that she felt moved to write in order to capture something of her experience and its effect on her. It is a simply written poem, but it expresses eloquently, I think, the feeling, tone, and imagery encountered by many near-death survivors who have deep experiences to relate. Accordingly, I shall pause here long enough to quote it.

THE VALLEY OF PEACE

One summer's night,
I was totally free.
High up in the room,
Looking down at me.

I went through a tunnel,
at a very fast speed.
I knew not what was happening,
But knew I'd soon be freed.

Then thru a door-like entity,
Into a valley of peace,
Where music played God's tune to me,
and made my fear release.

Colors bright, dancing lights,
Such a sight to see.
A figure is coming into view,
Oh, God, it's my grandfather talking to me.

Your time has not come yet,
Your family needs you still,
Enjoy your life to the fullest
I love you and always will.

I've had the chance to see a man
I did not even know.
I had the chance to stay with him
But decided I had to go.

It was so good to be free of pain,
It felt good to be so free.
The Land I saw so beautiful.
Death no longer frightens me.

I have presented these three narratives, and the poem, mainly to illustrate the different levels of depth I found in the many near-death accounts my staff and I encountered in the course of our interviews. Any careful reader can see how each successive example in this small series appears to present a richer, more profound experience than its immediate predecessor. Nevertheless, if we are to progress in our understanding of these core experiences, beyond the descriptive and anecdotal level already available in Moody's and Kübler-Ross's writings, it will be necessary to bring some conceptual order and statistical comparisons to bear.

THREE

Stages of the Near-Death Experience

In my investigation of near-death experiences, I found that the core experience itself tends to unfold in a characteristic way. In general, the earlier stages of the experience are more common, and the later stages manifest themselves with systematically decreasing frequency. Thus, it seems that not only are some of Moody's categories more common than others, but also that they are meaningfully ordered in frequency.

In Figure 1, I have indicated five distinct stages of the core experience, as suggested by our data, along with their corresponding frequency. In the sections to follow, these five categories will be described fully and amply illustrated by reference to specific interviews. As this discussion proceeds, it will be apparent that when these five categories are considered in sequence, they form a coherent pattern. What we will have, then, is the *basic thanatomimetic narrative*—the experience of (apparent) death in its developmental form.

The Affective Component: Peace and the Sense of Well-Being

The first stage, and one that is emphasized in many of our accounts, relates to the affective accompaniment of the core experience. The conscious experience of dying is heralded by a feeling of such peace and contentment that many respondents claim there is simply no way they can describe it. Nevertheless, some of the attempts to do so—which I will shortly quote—are themselves deeply moving and compelling even when the words do ultimately fail. As can be seen from Figure 1, about 60% of our sample report this kind of experience, including many who never get beyond this stage and a few who do not really conform to other aspects of the Moody pattern. If we confine ourselves just to these respondents who are "core experiencers," thirty-five of forty-nine, or 71%, explicitly use the words *peaceful* or *calm* to characterize the feeling-tone of their experience.[1] Most of the others in this category, as might be inferred, use various synonyms to describe how they felt.

Before presenting a full statistical breakdown of the different aspects of the affective component accompanying the core experience, it seems

Figure 1. Stages of the Near Death Experience

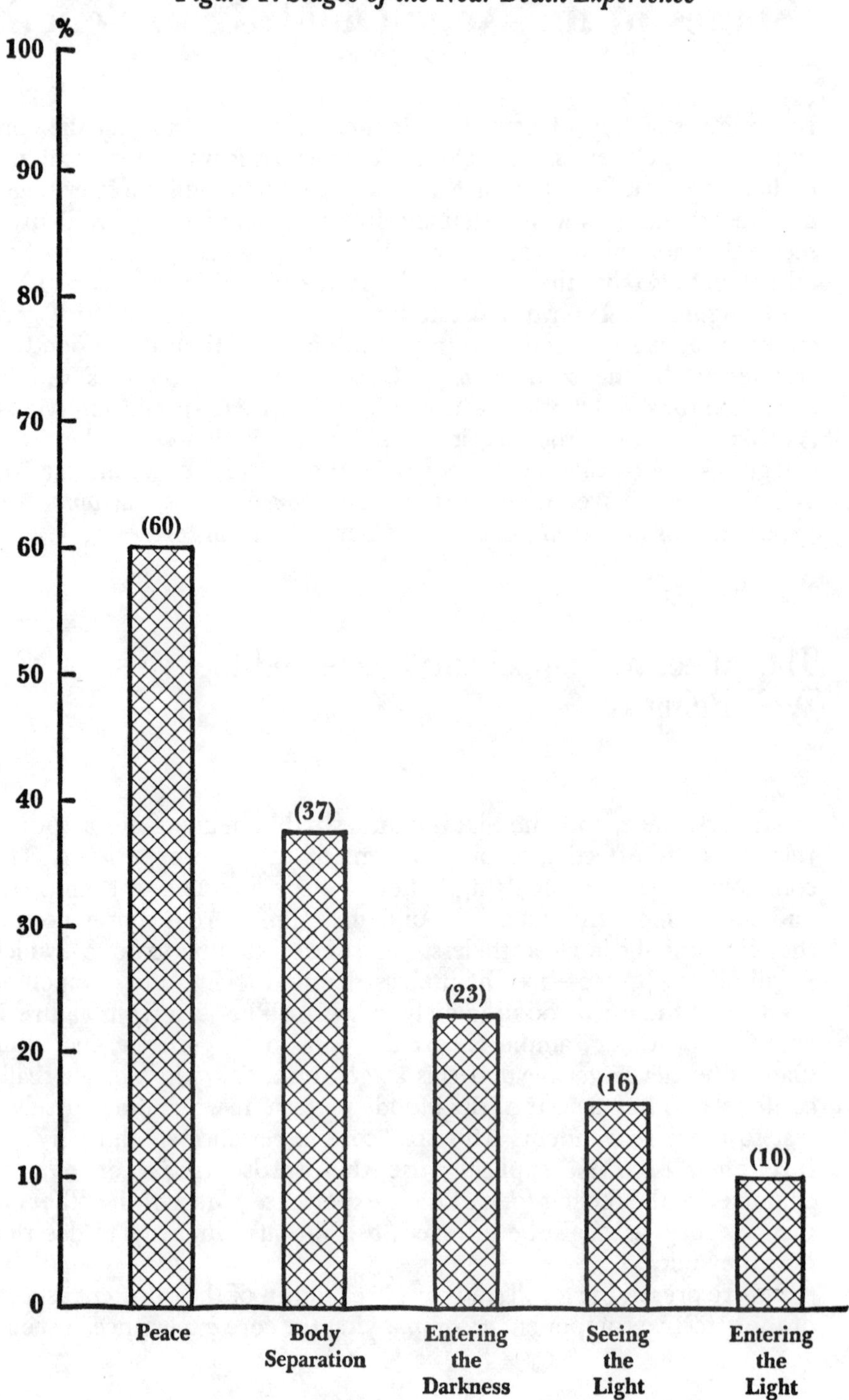

necessary to provide some qualitative descriptive accounts. The illustrations given below are meant to convey something of the range of the affective response to apparent imminent death. Enough excerpts will be cited here to give, as well, a sense of "the central tendency" of these statements.

A woman who nearly died of a ruptured appendix observed:

> I had a feeling of total peace. A feeling of total, total peace . . . it was just such a total peaceful sensation—I wasn't frightened anymore. *(30)*

Another woman who had a cardiac arrest said:

> [There was] nothing painful. There was nothing frightening about it. It was just something that I felt I gave myself into completely. And it felt *good*. . . . One *very*, very strong feeling was that if I could *only* make them [her doctors] understand how comfortable and how *painless* it is . . . how natural it is . . . I felt *no* sadness. No longing. No fear. *(20)*

A woman who had attempted suicide by hurling herself into the ocean and was badly smashed by the waves against the rocks of a nearby cliff recalled:

> This *incredible* feeling of peace [came] over me. . . . All of a sudden there was no pain, just peace. [Later in the interview she reflected on the sheer difficulty of describing how she felt.] I suppose it's because it's so completely *unlike* anything else that I've ever experienced in my life. So that I've got nothing to compare it to. A perfectly *beautiful,* beautiful feeling . . . to me, there's a definite feeling of sunlight and warmth associated with this peaceful feeling. [It should be noted that on the day this woman tried to drown herself the water temperature was 48°; she remembers feeling very cold in the ocean and was told that she shivered a great deal in the hospital afterward.] But when this feeling of peace came over me, I was warm. I felt warm, safe, happy, relaxed, just every wonderful adjective you could use. . . . This was perfection, this is everything anyone could possibly want and everything I could possibly want—is this, is this feeling. *(82)*

In case the reader may feel that these extravagant descriptions reflect a kind of feminine hyperbole, the following accounts from some of the men in my sample should prove sufficient to dispel that impression.

A racing-car driver commented:

> I guess the best description would be visualizing someone in a very strenuous, active sport, and when they got through with it, they take a sauna and have a massage. And if you can experience that feeling of relaxation, then multiply it times one thousand, that's how you would feel. It was just super, super-great. *(73)*

A young man who nearly died when a fever reached a temperature of 106.9° said:

> The mellowness and the passiveness that I felt in this state was just so intense . . . like I said before, it was a very, very strong—I can only use the words *mellow feeling, passive feeling.* There wasn't one bit of discontentment that I felt. I felt [pause] I can probably say the highest I've ever felt in my life. *(45)*

A man who tried to hang himself recalled:

> I felt really good. It felt, like when you wake up in the morning and you feel real good, you have a good feeling. *(100)*

A man who nearly died in a boating accident testified:

> It's tough. Use *euphoric.* Use *orgasmic.* Or use *high.* It was very tangible, very real. But it was doing magnificent things to me. You know, afterward I looked at that lake and I said, "That lake made love to me." It really did, it felt like that. *(66)*

A few more excerpts will perhaps add nothing except redundancy, but somehow I feel that repetition here is not wasted space, if it serves to convey just how frequently these powerful feelings are associated with the onset of (apparent) death.

A sixty-year-old woman who had suffered a heart attack observed:

> I think that probably the next thing I remember is total, peaceful, wonderful blackness. Very peaceful blackness . . . the only other word I might add would be *softness.* Just an indescribable peacefulness, absolutely indescribable. [This was] a total peacefulness, an ABSOLUTE [said very slowly and with great emphasis] peacefulness. *(4)*

A man who nearly died as a result of a motorcycle crash said that as he lay (apparently) dying in the hospital:

> I felt *peaceful.* I felt *calm.* No pain . . . extremely peaceful. *(68)*

And finally, a woman who clearly struggled to find the words to describe the ineffable. Her comments were perhaps the most passionate of any of my respondents, but that may be because she was one of the few who at least attempted to articulate for me a sense that most others despaired of ever being able to communicate to another with the power of speech. She had suffered a cardiac arrest in connection with a tonsillectomy.

> . . . the thing I could never—absolutely *never* forget is that absolute feeling of [pause] peace [pause] joy, or something. . . . I remember the *feeling.* I just remember this *absolute beautiful feeling.* Of peace . . . and happy! Oh! So happy! . . . The *peace* . . . the *release* [pause] the fear was all gone. There was no pain. There was nothing. It was just *absolutely beautiful!* [said with the strongest emphasis] I could *never* explain it in a million years. It was a feeling that I think everybody *dreams* of someday having. Reaching a point of ABSOLUTE [said slowly and with great emphasis] peace. To me *peace* is the greatest word that I can express. *(24)*

These passages should be sufficient to convey the feeling tone which seems to serve both as an initial cue for the core experience and as an affective background during its unfolding. A more detailed statistical picture of the range of affective reactions accompanying the core experience is offered in Table 5. For purposes of comparison, I have given the percentages for both experiencers and nonexperiencers.

Table 5

Comparison of Core Experiencers and Nonexperiencers on the Ten Most Common Affective Reactions (ranking based on core experiencers only)

Characteristics	*Core experiencers (49)*	*Nonexperiencers (53)*
Peace	59%	15%
Painless	49%	13%
No fear	47%	9%
Relaxed	29%	4%

Characteristics	*Core experiencers (49)*	*Nonexperiencers (53)*
Pleasant	27%	0%
Calm	20%	6%
Happy	20%	2%
Joy	20%	0%
Quiet	16%	2%
Warm	16%	0%

Even a casual inspection of Table 5 reveals several interesting facets. First, the general affective response of experiencers was *extremely positive.* In fact, of the total of 170 feelings and emotions named by the experiencers, only 8 (or 4.7%) were negative. Most of the 8 were some form of fear. And even of these, most were transient, occurring at the beginning of the experience or after its termination, upon recovering. Second, there is no clear pattern of affective responses for the nonexperiencers, even though in their case also the qualities of peacefulness, painlessness, and the absence of fear maintain the same relative rankings. Nevertheless, despite the identical ranking of the first three characteristics, it is obvious that the percentage values are drastically lower. Even then, because of the conservative nature of our core experience index (the WCEI), we may very well have included a few experiencers among our nonexperiencers category—a state of affairs which, if true, would mean the modest percentages for peacefulness, painlessness, and the absence of fear in the latter category are somewhat inflated. In fact, most of the statements of peace from the nonexperiencer category (namely, six of eight) come from one subgroup—female suicide attempt cases—and appear to reflect more a sense of *relief* that their lives were (apparently) over than the feeling of transcendent peace expressed in the quotes from experiencers. Finally, implicit in this table but not clearly shown is that where only one experiencer failed to report any feelings or emotions, fully thirty-five (or 66%) of the nonexperiencers disclosed or implied that they felt none. Thus, the modal feeling or emotion for the nonexperiencers was—nothing.

Summing up the results of this analysis of feeling, there is a consistent and dramatically positive emotional response to apparent near-death by experiencers, whereas an absence of any emotional response is typical for the nonexperiencers. The experiencers often report overwhelming feelings of peace as well as a transcendent sense of well-being. The nonexperiencers, for the most part, are not conscious of having had any emotions during their near-death episode.

Significantly, *no* person in our sample—including, of course, all our suicide attempt cases—recounted an experience that could be regarded as "a journey to hell." This is consistent with the findings of other large-scale studies.[2] Although some death experiences did include frightening aspects or moments of confusion and uncertainty, none was characterized by predominantly unpleasant feelings or imagery.

Body Separation: Leaving the Body Behind

The second stage of the core experience involves a sense of detachment from one's physical body. As can be seen from Figure 1, about three-eighths (37%) of our sample reached this stage. Most of these people reported a sense of being completely detached from their bodies, though they usually claim that they weren't actually able to see themselves or, at least in retrospect, they weren't sure. In addition, however, sixteen people did state that they had visually clear out-of-body experiences. (This figure represents approximately one-third of all those reporting a near-death experience.) Although these accounts do vary, it is typical at this stage in the experience for the individual to find himself in the room looking down on his physical body. Most of those reporting this commented that somehow they found it all very natural (at the time) and were aware of acute hearing and sharp but detached mental processes. Visually, they often describe the environment as very brightly illuminated.

At the most minimal level, respondents reported either no sense of bodily connection or no awareness of a body.

A suicide attempt victim commented:

> Mostly it was like a real floating sensation. I don't remember seeing anything. It's real weird. It's like I was detached from everything that was happening. . . . But I didn't see me. *(90)*

A man who had suffered a heart attack observed:

> It seemed like I was up there in space and just my mind was active. No body feeling, just like my brain was up in space. I had nothing but my mind. Weightless, I had nothing. *(33)*

The woman who had a cardiac arrest while undergoing a tonsillectomy found:

> I was *above.* I don't know above *what.* But I was [pause] up . . . it was like [pause] like I didn't have a body! I was [pause] but it was

me. Not a body, but me! You know what I mean? . . . It was a *me inside.* The real me was up there; not this here [pointing to her physical body]. *(24)*

At another level were several reports that indicated the respondent was aware of his "body" moving in some nonphysical dimension. Usually, the respondent stated that he had no bodily sense nor did he remember viewing his physical body from an external vantage point. "He" was just somewhere else. One individual (of the four cases in this subcategory), however, reported a kind of dual body perception—he not only saw "himself" moving through nonphysical space, but his physical body as well! One such report comes from the account of the man who tried to hang himself.

I also remember that I could see myself walking away. I was maybe twenty feet away. Everything was completely black and I could see me walking away. I was wearing this gray suit that I bought last year [he was actually attired differently] and I was walking away from myself hanging there. I could also see that from where I was in the suit I could see myself hanging there. I could see both people at the same time, more or less. *(100)*

Most commonly, an individual having an out-of-body experience would simply state that he was aware of seeing his body as though viewing it from outside and above its physical locus—often from an elevated corner of the room or from the ceiling. The following are typical accounts of this experience:

The young man who nearly died of a high fever said:

I experienced this type of feeling where I felt I had left my body and I had viewed it from the other side of the room. I can sort of remember looking back at myself—it was scary of course. . . . I can remember seeing myself lying there with a sheet and a hypothermia blanket on me. My eyes were closed, my face was very cold-looking. . . . It was like I was perched right up on a little level over near the side of the room. . . . I would be at the foot of the bed, but kind of more up onto the wall, closer to the ceiling, almost in the corner of the room. *(45)*

The woman whose case I cited earlier to illustrate a fairly deep core experience described her out-of-body experience this way:

I was up in the left-hand corner of the room, looking down at

> what was going on. *(Could you see clearly?)* I could see very clearly, yeh, yeh. I recognized it as being me. I had absolutely no fear whatsoever. That is one thing that is *very* definite, that there was no fear. *(25)*

A woman who had a very serious automobile accident told me that while in a coma:

> I had what *I* term a *weird* experience. It's where my husband was in the [hospital] room, it was very late at night and I remember looking at the clock—out of my body. It was 11:10 P.M. and it was where I was looking *down* at my body; I was actually *out* of it! *(Did you have any difficulty recognizing yourself?)* Nope. *(How did you look?)* Very pale. Just lying there, arms outstretched, the IV in. I can remember a nurse coming in and tucking in the blankets and everything and making sure I was all right and everything. And my hair was all over the pillow. *(Where were "you" in relation to your physical body?)* I was, like, over in the corner, and being able to watch people walk in the door and being able to see my husband sitting here [she later implies that she felt that she was "up" as well as to one side of her bed]. *(64)*

A man, also badly injured in an automobile crash, remembered a point when:

> At that time I viewed *myself* from the *corner* of my hospital room, looking down at my body which was very dark and gray. All the life looked like it was out of it. And my mother was sitting in a chair next to my bed looking very determined and strong in her faith. And my Italian girl friend at the time was crying at the foot of my bed. *(71)*

Lest the reader think that these apparently clearly perceived out-of-body episodes always occur within a hospital setting—hardly a surprising fact considering the source of most of our interviews—I will point out here that this same individual also reported an *earlier* out-of-body experience, occurring at the time of his accident:

> [I was] *outside* of my body. Because my body was damaged. I was down. I was looking at my body. I was trying to move it, like it was walking, trying to walk—I had a broken leg—and I kept trying to get up and going, "*No,* I'm all right," and all this weirdness. It seems . . . that I actually was outside of my body. *(71)*

Finally, a woman who nearly died while giving birth said:

> I felt like I was up near the light, up on the ceiling, or something, looking down. . . . I seemed to be above. I could see myself lying on the table. *(29)*

These representative out-of-body experiences will be sufficient, I think, to portray the observer's subjective sense of self relative to his body. This sense of elevation was a typical feature in the out-of-body descriptions of our respondents. There were, however, certain other features that occurred often enough to warrant illustration here. One had to do with the quality of illumination.

The fever victim:

> I can remember it being very, very bright, very bright, and also a very, very peaceful, mellow feeling that I had. *(Was the brightness from the illumination in the room?)* No, I don't think so, because, like I said, it was a private room and it had only one window that had a building next to it, so there wasn't much light coming in and I don't think the lighting in the room at that time was that bright. I remember it being very bright. And, like I said, that in combination with a very peaceful, mellow feeling. *(95)*

During an operation to remove a part of his stomach, another man suffered a heart stoppage. In connection with this event:

> I remember being up in the air looking down . . . and seeing myself on the operating table with all the people around working on me. I can remember, what sticks out in my mind mostly, were the colors. Everything in that operating room was a very brilliant, bright color. *(48)*

One of the women who nearly died in childbirth said:

> As I recall, everything seemed to be brighter. Everything seemed to be lighter and brighter. *(29)*

Thus, unusual brightness of the environment was one dramatic aspect of the out-of-body experience for several respondents. Another, commented on by at least three respondents, was the sense of viewing oneself as though from a great height.

> I seemed to be very high in the air. The people I was looking at were rather small. I couldn't tell you how high I was, but I was up,

> and I seemed to be looking through a hole in a cloud. It was like rainbows, it was bright rays shining down. *(48)*

> It seemed like my body was further away. I seemed to be *higher* than the ceiling. *(29)*

Another woman who nearly lost her life in an automobile accident recalled:

> Even though I was very close, physically, to the doctors, they seemed to be very far away while I was watching them operate on me. *(62)*

A final feature of these out-of-body experiences has to do with what may be called the "mind state" which accompanies them. The examples already cited have mentioned several *emotional* reactions, ranging from initial fear to the total absence of fear; we have also seen in them indications of a delicious sense of peacefulness. Nevertheless, from a reading of all the relevant interviews, the feature that clearly stands out as typical of the mind state of our out-of-body experiencers is the sense of *observerlike detachment,* often associated with a feeling that "all this is perfectly natural." One respondent said:

> Mostly, I think I was just observing. . . . It didn't feel as though it was happening to me at all. I was just the observer. *(29)*

A young woman who nearly died of complications resulting from a faulty exploratory surgery procedure observed:

> I was totally objective. I was just an onlooker. I was just viewing things and taking it in. But I was making no judgments—just waiting, I guess. Just waiting to die and realizing that all these things were going on. . . . I was the classic "fly on the wall." I was just there. *(22)*

> It was as if I was supposed to be watching it. It was part of what you were supposed to do. . . . It seemed very natural. *(25)*

> It seemed perfectly right. Everything about it seemed right. Perfectly natural. *(45)*

> It seemed very [pause] it seemed like it was the thing to do. . . . It wasn't a problem to me. *(64)*

In order to avoid possible confusion, let me emphasize that all of the people whose remarks I've just cited *also* reported the core affective response of peace and a sense of well-being. The emotional response itself usually pervades the entire experience. The *psychological* mind state of detached observation or reflection is typical chiefly of the out-of-body stage of the experience. Later I will return to the quality of thought processes (as distinct from the emotional responses) associated with the core experience.

Occasionally, I was to discover a feature that suggested a more elaborate out-of-body experience than any described so far.[3]

Various studies have provided examples of individuals who can later accurately report visual and conversational events that took place while they were unconscious and close to death.[4] Here is one such instance from our investigation—the account of a young woman who appeared to have "died" (that is, suffered cardiac arrest) three times while in a hospital following a severe automobile accident.

> [During this time] I heard Jack [the surgeon] saying to—the doctor's name was Cliff—"This is really too bad, the damage is severe. That liver's just about gone. But let's try to patch it up anyway, but the way it's been lacerated, I don't think it's going to function. Look at the pancreas, that's pretty well wrecked, too." I heard the conversation.
>
> About two weeks later, I said to Jack, "What went on in the OR?" He said, "Hon, you died on us there. You just went out. And we had to rush to get you back." And I said, "Well, when?" And he said, "Well, halfway through the operation, your pressure just gave out on us again and we cut you open and starting working on your liver and (you) just went." And I said, "Was that the part when you said, 'Look at that liver and it's just about gone?'" And he said, "How do you know, how do you know that? You were out totally." And I said, "I could *see* you operating on me. I was awake." And he said, "You weren't awake, you were sleeping, you were totally out." I said, "I *was* awake, I saw what you were doing, I saw you lean over to Cliff to get some instruments and I saw how you were pointing around and I could see you standing here and Cliff was standing on this side of the table. . . . Cliff was giving you this instrument and you were doing this to me and, all of a sudden, all these people rushed over to me and they started sticking needles in me and doing all these things." "That's when you died [said the doctor]. Come on, how do you know that? Did Cliff tell you that?" And I said, "No, that's the only thing I can remember." And he said, "That's really freaky." *(62)*

Since I have not been able to check the authenticity of this conversation with the woman's physician, I cannot vouch for its accuracy. Nevertheless, it is consistent with other accounts reported elsewhere, and I have no reason, given the remainder of this woman's case history, to suspect that it was either fabricated or unduly embellished.

In one case, not only did the respondent minutely describe the operating procedures while she was out of her body, but could also apparently, visualize scenes taking place *outside* the room itself. This kind of account has also been reported elsewhere,[5] and I furnish this material here mainly for its suggestion that in near-death states of consciousness, apparent spatial limitations may be transcended. Again however, I am not in a position to authenticate the claim of this respondent:

> As my pressure dropped, it felt like an out-of-body experience. As I went out they kept calling my name. . . . I could see them with my eyes closed. I could see them vividly. . . . I could also see my sister, who was a nurse at ——— hospital [where the respondent was]—we're very, very close and if anybody should be close at the time, I'd want her—I could see her coming into the hospital to work. It was her time to be coming in. And I could follow her movements. . . . She walked in shortly after the alert was sounded and got to the emergency room where she worked and someone told her what was going on and she came ripping upstairs. I could see her doing it, I could see her coming up the elevator, telling people that they couldn't—and she told me all this afterward and I shared that with her—get off the floor, that she used the emergency elevator and she went straight up to the floor. *(So you were able to confirm the details of what you were aware of during the time you were unconscious with her afterward?)* Right. *(And you essentially confirmed what you had witnessed?)* Yes, yes. Many of the things she came out with first, but there were things that I told her that she didn't tell me that I could not have known. *(Could you give me an example?)* The elevator was one of them. *(22)*

She also told me that she could plainly see someone operating a defibrillator. She was aware that it was not functioning properly, she could hear the medical team shouting. She described all this as if she were a spectator. In addition, she said she was able to see her mother waiting outside her room and could experience her mounting anxiety In short, this respondent, during the time she perceived herself to be out of her body, claimed to be able to see the actions and to experience the mental states of two people in remote locations outside the room, with whom she had strong emotional ties. As such, this case was unique in my files—though it is not rare in the literature on parapsychology.

Before turning to the next stage of the core experience, we need briefly consider two issues that concern researchers into out-of-body experiences. The first is: When individuals claim to be out of their body, are they typically aware of having "another body?" The answer is: No. Most persons are simply aware of the scene before (or below) them. When asked about "another body," they usually respond that they were unaware of having one or that they felt they existed, in effect, as "mind only." Only two people suggested some vague perception of a "second body." That "body" was sensed as incomplete. The most detailed description of this alleged "second body" was:

Interviewer: Were you aware of or did you feel you had *another* body? Or did you just feel that you had a kind of awareness of what was going on, without a body?
Respondent (64): I felt I had another body.
Interviewer: Could you see it?
Respondent: It's like I didn't even have to see it; I didn't have any real feeling in it. All I felt—I had a piece of clothing on; it was very, very loose. And I remember [having bare feet].
Interviewer: And did this body *seem* like your physical body, only somehow it wasn't your physical body? I mean, like the same shape and so on?
Respondent: No, it was very different. It was very thin, very delicate. Very light. Very, very light.
Interviewer: Could you see anything that was connecting your physical body on the bed with the body you felt yourself to be over in the corner of the room? Was there any kind of connection between the two that you can recall?
Respondent: [Misunderstanding the intent of the question] Just that I felt that my face and hand were the same. Because I remember trying to touch my face to make sure that everything was okay.
Interviewer: And could you feel it?
Respondent: I could feel it.

The second issue is the nature of the connection, if any, between the two "bodies"—a point that was raised with, but not answered by, the respondent just quoted. As is well known in occult literature[6] and in the literature on out-of-body experiences,[7] mention is often made of a "silver cord" (or tube, thread, rope, and so forth), which is said to unite the two "bodies." Did any of our interviewees report this phenomenon?

Unfortunately, the question was not systematically asked of all who reported an out-of-body experience, but *none* of those who were queried about it gave a positive response. One person, who was familiar with the notion from his reading, thought that he "might have" seen such a connecting cord, but even he was very unsure of it. The fragmentary data we have that bear on this question, then, must be regarded as negative.[8]

Entering the Darkness

The next stage of the experience seems to be a transitional one between this world and whatever may be said to lie beyond. I call it entering the darkness. This space is usually characterized as completely black or dark, very peaceful, and, at least in the majority of such accounts, without dimension. Most people have the sense of floating or drifting through it, though a few respondents reported that they felt they were moving very rapidly through this space.

Figure 1 demonstrates that slightly less than one-quarter (23%) of our sample encountered this feature of the core experience.

Moody's work implied that many individuals experience this phenomenon as traveling through a dark tunnel. We found some evidence for this interpretation, but only among a minority of our respondents who "entered the darkness." Specifically, nine people described their experience here in ways consistent with the Moody tunnel concept. These did, in fact, choose the word *tunnel* most frequently to designate the space they found themselves in, although occasionally other similar terms were used (for example, *funnel, pipe, culvert,* and *drum*).

A few brief excerpts will suggest the qualities of this kind of experience of the "darkness."

A woman who suffered a cerebral hemorrhage and temporary blindness told me:

> I remember going through a tunnel, a very, very dark tunnel. . . . *(Did you feel the tunnel was vast?)* Yes, *very,* very. It started at a narrow point and became wider and wider. But I remember it being very, very black. But even though it was black, I wasn't afraid because I knew that there was something at the other end waiting for me that was good. . . . I found it very pleasant. I wasn't afraid or anything. There was no fear attached to it. I felt very light. I felt like I was floating. *(17)*

Another woman who almost died during open-heart surgery remembered:

> I was—it was—a great big drum and this drum was black. In my mind I says, "The Bible says we walk through a dark tunnel until we reach light." And I says, "When am I going to reach the light? *(You felt you were in the tunnel?)* I was in the tunnel, yeh. I was in this great big tunnel and I walked and I walked and I walked and I says, "When am I going to see the light? I'm dead, but when am I going to see the light." *(You felt you were dead?)* I was dead, yeh. . . . It seemed like [pause] there was no light. I never saw the light. *(21)*

A young woman who experienced a near-fatal asthma attack observed:

> I do remember thinking to myself that I was dying. And I felt I was floating through a tunnel. . . . When I say *tunnel,* the only thing I can think of is—you know, those sewer pipes, those big pipes they put in? It was round like that, but it was enormous. I couldn't really see the edges of it; I got the feeling that it was round. It was like a whitish color.[9] I was just smack in the middle. My whole body, you know. I was lying on my back. I was just floating. And smoke or white lines or something were coming this way [toward her] and I was going the opposite way. *(What kind of feeling did you have as you were floating through this tunnel?)* Very peaceful, almost as if I were on a raft in the ocean, you know? *(2)*

A cardiac arrest victim's description:

> Well, it seemed at that particular time, when my heart died, I seemed to go up into a spiral in a deep black, pitch black tunnel. . . . I saw nothing. It was just *pitch* black. I mean, you never saw anything so dark in your life. *(33)*[10]

More commonly, the experience of "entering the darkness" was phrased in terms of a journey into a black vastness without shape or dimension. An account that is seemingly a combination of the tunnel and the black dimensionless domain comes from a woman who experienced an immediate postdelivery embolism:

> It's just like a void, a nothing and it's such a *peaceful*—it's so pleasant that you can keep going. It's a complete blackness, there is no sensation at all, there was no feeling. *(Did it have any kind of*

> *form to it?)* No—sort of like a dark tunnel. Just a floating. It's like [being] in midair. *(5)*

More typical expressions of this dark dimensionless space are given next. From a young man, badly injured in a motorcycle crash:

> I felt as though I was—well, that's the hard part to explain—like you're floating. Like you're *there* and, believe it or not, the color is—there *is* no color [pause] it's like a darkness. *(Did the darkness have a shape of any kind?)* It was empty. Yeh, that's it. Space. Just nothing. Nothing but something. It's like trying to describe the end of the universe. *(68)*

An eighteen-year-old man, intent on committing suicide by jumping from a cliff in midwinter, lost his footing and sustained a head injury resulting in unconsciousness. While in this state, he found himself in

> . . . a darkness, it was a very darkness . . . it was a total nothing. *(79)*

The woman who suffered a cardiac arrest while undergoing a tonsillectomy recalled:

> Well, it was like night. It was dark. It was dark. But it was like, like [pause] like in the dark sky. Space. Dark. And it was—there weren't any *things* around. No stars or objects around. *(24)*

The woman whose remarks I cited earlier to illustrate the affective tone of the core experience provides a useful quote here also:

> I think that the next thing I remember is total, peaceful, wonderful blackness. Very peaceful blackness. [She then heard her name called as though from a great distance.] I remember distinctly thinking to myself how easy it would be to slip back into that nice peaceful blackness. [Afterward, while still in the hospital, she was intensely happy, so much so that people commented on it.] My happiness had no connection with the fact that I was alive again; my happiness seemed at that time to be connected with that total peaceful blackness. *(4)*

Finally, let me quote a woman whose case is most unusual in our sample for two reasons. First, she had *recurrent* near-death episodes—she estimates twelve to fourteen of them—as a child between the ages of nine and sixteen as a result of heart stoppages resulting from rheumatic fever. Second, since at the time of her interview, she was a woman in her mid-fifties, she was describing experiences that, in some cases, took place nearly a half century before! Needless to say, reasonable questions can be raised concerning the accuracy of her recall of these childhood memories. She herself emphatically stated that the *form* of her experience was *identical* on the occasion of each such near-fatal episode. However that may be, her observations here are of some interest, if only because they seem to square with other, much more recent, accounts:

> [During these attacks she would reach a point where she would] go over is the only—descend into this feeling of soft velvet blackness. It wasn't like going into a tunnel [She had recently read Moody's first book]; I had no feeling of going into a tunnel. I just seemed to be surrounded by a velvet blackness and a softness and I would have absolutely no fear and the pain would disappear when I entered into this other state. *(16)*

Whether the experience is described as floating through a dark tunnel or as entering into a black spaceless void, it is clear that those who have reached this stage of the core experience have begun to encounter very nonordinary realms of consciousness. In the next stage, these realms reveal a distinctly transcendental quality, leading to the culminating phases of the core experience.

Seeing the Light

The passage from the third to the fourth stage of the core experience is marked by one singular feature: the appearance of light. It is usually described as a brilliant golden light. This light, however, almost never hurts one's eyes[11] but is, on the contrary, very restful, comforting and, apparently, of ineffable beauty. Some of our respondents told me they felt enveloped by this light, and virtually all who experienced it felt drawn to it. Figure 1 shows that sixteen people—or about one-third of our experiencers—reported seeing this kind of light.[12]

For many respondents, though not all, the golden light brings to an end the "time of darkness" and thus seems to signal an entirely new stage of the experience. In the minds of at least some of our respondents, the transition from darkness to light is packed with symbolic meaning: phenomenologically, if not ontologically, it is taken to signify the termination of the experience of dying and the beginning of new life.[13] Of course, for religiously minded individuals the golden light is sometimes interpreted as the visual manifestation of God, and two of our respondents appear to have had a vision of Jesus, in connection with their near-death incident, in which he was surrounded by this light.

Sometimes the transition from darkness to light is stated very simply, as it was by the woman who had recurrent near-death episodes as a child:

> I just seemed to be surrounded by a velvet blackness. . . . And then, sort of at the periphery of the velvet blackness, there was a brilliant golden light. And I don't remember feeling frightened at all, just perfectly at peace and perfectly comfortable, as if this is where I should be. *(16)*

In some cases, the transition from darkness to light is associated with a "presence" as it was in the following example when a voice told the respondent that she was being sent back:

> It was dark and it was like—hard to believe—like you were going from dark to light. I can't explain it . . . all of a sudden there was light. . . . And then when the voice was coming to me . . . it was just like light. *(Was the light bright?)* Not piercingly. *(Did it hurt your eyes?)* No. *(28)*

In other cases, the experience of the light is described in a more detailed way and in a definite "tunnel" context. The following is taken from an account from a seventy-year-old woman who was in ill health at the time I interviewed her. She had had a near-death episode stemming from a respiratory failure two years earlier:

> [After having had an out-of-body experience, she said, mentally, to herself] "I'm going to go over to the other side. There's a culvert over there. I want to go through [to] see what's in that culvert." I can see the culvert now. It was just like one of these big water culverts. Great big one. But when I went over there and walked into it, I could stand up. And I says, "Geez, that's funny, I never could when I was a kid." We'd crawl through them. Here I could stand up and walk. And as I started to walk, I saw this beautiful, golden light, way, way small, down the tunnel. I said, "That's a funny light. It doesn't even look like gold and yet it is gold and it isn't yellow. I'll go see what's on the other side. Maybe it—it must be pretty over there." And I kept thinking, "Well, yeah, I'll go, I'll go see." *(18)*

Another illustration of the magnetic pull of the light is taken from the testimony of a woman who had a cardiac arrest:

> [She found herself walking on a path] and as I was walking down . . . there was a wee bit of a light down at the extreme end of it and as I kept walking down, that light kept getting brighter and brighter all the time. Really, it was *beautiful* while it lasted, but it was such a short time, because then they gave me a shot . . . and I was out. *(10)*

In other instances, as I have already indicated, the light does not merely beckon from a distance, but appears to enfold the individual in what can only be described as a loving way. The following examples will serve to justify this subjective-sounding characterization.

> *Interviewer:* Were you ever aware at any point of a light or glow or any kind of illumination?
> *Respondent:* A light glow. There was a glow.
> *Interviewer:* Was it in the room itself, or was it somewhere else?
> *Respondent:* In the room.
> *Interviewer:* Different from the illumination that was provided naturally?
> *Respondent:* Oh, yes. Different, very different. It was like [pause] a tawny gold. It was just like on the outer ridges of where I was at. It was just like me looking through—and being apart from everything and just looking. And it was really, really [pause] I felt warm from that.
> *Interviewer:* So that was a positive aspect?
> *Respondent:* It was peaceful. *(64)*

> I can remember it being very, very bright, very bright, and also a very, very peaceful, mellow feeling that I had. *(Was the brightness from the illumination in the room?)* No, I don't think so, because, as I said, it was a private room and it had only one window that had a building next to it, so there wasn't much light coming in and I don't think the lighting in the room at that time was that bright. I remember it being very bright. And, like I said, that in combination with a very peaceful mellow feeling . . . *(Tell me more about the light.)* Very, very bright, like the sun was right in my room shining down. And it seemed like, if there was any color, all the colors were their brightest. You know, everything just magnified a lot of light, it seems like. *(Did the brightness of the colors hurt your eyes?)* No, I could just see the colors so perfectly. *(What did you make of this?)* Well, I look at the whole thing as being like a kind of utopia. Like

this is the way the colors are in Utopia, perfect. Perfect to their natural color. *(45)*

I had the sensation of a warm, a very warm sensation, of a very [pause] it was like a light. You know, I can't explain it, what the light looks like, but it has a very—and I can see it, just like I'm going through it right now—like a very warm, comforting light that I had. And it wasn't centered on anything; it was, like, all around me. It was all around me. *(It enveloped you?)* Right! It was all around me. And the colors, the colors, were very vivid—very vivid colors. I had a feeling of total peace. A feeling of total, total peace. . . . *Tremendous* peace. Tremendous peace. In fact, I just lay there—my bed was right near the window—and I remembered I stared out the window—and the light, and everything, was even outside! *(Did that light hurt your eyes?)* No. *(Was it bright?)* No. Not bright, it was not bright. It was like a shaded lamp or something. But it wasn't that kind of light that you get from a lamp. You know what it was? Like someone had put a shade over the sun. It made me feel very, very peaceful. I was no longer afraid. Everything was going to be all right. *(30)*

Although quite a few of our respondents felt they talked directly with God (see Chapter Four), *visions* of religious figures were actually reported very rarely.[14] When they were, however, the figures were usually described as though light radiated from them. One respondent specifically implied that the light she saw in connection with a vision of Jesus was similar to the golden light seen earlier while "in the tunnel." The number of these instances is entirely too small, of course, to justify any conclusions about the possible similarity or identity of the light associated with near-death religious visions and that which occurs without any particular form. Nevertheless if only for the sake of its intrinsic interest, I shall conclude this section with the clearest instance of a vision of Jesus reported by our respondents. It comes from the interview with the seventy-year-old woman whose record I cited at the beginning of this section.

This particular incident occurred *after* the respondent had survived her near-death episode, brought on by respiratory failure, but while she was still hospitalized for it. At this time, because of a medical implant in her throat, the doctors had told her that she would be unable to receive Communion that week.

I told [a friend] that I wanted to receive Communion. I [laughing a little with embarrassment] saw Jesus Christ. . . . I was crying. . . . All of a sudden, I was crying so, I felt something funny and I looked up and there I saw this light again. And it was almost the same light as it was at the end of the tunnel. It was this vivid gold, yellow. And then I saw a form there. And I can see that form now: It had blond-gold hair and it had a beard, a very light beard and a moustache. It had a white garment on. And from this white garment there was all this gold shining. There was a red spot here [she points to her chest], on his gown, there was a chalice in his hand, and it said to me, "You will receive my body within the week." And he went. And I thought to myself, "Well, that's funny, that can't be. Did I see something that I shouldn't see? Am I going crazy?" And I told my husband I saw Jesus. He said, "Don't tell anybody; they'll think you're losing your mind." And I never did. And then, that Friday [within a week of her vision—the doctors removed the implant after all], Good Friday, I received Communion."

[Later she commented on her vision] I'll never forget it. I can still see it so plain. *(18)*

The various manifestations of the light bring us to the threshold of the last stage of the core experience. From this point, the light no longer serves as a beacon or a warm, enveloping effulgence. Instead, it becomes the preternatural illumination of what to our respondents is perceived to be the world beyond death.

Entering the Light

The difference between the preceding stage and this one is the difference between seeing the light and entering into a "world" in which the light appears to have its origin. For, according to the reports indicative of having reached this stage, one does indeed have the sense of being in another world—and it is a world of preternatural beauty. The colors are said to be unforgettable. The individual may find himself in a meadow or see unusual physical-like structures, which, however, do not seem to correspond exactly to anything in *our* world. This is the stage where respondents report being greeted by deceased relatives. Five people claimed to see beautiful flowers here and four were aware of lovely music. Although resentment for being brought back from imminent death was not frequently expressed by our respondents, that sentiment was particularly evident for several people who were "returned to life" after experiencing this stage.

Figure 1 reveals that only ten people—or about one-fifth of our experiencer sample—gave evidence of penetrating into this final stage. Indeed, it is typically the case—at least among our respondents—that only a glimpse, rather than a protracted visit, is vouchsafed those who come this far. One person whose experience and reaction were representative of this group said that she was afforded "just a peek" into what she felt was "the hereafter." Accordingly, with only a few exceptions, the descriptions we have of this domain tend to be decidedly, perhaps disappointingly, pithy.

I will begin with a sampling of typical statements and conclude this section with excerpts from the interview that provides the most extensive impressions of this stage.

From a cardiac arrest victim:

> I happened to go down this path and it was *beautiful.* Beautiful flowers and the birds were singing, and I was walking down. . . . [After she was resuscitated] I did reprimand my surgeon and my cardiologist. I said, "Why, in heaven's name, did you bring me back? It was so beautiful." *(10)*

From a woman who suffered a respiratory failure:

> I was in a field, a large empty field, and it had high, golden grass that was very soft, so bright. And my pain was gone and it was quiet, but it wasn't a morbid quiet, it was a peaceful quiet. [Afterward] I said to Dr. ———, "Why did you bring me back?" I didn't want to come back. So I was really very happy in that place, wherever it was. [She later further described the field she found herself in.] Soft, silky, very brilliant gold. *(What was the quality of the light?)* Just bright, but restful. The grass swayed. It was very peaceful, very quiet. The grass was so outstandingly beautiful that I will never forget it. *(3)*

A man who appears to have come close to dying as a result of being ill during a tooth extraction[15] gave the following statement:

> I took a trip to heaven. I saw the most beautiful lakes. Angels—they were floating around like you see seagulls. Everything was white. The most beautiful flowers. Nobody on this earth ever saw the beautiful flowers that I saw there . . . I don't believe there is a color on this earth that wasn't included in that color situation that I saw. Everything, everything. Of course, I was so impressed with the beauty of everything there that I couldn't pinpoint any one thing. . . . Everything was bright. The lakes were blue, light blue. Everything about the angels was pure white. *(Tell me what the angels*

> *looked like.)* I can't. *(Did the colors hurt your eyes?)* No. *(Was it restful?)* It was. Everything about the whole thing was restful. *(53)*

A woman who nearly died as a result of a cerebral hemorrhage described a part of her experience:

> There was music, very, very pleasant music. . . . The music was beautiful. . . . [Later] And then there was another part to it where two aunts of mine—they're dead—and they were sitting on a rail and it was a beautiful meadow and they started calling me. They said, "Come on, Giselle, come on." . . . And I was very happy to see them—it was a meadow lane. Beautiful grass, and they were sitting on this railing and calling me . . . and I went halfway and then stopped. And that's probably when I came to. *(17)*

The woman whose near-death episode was used to illustrate a deep core experience (see pages 36–38) also reached this last stage. The excerpts from her interview, already cited, disclose that she, too, heard music she characterized as "spiritual" during an episode in "a very *pretty* valley." At this time, she encountered her deceased grandfather, who instructed her to return to life, saying that she was "still needed." I will quote further from her interview in order to amplify her description and interpretation of her surroundings:

> *Interviewer:* Could you describe the valley for me a little bit more? You said it was like the valley of the shadow of death.[16] Are there more things that come to mind in terms of what you can recall about it? How you felt? What you were aware of? What you saw?
>
> *Respondent:* I think I should say that the psalm happens to be my favorite psalm. And while I've never seen the valley of the shadow of death before, it was just a very beautiful, crystallike place, and it just gave me a very good feeling once I realized where I was.
>
> *Interviewer:* And you did have this realization at the time? It wasn't something that you had come to *after* the experience, but at the time it occurred you said, "This is where I am." Was it like—was it comparable to any place that you've been to? Was it earthly? Was it—
>
> *Respondent:* No. It wasn't earthly. I can't say if it was heavenly because I really don't know what heaven is like, but it didn't seem earthly at all.
>
> *Interviewer:* Can you say anything about the illumination of the valley? Could you see it clearly?

Respondent: It was very bright. Very bright.
Interviewer: Did the bright light hurt your eyes?
Respondent: No. Not at all. *(7)*

The last passage is taken from the interview with a woman, who, on the basis of both my own judgment and her score on the WCEI (24), had the deepest experience of any respondent. In her case, she not only had a glimpse of the world that appears to individuals in stage V, but, in addition, received some quite detailed visual impressions. For the purpose of coherent exposition, I have had to rearrange some segments of this interview, but the order of the excerpts in no way distorts the substance of her account. She came to this experience as a result, apparently, of suffering cardiac failure at home, where, owing to some unusual circumstances, she lay comatose and undiscovered for three days. Finally, she was brought to a hospital, where she had a cardiac arrest before eventually recovering.

> The first thing I remember was a tremendous rushing sound, a tremendous [searching for words]. . . . It's very hard to find the right words to describe. The closest thing that I could *possibly* associate it with is, possibly, the sound of a tornado—a tremendous, gushing wind, but almost pulling me. And I was being pulled into a narrow point from a wide area. *(Sort of going into a funnel?)* Yes! Yes. And it was [pause] nothing painful. There was nothing frightening about it. It was just something that I felt I gave myself into completely. And it felt *good.*
>
> Then, suddenly, I saw my mother, who had died about nine years ago. And she was sitting—she always used to sit in her rocker, you know—she was smiling and she just sat there looking at me and she said to me in Hungarian [the language her mother had used while alive], "Well, we've been waiting for you. We've been expecting you. Your father's here and we're going to help you." And all I felt was a tremendous kind of happiness, of pleasure, of comfort. And then somehow she took me by the hand and she took me somewhere [pause] and all I could see was marble all around me; it was marble. It *looked* like marble, but it was *very beautiful.* And I could hear beautiful music; I can't tell you what kind, because I never heard anything like it before. . . . It sounds—I could describe it as a combination of vibrations, many vibrations. *(How did that music make you feel?)* Oooh, so *good*! The whole thing was just very *good,* very happy, very warm, very peaceful, very comforted, very—I've never known that feeling in my whole life.
>
> [Yet] somehow, I was never right there with her [her mother].

She was always at a distance. And she seemed to be just smiling and saying or implying, "Wait." She was saying this in Hungarian, and smiling. And then I would see my father. There were many people or beings or whatever they were [pause] I never *saw* and yet I *knew* that I knew them.

Interviewer: They were familiar to you?

Respondent: Yes.

Interviewer: But the only persons that you specifically recognized were your mother and father?

Respondent: Yes.

Interviewer: What did they look like?

Respondent: The way I always remembered them looking; somehow they always looked the same. . . . I always remember [my mother] as being very dignified and very tender and quiet, and my father was just the opposite—very jovial, poetic, and artistic; and they were just that way. They were the way I always remember them.

Interviewer: Were you able to see them clearly?

Respondent: Oh, very clearly. Very, very clearly.

Interviewer: Did your father communicate anything to you?

Respondent: [Laughs] It's a funny thing because I've thought about it after and I remember when I was thinking about it later, as I was regaining consciousness, I kept saying, "Now why did he ask me that?" He asked me, "Did you bring your violin?" And I thought that was so funny. And I don't know if he really said that or if I imagined it, you know; it's really hard to tell.

Interviewer: Did that question make any sense to you afterward?

Respondent: Yes, it did. My father loved music and he played the violin, beautifully. I've always wanted to play the violin, but never could. I have a violin, but—

Interviewer: The other people there did not communicate anything to you?

Respondent: Yes, they did. They were all talking to me but I don't remember what they were saying. It was all, it was as though they were all—when I saw the groups of people, it was in sort of a *marble* [pause] something I've never seen in my whole life. I've never seen it in a movie, a picture—

Interviewer: Was it a building of any kind, a structure?

Respondent: Yes, it was and yet it seemed to have no walls. And yet there was a lot of marble and music and people were walking by and working and doing things, and just smiling. They weren't talking. They were not speaking to me and yet they were. I was hearing; they were communicating with me.

Interviewer: What were the people doing?

Respondent: [Pause] It seems that I saw one person carrying what looked like a *saw;* another was carrying a hammer, woodworking tools, but everyone was smiling. There was a great feeling of happiness around me. And everyone was [pause] not really walking. They seemed to be, you know, kind of floating.

Interviewer: Were they dressed in ordinary attire?

Respondent: [Pause] I wasn't aware of it.

Interviewer: I'd like you to describe as much of the scene as you can now recall.

Respondent: You know, I've tried to sketch this, but it's too difficult. I know I've never seen anything like it. The closest thing I could compare it to is possibly a mausoleum. But somehow there was a lot of marble. . . . It was *immensely* filled with light, with light. . . . I felt it surrounding, totally surrounding me and it surrounded everything—my mother, when I saw her, and my father—

Interviewer: You mean it was there sort of as a permanent but shifting background to your experience? You were just aware of this light?

Respondent: Yes, and it was especially powerful when I describe this building or whatever it was. . . . It was just so *illuminating*!

Interviewer: Did it hurt your eyes?

Respondent: No!

Interviewer: Could you see anything else besides this marble—whatever it was without walls? Were there any other features of the surroundings?

Respondent: Yes. There was one thing. It seemed like, like—and this was what puzzled me—it seemed like it was a big [pause] crypt. It was very beautiful and very ornate and somehow I was talking to someone—I don't know who it was. And I had the feeling that, well, this is where my mother and father were and I was to meet them right there. They weren't there at the moment, but I was to meet them right there. And I was waiting for them.

Interviewer: Was this after you had seen them or—?

Respondent: Yes, after I had seen them. And I was waiting for them. Suddenly, it was all gone.

Interviewer: Did that scene just end all of a sudden? Or did it fade out? Did it dissolve like they do in the movies?

Respondent: It ended very abruptly. It seemed, in my trying to understand it and comprehend it because I felt it was *so* important, to end just like that. But it was at the moment I felt . . . *tremendous* pain and that feeling of being torn away from something. . . . I think that I *really* made a decision, I can't tell

> you how or when or what, but I reached a point where [pause] I *knew* that I *had* to come back. . . . I cannot tell you exactly *what* happened—whether I heard *my* daughter or my children speak to me [at this time, several of her children were with her in the hospital room] and when they said, "We *need* you!"—suddenly, the immensity of what I had experienced made me realize I *had* to. I *have* to make them realize that death is not a frightening or a horrible end. *It is not. I know* it is not! It's just an extension or another beginning. *(20)*

A casual perusal of all the accounts presented in this section—even the very brief ones—will be sufficient to reveal that each of them, *without exception,* uses the adjective *beautiful* to describe the sensed features of the "surroundings" where these respondents found themselves. If, for the time being, I may take the liberty of speaking about this realm as a "world" of its own, then, plainly and without equivocation, it is experienced as a surpassingly beautiful one. Reading these accounts, it is understandable why a person entering such a world would be reluctant, even unwilling, to return to the world of ordinary experience.

Nevertheless, all those in my sample who reached the threshold of this world were obliged to return and no one reported venturing into any further realms that might be construed as transcending this one. With the description of this stage of the core experience, then, we have followed the phenomenological path of the dying as far as these accounts will take us. As Moody has implied, it seems to be the *same* journey, with different people encountering different segments of what appears to be a *single, common path.*

At this point, however, I must admit that I have deliberately omitted from this account one singular and extraordinary phenomenon which *crosscuts* the stages of the core experience and brings it to a resolution. Indeed, this aspect of the core experience appears decisive in determining whether an individual is to return from the journey upon which his near-death episode has launched him. Because of the crucial and unusual nature of this phenomenon, it is best discussed with all the stages of the unfolding core experience clearly in mind.

FOUR
The Decision to Return to Life

For the majority of the core experiencers, there is a point in their passage toward (apparent) death when they become aware that a decision has to be made concerning their future: Are they to return to life or continue toward death? Awareness of reaching this point of choice is usually signaled by one of several remarkable phenomenological features. Because of their similarity from case to case, these features, taken in their totality, are unquestionably among the most provocative of any of the elements regularly associated with the core experience.

The life review. A person may experience the whole or selected aspects of his life in the form of vivid and nearly instantaneous visual images. These images usually appear in no definite sequence (though they sometimes do), but rather as a simultaneous matrix of impressions, like a hologram. In some instances, they appear to include *flash-forwards* as well as flashbacks. They are usually overwhelmingly positive in emotional tone, even though the individual viewing them ordinarily (but not always) experiences them with a sense of detachment. Twelve people—or about one-quarter of our experiencer sample—reported this phenomenon.

The encounter with a "presence." Sometimes in association with the life review, sometimes independent of it, the individual may become aware of a "presence."[1] Among our respondents reporting this experience, the presence is never actually seen, but is always sensed, inferred or intuited. On occasion, however, it is *heard* to speak—though sometimes this is described as a "mental understanding"—and then it speaks with a voice both clearly audible to the experiencer and identifiable as to gender.[2] The respondent usually feels as though there is mutual direct communication between the presence and himself. Although there is some variation here, the presence usually states or implies that the individual is at a choice-point in his life and that it is up to him to elect whether to return to it (that is, physical life). At this point the individual seems led either to reflect on his life or to reexperience it in the form of the panoramic life review just described, as he attempts to make up his mind. In some cases, the individual seems to be given information about his future physical existence, should he decide to live. Altogether, twenty people in our sample—or slightly more than two-fifths of our experiencers—indicated that they were aware of what I have called a presence.[3]

The encounter with deceased loved ones. In a few cases—there were eight clear instances of this—the respondent becomes aware of the "spirits" of dead loved ones, usually relatives. In contrast to the phenomenon of the presence, these spirits are usually seen *and* recognized.[4] Typically, they greet the individual in a friendly fashion, while the respondent himself usually experiences a combination of surprise and great happiness at this apparent reunion. Nevertheless, these spirits usually inform the respondent that, in effect, "it isn't your time" and that "you must go back." Thus, while the presence usually appears to give the respondent a choice whether "to stay," the spirits usually urge the individual "to return."[5] This difference between the encounter with a presence and an encounter with spirits, especially when one bears in mind the (near) mutually exclusive relationship between them, suggests that they represent two quite distinct and independent phases of the core experience decisional process.

Making the decision. The result of the events just described is a decision, made either by or for the individual, whether to return to life or to continue further into the journey beyond this life. Not surprisingly, virtually all experiencers feel that either they themselves decided to "come back" or that they were "sent back" (in a few instances, apparently, against their own preferences). Sixteen people—about one-third of our experiencers—testified that they either chose, bargained, or willed themselves to return. Five stated that they felt they were sent back. For the remaining respondents—seven in number—who appear to have experienced at least one aspect of the decisional process, how the decision was made is not clear. In a few cases, however, a decision is apparently arrived at without any of the three features occurring in a clear-cut fashion.

Whether the individual feels he chose to return or was sent back, the reasons given usually have to do with one or the other of two nonindependent considerations: (1) the "pull" of loved ones—usually children or spouses—who are felt to have need of the respondent or (2) a sense that one's life's tasks and purposes are not yet accomplished—a feeling of "unfinished business."

In any case, reaching a decision is usually the last event of which an experiencer has any recollection. The decision appears to reverse the dying process and returns the individual to the world of ordinary reality.

The components of the decision-making process reveal themselves during various stages of the core experience. They may, in fact, appear in conjunction with *any* of the stages of the core experience (since they crosscut these stages), but they *tend* to occur in association with the intermediate stages, namely II, III, or IV. Altogether, by a conservative count, twenty-eight experiencers (or 57%) appear to have passed through a decisional phase, nineteen in a very marked way, the remainder to various lesser degrees.

In order to recreate the sense of these decisional episodes, it will be necessary here to reproduce some long passages from the interviews. This phenomenon is as complex as it is unusual, and the effort to grasp its meaning requires that these episodes be presented, as much as possible, in their full context.

The first involves a man who nearly died in a motorcycle accident at the age of eighteen:

> During the time I was supposedly dead—according to *them* [the doctors], supposedly I was dead—during this time it was like I was talking to someone that—I never knew who they were; that was strange. I asked, but I never got an answer. The only thing I can remember is like a voice say, "Well, you've made it. You've finally made it." I say, "No, this is too early. What are you talking about?" He says, "Well, you've finally left; you don't have to suffer anymore." I had been sick as a kid and it hurt. And he says, "You don't have to suffer anymore. You made it." I say, "What do you mean? I want to go *back*. I can't [pause] I can't—I haven't *done* anything. I'm still trying to go to school. And work. I've got people that *need* me. And things I've *got* to do. And I'd like to go back—if that's possible." And then the voice says, "Well, it's up to you. If you go back, you're going to suffer. And you're going to have to endure some *real* pain." [Indeed, the respondent reports having suffered intense pain for the next year during his recuperation.] And I say, "Well, it doesn't matter to me. *That* I can handle. Just let me go back." And he said, "Well, okay." And at that instant, I felt a drop of water hit my—and then the doctor screamed, "He's alive, he's alive!"
>
> *Interviewer:* Do you remember being aware of any unusual noises or sounds?
>
> *Respondent:* The *only* sound I was aware of was the voice. And it sounded—it seemed to be a *man's* voice. It seemed to be soft, yet harsh. . . .
>
> *Interviewer:* Were you aware of any other persons, voices, presences?
>
> *Respondent:* Just one. Just the one voice and it was like an entrance.
>
> *Interviewer:* Like an entrance?
>
> *Respondent:* Yeah, it was like a walk-in person. Like a voice that says—like a *greeting* voice. Or like, "Well, here you are. You finally made it."
>
> *Interviewer:* Now, this wasn't a voice of anyone you recognize—anyone in your family?
>
> *Respondent:* No. This is why I tried to describe it as being a harsh voice yet soft—but sure.

Interviewer: You said before [referring to a portion of the interview not quoted here] that you kind of felt reassured when you heard this voice.

Respondent: Comforting. It was a comforting voice.

Interviewer: It essentially said, "You've made it now. You're not going to have any more pain." And then you kind of bargained to get back.

Respondent: Right. It gave me a *choice.* I had a choice of staying or going back. *(68)*

The next case is that of the woman who suffered a cardiac arrest during a tonsillectomy. According to her own account, she was told afterward that she was "clinically dead" for nearly three minutes.[6]

[At this point in the interview, the respondent is describing her sense of "being up," that is, elevated in space.]

Respondent: And I was *above.* And there was—a *presence.* It's the only way I can explain it—because I didn't see anything. But there was [pause] a *presence* and it may not have been talking to me, but it was, it was like [pause] like I *knew* what was going on between our minds.

Interviewer: Sort of like telepathy?

Respondent: Well, I *guess* so. It wasn't that I remember him *telling* me that I had to go down, but it was as if I *knew* I had to go down. And I didn't *want* to. Yet I *wanted* to. And it was like being *pulled* without being pulled. My feelings, I guess, were [pause] pulled apart. *I wasn't afraid to go that way.* This is the only way I can explain it. I wasn't *afraid* to go that way. I *wanted* to go that way. I *really did.*

Interviewer: In this upward direction?

Respondent: That way there [pointing upward, on a diagonal]. I wanted to go there. *Something* was there. . . . I remember that there was *something* there—a presence there. And I had no fear of it. And the *peace* . . . the *release* [pause] the fear was all gone. There was no pain. There was nothing. It was just *absolutely beautiful*! I could *never* explain it in a million years. It was a feeling that I think everybody *dreams* of someday having. Reaching a point of ABSOLUTE peace. To me peace is the greatest word that I can express. . . . That's all I can *really* remember—that I was being *drawn* back. It was a choice, evidently, that I made.

Interviewer: Do you feel that *you* made the choice?

Respondent: Yes, I *think* so. I wasn't afraid to go that way. And yet I'm sure it was my choice to come back.

Interviewer: Why do you feel you came back? Why did you choose to come back?

Respondent: I don't know. I think it's because I had two little children. And I felt they needed me more than—up there. And I think going up there meant *my* peace and joy, but it meant misery for my children. And I think *even then* I was *thinking* of these things—*weighing* things. I wasn't feeling any *pain* or *sorrow* or anything, but I was thinking *calmly* and *rationally,* making a decision—a rational decision, a logical decision—*without emotions involved.* Do you know what I mean? . . . I didn't make that decision *emotionally.* I made it *logically.* And the choice, both choices were—I mean, I wasn't afraid to die so *that* choice would have been just as easy for me. But the choice was made *logically.* And I'm sure it was *mine. (24)*

In the following instance, the respondent is unusual in that he reports that his experience came back to him bit by bit, like fragments of a forgotten dream, only after several years had passed since his near-death episode, brought about by an automobile accident:

Respondent: It was like I got to view my whole life as a movie, and *see* it and get to view different things that happened, different things that took place. [Pause] I think I got to see some things in the future; I might even have gotten to see how my whole life *might* have turned out or *will* turn out—I don't know—as far as the future destiny of it. It's hard to say. Sometimes I recognize things when I get there and go, "Wow!" . . . So anyway, I got to see, basically, what was a whole view of my life. Now, after I was shown a lot of things, which somehow it's very hard on words on describing . . . basically, it was like watching a movie. But this movie, although it is speeded up, probably to show you it all—it only seems to take a second—and the next thing was a voice coming to me after all this and saying, very compassionately—it was like an *all-knowing* voice, something that at the time I took to be the voice of Jesus, but I can take it to be the voice of any one God as far as the whole universe is concerned. I don't *know* who that person was. It was like a voice that I *knew* and it said to me, "You really blew it this time, Frank."

Interviewer: Did it actually use those words?

Respondent: Yes. Actual words, "You really blew it this time, Frank" . . . Right there it was like I was shown this movie and then the voice said that to me—and at that time I *viewed* myself from the *corner* of my hospital room, looking down at my body, which was very dark and gray. All the life looked like it was out of it. And my mother was sitting in a chair next to my bed, looking very determined and strong in her faith. And my Italian girl friend at the time was crying at the foot of my bed—in beautiful form—it was beautiful. But, anyway, at this time the voice said, "You really blew it this time, Frank." And I looked down at this scene and that scene compared with the fact that I had seen this view of my life and I said, "No! I want to live." And at that saying, it was almost like, it seems like, it was a snap [he snaps his fingers] and I was sort of inside my body. And the next thing . . . I was waking up and looking down at my girl friend and saying, "Jesus Christ, it's bad enough that I'm dying and you got to sit there and cry!" [He laughs.]

Interviewer: Those were the first words out of your mouth? You actually said that?

Respondent: Yup. First words.

Later, this respondent talked about the sense of choice he had and his feelings at the time:

Respondent: . . . looking at [my body] from the end of the bed, it looked dead to me. It was a choice of right at that split second—was the choice of, okay, do you want to go back to your body or not?

Interviewer: Did somebody give you that choice or did you feel that you had to make it yourself? Who gave you that choice?

Respondent: The voice that said, "You blew it." Like I said, I got to see a movie of basically my life, of what *had* happened and what *was* happening. It was like, I have a *mission* here to do, let's say, and I had a choice of what basically I call going on with the physical body or starting over again with a new one.

Interviewer: Can you remember what it *felt* like to be in that state? At the choice point?

Respondent: . . . how I felt—was I worried? Scared? It's good you asked that question. . . . In the beginning, it *is* scary for a little while. But then, all of a sudden, there's *such* love and great warmth and [pause] and security and strength in that . . . that . . . that All-Being, that All-Presence that is *there.* Whatever it is that's out there, that's the presence. There's great *comfort.*

Finally, I asked him to tell me more about the "movie" of his life he had viewed and what kind of response he had to it:

Respondent: I don't know if I actually did see *all* of my life—that's too hard to say—but I can remember it was like going to certain little things. Some of them seemed very insignificant . . . you wouldn't think that they had any significance in your life. . . . It was like I got to see some good things I had done and some mistakes I had made, you know, and try to understand them. It was like: "Okay, here's why you had the accident. Here's why this happened. Because so and so and so." . . . it all had meaning. Definitely.

Interviewer: Were most of [the things you viewed] positive? Negative?

Respondent: The interesting thing about that: They were *both.* But there was *no feeling* of guilt. It was all *all right.*

Interviewer: You weren't involved? I mean, it wasn't like you were *watching* them.

Respondent: That's why I say it was like a movie.

Interviewer: But you were watching like a spectator. But somehow you were understanding your life in a way that you've never been able to understand it before.

Respondent: Yeh, in a new context. A whole new context. *(71)*

In the next case, a woman recounts her decisional crisis, which appeared to take place while she was out of her body, in her hospital room, following an automobile accident. At the time of her experience, she had been in a coma for four days.

[While she was out of her body] I was trying to make up my mind whether I was going to live or die. So I went back through my childhood and I came back. It was like I could recall instances out of my childhood and I was trying to decide whether I wanted to live or die, because I had just gotten married. . . .

Interviewer: Can you reconstruct that [how she went about making up her mind] for me as best you can?

Respondent: Well . . . I had a very tough childhood. And I had been afraid even of getting married. And it was where I had to make a decision. I was going to trust my husband enough to go on to be here [i.e., to remain alive]. And it was where I was visiting all the painful places in my childhood and saying, "Well, am I going to experience this with a husband?" It was really *vivid* to me—all the different places that I had to go to. But yet I went to visit two places where I remember that I had a good time. One was on a playground when I was a child about eight years old, and one was on a Halloween night and it was where all my brothers and sisters were with me. And it was a really *good* time. What made the decision for me was, I said, "I have all the time, the rest of my life to find out if I really love this man. And

I really do love him so I think everything will be different." . . . and I saw him so worried and it was just like he was—I don't know—he was patting my hand and saying, "Come on, come on. You've got to come out of this." And the next thing I remember is, it was about two A.M. and I decided that I was going to live and the next thing, I was sleeping. I woke up about eight-thirty that morning. And I was out of the coma.

Interviewer: You said you felt the choice was yours as to whether to live or die at this point, and because you felt that your feelings for your husband were trustworthy, you could trust him—was that what decided you that you were going to live?

Respondent: Right. There was no religion or anything connected with it. It was just like [pause] *I* had that decision to make and that it was *totally* up to me. And I never gave a thought about God or anything else. It was totally up to me. And it was *my* decision to make. And I felt *really good* about this.

Later she spoke about how she viewed the scenes of her childhood and of how (possibly) images of her future manifested themselves to her.

Respondent: Some [images] I watched in a very detached way. Because I could see the stuff going on was like opening up a door and just watching everything going on, and me stepping back away from it and leaving it there. But some of the things I got emotionally caught up in. Then I stopped and I said, "I don't want to be here anymore; I don't like that situation."

Interviewer: The things that you saw—can you describe the quality? Were they vivid, indistinct, fast, slow, and so forth?

Respondent: I would say most of them were not vivid, but not indistinct. They were there, like they were all going on and they were at a pace where they happened, but, like, all the garbage got left behind. If that experience happened to me, I skipped some of the things, and I just went on from the beginning until I came to the end.

Interviewer: More or less in a chronological sequence? But you could delete a lot of the stuff?

Respondent: Right.

Interviewer: Was it like, in a sense, that a tape of your life was playing and when you got to a boring part you could just skip it?

Respondent: Right, and go on to another part.

Interviewer: Was it like your whole life was being laid out before you; that you could look at it selectively in terms of what parts seemed to be particularly relevant in the decision you had to make?

Respondent: Yeh. I would say yes. . . .

Respondent: [Speaking of other imagery she had] It was like . . . I saw my husband there and I had an image of us five years later. I had an image of us with our children. And it was like I had images and like [pause] I had knowledge [pause] of what children I was going to have.

Interviewer: Did you in fact have children?

Respondent: Yeh. And I had two boys.

Interviewer: What was contained in the image that you saw? Was it two boys?

Respondent: I saw two children, with their backs. That was all I saw.

Interviewer: So there was a sense in which you could not only review your past but also [see] scenes from the future?

Respondent: Right, and it was very close; it wasn't foggy. *(64)*

In this case, of course, there is only the suggestion of paranormal knowledge of the future, not any convincing evidence of it. The respondent's image of the children (assuming it was faithfully described) was not specific enough for any definite conclusion to be drawn. Nevertheless, the reader may recall case *(25)* mentioned on pages 35–36, which presents rather more striking data consistent with the assumption that near-death experiences can sometimes disclose precognitive information. In that instance, the respondent also reported an awareness of an external source of her thoughts that she must return to her body, though she did not actually term this source a "presence."

In the next case, we shall find another hint of paranormal knowledge of the future—again concerning an unborn child—but this time the source of this datum is very clearly linked in the mind of the respondent to an unmistakable "other." This material is drawn from the interview with the young man who tripped and accidentally knocked himself unconscious as he was about to commit suicide.

> The first thing was, when I was out, I had a really weird feeling like [pause] I was *going* somewhere. I don't know *where* I was going but [trails off] . . . I don't know where I was going but I was moving to an emptiness. And then, all of a sudden, I heard this *voice*. And it was a really, a really [pause] calm; and it was just a great—it was a male voice. It was just really great. It was just a really—like someone talking to me as a *real close friend* or something like that. It was a really nice tone of voice, you know what I mean?

Interviewer: Compassionate?

Respondent: Yeh. It was *great.* Yeh. And, and, the first thing he said was, "Do you really want to die?" And I said, "Yes. Nothing has been going right all my life and at this point I really don't care if I live or die." And he says, "What about your mother? She cares about you. What about your girl friend?" And then it got kind of hazy and he said something about a *daughter* but—I don't *have* a daughter! So I think it's sort of like, like, you know, sometime in the near future I'm going to have a daughter and she's going to be something *important,* because if God wants me to live, there must be some *purpose* in my life. And my daughter is going to be something *important*—maybe she'll find a cure for cancer or maybe she'll [pause]—something like that. Or make something very important like—maybe she'll solve ecological problems or maybe the population or something very important that will help prolong the existence of mankind, which is coming very short, you know? And so, anyhow, then he said, "Do you want to go back?" And I says, "What do you mean, go back?" And he goes, "Finish your life on earth." And I go, "No. I want to die." And he goes, "You are breaking my *laws* to commit suicide. You'll not be with me in *heaven*—if you die." And I says, "What will happen?" And then after this I started coming to. So I don't know what happened after this. So I think that God was trying to tell me that if I commit suicide I'm going to hell, you know? So, I'm not going to think about suicide anymore [nervous laughter].

Further into the interview, he offered some illuminating observations concerning how the voice of the presence is experienced. His comments here are, to the best of my knowledge, very indicative of the *form* that this kind of "communication" takes in most cases.

Interviewer: Okay, let's focus on the voice then. You never saw anything?

Respondent: No, it was still. The whole time it was in complete darkness.

Interviewer: Even during the time that the voice was speaking to you?

Respondent: Yeh.

Interviewer: When you heard the voice, you heard it as a male voice. Did you actually hear the *words,* or—

Respondent: It was like it was *coming into my mind.* It was like I didn't have any hearing or any sight or anything. It was like it was *projected into my mind.*

Interviewer: What you told me before—is that the gist of what the voice said? Or is it pretty much the actual words?

Respondent: It was mostly *thoughts,* you know? It was mostly thoughts. It wasn't like somebody—you know, like you and I are communicating with words. It was mostly thoughts—like, I would picture in my mind my mother crying and my girl friend crying and then when there was the thought about a daughter, she [his girl friend] was holding a baby. It was like—the more I think over it, the more it comes out as words, but when it happened it was more like symbols—symbolic, you know?

Interviewer: So what you're doing now is trying to translate it into words?

Respondent: I'm trying to change it into English, yeh. It was very specific.

Interviewer: But the message to you was very clear?

Respondent: Yes. It was *very* clear. That my life isn't ended yet and that I shouldn't be trying to fool around with my life because it isn't under my control, you know?

Later, I asked him to describe to me his sense of choice in returning and to tell me how he interpreted his experience.

Interviewer: Was it your understanding that it was up to *you* to choose, or did you feel you were *sent* back?

Respondent: Whether I wanted to live or die? I feel that I was more or less *forced* back. Because, still in my mind, I *wanted* to die. I had some *doubts* about it but I still wanted [trails off]. Everything had been going so bad to this point in my life that it didn't seem worth it—that my earthly existence was no longer any good.

Interviewer: Do you think that you *could* have chosen to die if you were prepared to pay the consequences—of not going to heaven?

Respondent: Like, see, I didn't want to go to hell. When I saw the picture of—well, probably in my upbringing about hell being fire and all this and suffering and whatnot, I've gone through enough suffering in my life. I thought, maybe it's time for a change. So that's what probably changed my mind about dying. So I guess I *did* have a choice in a way.

Interviewer: You interpret this voice as God? You think God was speaking to you?

Respondent: I really do think it was, yeh.

Interviewer: What do you make of the image of your girl friend . . . and being told about your daughter—that she'd miss you or need you or something like that?

Respondent: It's a weird feeling, like, like [pause] knowing the future. I had already had thoughts of marrying this girl at this point and I had just a couple of months earlier given her a preengagement ring. And, you know, it was just like, like [pause] a *prediction* of the *future.* Like, I'm really going to marry this girl—because I saw her with the baby. It'll be *my* daughter. I mean, wow, I'm really going to marry this girl. And I didn't know if this was the real thing or not. I'm so young [18] still, I didn't know if I had found the right girl or not. But I guess God wants me to marry her! I mean, I guess she's the one. *(79)*

As I mentioned earlier (see footnote 2) several people, in addition to the young man just quoted, identify the presence with God and believe when they hear a voice speaking to them, that it is His voice. Although in most cases in which a presence is felt or heard the respondent believes that the choice to live or die is ultimately up to him, in those instances where the individual feels he is in direct communication with God the entire range of decisional possibilities seems to be represented: One may either choose to go back, bargain to get back, or find oneself sent back.

A woman who suddenly incurred a very high fever (106°) found herself "talking with God."

During this time, a feeling of complete calmness—the only way I can describe it is like a blanket being pulled up from my feet, gradually coming up. And a voice—and I believe the voice was God—telling me, "If you want, I'll take you now." And I recall thinking about it at this time. And I said, "No, I want to stay with my children." And I felt the same cool blanket being slowly removed.

Interviewer: How did you feel at the time?

Respondent: Total relaxation. Complete calm. It was more like a logical decision. I wanted to remain because my children were very small. And there was no anxiety. Cool, calm.

Interviewer: And logical?

Respondent: Logical. Yes, this was very definite.

Interviewer: You feel that you made this choice?

Respondent: Yes. Definitely. I feel that I was given the choice.

Interviewer: Can you tell me more about the voice?

Respondent: I would say it was very definitely God.

Interviewer: When you heard the voice, did you hear it mentally or actually?

Respondent: I heard the voice. It was a masculine voice. The voice was [pause] almost like over a megaphone. Amplified, but not echoing. Very clear. *(26)*

A person who felt she bargained her way back to life is the woman who nearly died of a ruptured appendix:

It was during that time that I came to, first with a lot of fright—I was scared to death—then, I got a very, very funny sensation. And the feeling was, like, almost like rebirth. Almost like rebirth. I lay there and I thought about things that I had planned to do, that I had better start making moves towards. For about two days—I didn't sleep—I had the sensation of warm, a very warm sensation, of a very [pause] it was like a light . . . I had a feeling of total peace. A feeling of total, total peace. [She felt she was conscious during this time.][7] . . . [And then] I was thinking to myself, my children—I've got these four children I've got to raise—and I remember thinking, "What's going to happen to my kids?" I definitely didn't want my mother-in-law to have 'em, you know? And my mother couldn't handle 'em.

Interviewer: It sounds as though you had to live.
Respondent: I had to. I had to! My kids were young, you know? And I said, "I can't leave 'em. I can't leave 'em. They're not ready for me to leave 'em yet."
Interviewer: When you were thinking about your kids, did you have any images of your kids?
Respondent: Yeh, mm-hmm. I had a very clear picture of them. Some of the things we had experienced together. Some of the things that my husband and I had experienced together. I felt a tremendous, *tremendous* love for my mother. Like if I'd been able to, I could have just hugged her, you know? Held on tight to her.
Interviewer: What were these images like?
Respondent: They were vivid. They were vivid. Lots of scenes.
Interviewer: Were they like flashbacks?
Respondent: Right, it was. It was. It was. It was.

Later, I asked whether she had been aware of "the presence of anything" during her decisional crisis:

I felt very close to God. I felt very, very [pause] like I was having a personal conversation with Him. Even though I wasn't saying it verbally, He knew what I was saying. He heard me.

Then I asked her to describe for me who made the choice:

Respondent: When I came to in the evening, it was like I was holding on. And that was what the whole, *whole* mental conversation was. "Cause I can't go now."
Interviewer: Who decided that you would live?
Respondent: I think I bargained. I think it was just a bargain that I had struck.[8] [She promised to accomplish certain things she felt she had a talent for, to raise her kids to be decent and loving human beings, and so forth] [And] I was no longer afraid. Everything was going to be all right. *(30)*

Finally, to take an example of a person who felt she was "sent back" by God, we have this testimony from a woman who suffered massive internal hemorrhaging two weeks after giving birth to her first child:

I could feel myself just slipping away. I could feel myself in a chamber [apparently like an echo chamber]; I could hear them [the medical team] say that I was in shock. I could hear the nurse say, "I can't get a pulse. No respiration. She's gone." [She says she was told later that she was "gone" for more than a minute.] . . . It was all echoey. Meanwhile . . . I felt very detached and very at ease. I was completely panic-stricken before when I was going in, I was terrified, but when I was in there, it was the most *peaceful,* happy time. I never saw God. No one ever came walking up to me. But I did hear somebody say, "You're needed, Patricia, I'm sending you back now." *(Was it a male or a female voice?)* It was a man's voice, a male voice. And I opened my eyes. *(28)*

This respondent later observed, "I guess I know that there really is a God."

Feeling ushered back to physical life by God is not, of course, the only means by which a person can find himself again in the world of ordinary reality. Sometimes, an individual is enjoined to return to life by the exhortations of a "visible spirit" rather than an "audible presence." An example of this kind of "forced re-entry" can be found in the case history given to illustrate a deep core experience near the beginning of the book (pages 36–37).

To round out my exploration of the decisional process, I will give just one additional and detailed account of this effect. In this case, a woman, while hospitalized, was experiencing severe respiratory problems, owing to a chronic asthmatic condition:

[She had been feeling extremely uncomfortable, unable to

breathe, move or talk, but then became aware that she was feeling comfortable. Apparently without moving, she saw a room monitor go flat.] I thought, Gee, I feel so comfortable. And then I heard, I heard Mrs. Friedrich [a wealthy woman for whom the respondent had once worked. The respondent described Mrs. Friedrich as a very loving and much respected woman. She, herself, loved her and felt loved by her]. She had been dead for nine years at that time. I heard, in her very distinct voice—she spoke slowly and every word was brought out strong—and she had a low voice, and she said, "Miss Harper . . . *Miss Harper* . . . MISS HARPER [with gradually increasing volume and emphasis], I want you to live." And she appeared, not distinctly, but . . . it's hard to explain. . . . I don't think I saw her face; it was there but it was more of a [pause] . . . she was dressed in black. I don't think I could see her feet, but I could see the middle part of her, and it was almost as if you would look at the side of a tree, a straight tree. And I saw this simple black dress and it just sort of faded out, top and bottom. But she was there and she said, "Miss Harper. Miss Harper! I want you to live!" [This was repeated many times.] And she said, "I didn't build this hospital for my family to die in; I built this hospital so that my family could live!" She said it many times and distinctly. It was the wing of the hospital she had built. And finally I answered in my mind, "I'll try, Mrs. Friedrich, I'll try [said weakly]." And she said [forcibly], "Miss Harper. Miss Harper! I want you to live!" *(6)*

It is tempting to quote from additional interviews to illustrate further nuances of the decision-making process,[9] but perhaps enough men and women have already been seen to convey something of the sense of awe, wonder, comfort, and peace that usually accompanies the decision to return to life. Clearly, the decision whether to return to life is usually made in an atmosphere that has a very definite otherworldly ambiance. A specifically religious interpretation is given to it by many, though not all, of the experiencers. Although the phenomena described in this section do indeed cry out for interpretative commentary, this must be postponed until after we have completed the presentation of all our findings on the core experience. Despite the patterned coherence and consistencies among our accounts, there remain many aspects of these experiences that require clarification before any conclusions, however tentative, may legitimately be drawn.

Five

Qualitative Aspects of the Near-Death Experience

I have so far tried to delineate certain sequential features of the core experience in order to show something of its uniformity of content in different men and women. Now, I want to move to some characteristic features of the experience that will serve to deepen the reader's understanding of its feeling-tone, sensory qualities, and cognitive processes. Several of the factors I will be discussing here refer to qualities originally identified by Moody as constituting part of the core experience pattern.

Is It Like a Dream?

One of the first questions usually raised about the core experience is whether it has a dreamlike quality. Or whether it could, in fact, have actually been a dream. Quite apart from the improbability that at the moment of (apparent) death everyone should dream fragments of a common dream, the subjective reports of near-death survivors provide almost no support for the "dream interpretation."

Unfortunately, we did not incorporate a question relevant to this interpretation until our study was already underway. Nevertheless, we did raise the issue with twenty-two of our core experiencers. Of the nineteen who responded unequivocally to this point, only one claimed that her experience was like a dream; the rest denied it—usually, as the reader will see, emphatically. Three people gave equivocal or irrelevant responses to the question. Thus, of those who addressed this issue, 94.7% stated that their experience was *not* like a dream. Instead, you will see, they typically claimed, it was very *real:*

> *(Was it like a dream?)* No. It was too real. Dreams are always fictitious. *This* was *me,* happening at *that* time and there was no doubt that it was reality. It was a very real feeling. *(25)*

> Now, this *could* have been a dream. Or it could have been for real. I more or less feel it was real. *(It wasn't like your ordinary dreams?)* It was *not* an ordinary dream. No way . . . it was *real. (68)*

> *(Did this experience seem a dream to you? Or did it seem different?)* Very, very *different* from a dream. In fact, it felt like actual reality happening. *(So that when it was happening . . . it* did *seem real to you?) Very,* very real. *(Was it more vivid than a dream?) Much* more. It was where I could recall colors, places, things [referring to a flashback phenomenon], just everything altogether. And it was very, very vivid. *(64)*

> *(Was it like a dream?)* Yes [pause] it was. It was, in a way, but, then, in a way, it wasn't. It was very *real. (20)*

> *(Was this experience like a dream? Or was it different from a dream?)* I wasn't sure at first. But to think back—recently, I've been dreaming a lot and there's a different quality to it. It was *more realistic* It was very *real* to me . . . The more I thought about it, the more I felt it was real; it really happened to me. *(79)*

> *(Was it like a dream?)* No. I thought to myself for a while [afterward], it didn't really happen. But then I thought to myself, Boy, you were there and it really did happen. *(28)*

> *(Was this experience like a dream in any way?)* No. It was very real. It's as real as you and I are. *(26)*

A related question is: Is the experience an hallucination? The preceding testimony, of course, offers no support for this supposition. Nevertheless, I did find some evidence for the occurrence of hallucinatory-like images among a small number of our respondents—there were perhaps a half dozen such cases—including both core experiencers and nonexperiencers. In every case, however, the hallucinatory images were completely *idiosyncratic* and were regarded afterward by the respondents as having been hallucinations, that is, not real. In the few instances where a core experiencer also reported having had hallucinations, these could be *distinguished* from the core experience itself as having had a distinctly different quality. Perhaps the most definitive comment was delivered by one of our core experiencers, who was herself a psychiatrist and who, accordingly, should know something both about dreams and hallucinations. She told me, without qualification, that, in her judgment, her own experience was neither the one nor the other.

The data here, then, are quite unambiguous: In the opinion of the respondents themselves, their core experience was not a dream nor an hallucination—it was real.

The Question of Ineffability

According to Moody, many near-death survivors find that their experience is, at bottom, ineffable—it cannot really be communicated in words. What do our respondents have to say on this point?

Table 6 presents the relevant data.

Table 6

Core Experiencers' Responses to the Question:
Is Your Experience Difficult to put into Words?

	No.	%
Yes	24	49
No	15	31
Equivocal/irrelevant	7	14
Not asked	3	6
Total	49	100

Percentages of unequivocal responders only

Yes	61.5%
No	38.5%

Inspection of the table discloses that there is considerable support for Moody's claim from the data furnished by our respondents. The bulk of those who answered the question directly admitted that they have difficulty in conveying their experience to others because of their inability to find the right words. Still, it should be noted, nearly 40% of those who responded unequivocally reported no particular problems on this score. This group, incidentally, includes a number of people who had "deep" experiences, so the apparent ineffability of the experience does not seem to be a simple function of its complexity or richness. Thus, on the question of ineffability, the data are by and large consistent with Moody's contention, but not overwhelmingly so.

When the experience *is* said to be ineffable, however, one can ask why is it so? On this point, our respondents are sometimes quite emphatic about the reasons for their frustrating inability to translate their experience into ordinary speech:

(Do you find it hard to convey this experience in words?) There are not

> *words.* There are not words. . . . It can't [be conveyed]. And it cannot be fully understood. *(20)*

> Yeah, it was like—it was *such*—I've *never* had an *experience like this.* I mean, like, there's, like, *no,* no words—to convey it. Like when I was trying to tell you how the voice was and how the *feeling* [pause] of just *drifting,* you know, it was [pause] it was *really weird.* It's hard to explain in words. *(79)*

> It's very hard because there's nothing like it. There's nothing on earth, I think, that can compare to this feeling of total peace. *(5)*

> Yeah, because I can't explain to you the feeling, the sensation. You know, I can't tell you what the sensation was. *(30)*

> I'm not coming across at all as I want to. Maybe just the feelings that were felt at the time, being totally brand new, unable to put a label on them . . . *(32)*

> It was just *absolutely beautiful*! I could never explain it in a million years. . . . I can *never* tell you what the feeling was like. *(34)*

> I remember at the time, when I was in the hospital, trying to explain to one of the technicians how I felt. And I just couldn't get it across; I always felt like the words were *lacking.* You just couldn't describe it. *(99)*

> This was different from a dream. And different than being on this physical planet. So it was something *other* than [pause] than what words can express on this planet for sure. *(77)*

The answer is repetitively clear: Over and over, the respondents state that there simply *are* no words that *can* be used to describe their experience adequately. Not only do their perceptions, while in this state, defy linguistic expression, but so do their feelings. Usually, the respondent's very *struggle* to communicate his experience to me was dramatic evidence. This was no mere matter of verbal fluency. When the woman said, "I'm not coming across at all as I want to," she was, in fact, voicing a common frustration.

There is still another and very different reason why the experience sometimes tends to remain private. This has nothing to do with the problem of ineffability, but rather with the fear of ridicule. Recall that Moody's account of the prototypic near-death experience includes an observation that survivors find that people often scoff when near-death experiences are related. This ridicule gradually leads to the experiencers suppressing their accounts. Although I did not systematically inquire into the reactions of others on hearing these accounts, enough respondents unburdened themselves on this point to make it clear that *fear* of ridicule was a powerful deterrent. In some cases, I was the first person to be told about these experiences. In most cases, respondents did not want to be regarded as "weird" or "nuts." As one young man put it:

> . . . If you go talk to people about this, they look at you like you're *weird.* Because they can't [pause]. How can you explain something to somebody that they can't believe? or visualize? or whatever it is? A lot of people have trouble with that. [He goes on to say that he believes this is changing somewhat as a result of the publication of *Life After Life.*] *(71)*

Another woman, who had had her experience seven and a half years before my interview with her, told me that only recently had she told anyone about her experience and that was her therapist. When I asked her why she had waited so long, she replied, ". . . I thought I was weird. . . . I thought I was off-the-wall." *(64)* Her reticence stemmed from her fear that others would confirm her own suspicions.

And in fact, such fears are not altogether insubstantial.

> I don't find it difficult [pause] to communicate this in words. But I find that people are very standoffish when you start talking about it. You know, they'll say, *"Oh, really?"* And they'll kind of hesitate away from you. I mean, it happened with the doctors at ——— hospital after the incident *did* happen to me. *(You described that to them?)* I *tried,* and they wouldn't listen. . . . For a while, I really felt that I was a little *crazy,* because every time I did broach the subject, somebody would *change* the subject, so I felt the topic probably shouldn't be discussed. *(7)*

Afterward, this woman tried to discuss her experience with her rabbi and again felt she received a response that indicated neither understanding nor acceptance. It was not until she came across *Life After Life* that she realized her experience was *not* unusual, given her closeness to death. She has since been emboldened to discuss it with many others and has even agreed to be interviewed by journalists and radio reporters.

In summary, Moody's assertion that the disclosure of near-death experiences tends to be inhibited because of anticipated ridicule or scoffing does receive some support from the spontaneous comments of a number of my respondents.[1] His claim that many near-death survivors believe that their experience is essentially ineffable receives even stronger and more systematic support. Together, these two factors operate to keep these near-death episodes in the domain of private events.

Perception of Death or Dying

When a person is apparently on the brink of death or has gone temporarily over that brink into "clinical" death, is he aware of his condition? I have already mentioned (see footnote 7, page 288) that with only two exceptions all our core experiencers were apparently or clearly unconscious or comatose at the time of their episode. It is during these periods, then, that the question of perceived death or dying is applicable.

A preliminary answer to this question can be obtained by comparing the perceptions of core experiencers with nonexperiencers:

Table 7

Perceptions of Dying and Death by Core Experiencers and Nonexperiencers

	Did not perceive themselves to be dying	Perceived themselves to be dying	Perceived themselves to be dead	
Core experiencers	11	19	10	40
Nonexperiencers	21	17	0	38
	32	36	10	78

$\chi^2 = 13.28$ ($p < .01$)*

Data on this question were available for 87 of our 102 respondents. Nine respondents—6 core experiencers and 3 nonexperiencers—whose responses were either indeterminant or uncertain were dropped from this analysis.

*χ^2 is the statistic used for evaluating the significance of the differences between rows; in this case, between core experiencers and nonexperiencers.

Core experiencers are significantly more likely to perceive themselves as dying or as already dead compared to nonexperiencers. Indeed, all ten cases where an unequivocal perception of death is reported come from core experiencers.

It is difficult to judge whether the impression that one is either dying or dead should be regarded as an inference or as a datum. How, after all, does one "know" that he is dying when he has had no comparable prior experience? Does one merely infer that he is dying or dead from the apparently overheard remarks of members of the medical team who often observe that the patient is dying or has died? Are experiencers more likely to form these impressions precisely because they have otherworldly experiences on which to base such an opinion? Is it the qualitatively discontinuous feeling of peace and the sense of well-being that accompanies it which leads a person to conclude that he has died? These questions do not lend themselves to facile answers, and the exact determinants of the inference or knowledge of one's own dying or death cannot be stated with certainty.

Nevertheless, we can still examine this aspect of the core experience in the hope of arriving at some tentative conclusions. The fact is, the overwhelming proportion of experiencers claim they knew that they were dying or had died. Perhaps if we listen again to their own comments, we shall gain a valuable insight into this feature of the experience.

The woman who nearly died of massive internal bleeding two weeks after giving birth to her first child recalled:

> [In the emergency room she said inwardly] I'm leaving. Goodbye. I felt myself just slipping away. I could feel myself in a chamber [like an echo chamber]; I could hear them say that I was in shock. I could hear the nurses say, "I can't get a pulse." "No respiration." "She's gone." And I could hear a nurse saying, "Get a line through her," but it was all [echoey]. . . . Meanwhile . . . I felt very detached and at ease . . . it was a, the most *peaceful,* happy time. [Soon thereafter she heard a voice saying she was being sent back.] *(28)*

It was her sense that she was definitely dying, although she wasn't sure that she was actually "dead" (even though she was told that she was "gone" for over a minute).

The man who suffered a cardiac arrest and found himself spinning up into a "deep black, pitch black tunnel" was soon confronted with a "mental question": Did he want to live or die? He said that during that time:

> I just thought I was dying at that particular time. It didn't even affect me as far as being scared. Of course, being up there and knowing your mind was alive, but my mind was very much alive. I could think very clearly, even though I was considered dead [laughs]. *(33)*

The young man who fell on a rock while contemplating suicide also found himself drifting in a dark space:

> *Interviewer:* Did you actually think at any point that you *were* dying?
> *Respondent:* Yes, I did. I did at first. When I first started feeling that drifting, I thought to myself, Maybe I'm on my way to heaven.
> *Interviewer:* Did you actually think that you *were* dead?
> *Respondent:* I wasn't sure. I wasn't sure. *(79)*

A man, badly injured in a motorcycle accident, was taken to a nearby hospital, where he was declared "dead on arrival":

> *Respondent:* [I felt] no pain. Extremely peaceful. No sense of actual touch or anything of that sort. . . .
> *Interviewer:* You actually had this sense, then, that . . . you were actually dead?
> *Respondent:* Absolutely. To tell people this, they think I'm nuts. Okay, let them think so.
> *Interviewer:* The next thing that you were aware of was the doctor saying, "This man is alive." Did you hear anybody say, "This man is dead," or anything like that?
> *Respondent:* No. No. *(68)*

A woman involved in a severe automobile crash was in intense pain when she was brought to a hospital emergency room. Like the previous respondent, she also claims that she was and felt dead.

> Then the blood pressure started to drop really fast and they were losing me rapidly. At this point there was no pain. I felt *very*

> comfortable, very euphoric, just *really* like it was okay and everything was still and calm. At that point they said I died, right there. . . . It was funny, at the point when I really died, it just felt so good. I don't know why the pain stopped. It was just such a peacefulness, it was just really strange. *(62)*

Finally, I will again cite the case of the woman who had the deepest core experience. She had been comatose for three days at home after an apparent heart failure. She was then taken to a hospital.

> *Respondent:* I *know* that I had died. I know that I had died.
> *Interviewer:* Do you know that according to your medical records if you were declared clinically dead?
> *Respondent:* I've talked with Dr. ——— about it. He said, "Margaret, I wouldn't have given two cents for your life. We were ready to give up so many times. . . ."
> *Interviewer:* You felt at this time that you *were* dead, would you say? That you *had* died? This was your subjective feeling?
> *Respondent:* Yes. Yes. I did. I did.
> *Interviewer:* Did you hear anybody say, at the time, that—
> *Respondent:* Yes, I did. . . . [She then recounts several such comments exemplified by the following remark, made, she says, by one of her physicians: "No *way* are we going to keep this woman alive."] *(20)*

From these brief excerpts, it may seem impossible to draw any firm conclusions about the factors associated with the perception of dying and death, but my examination of all of the relevant cases in their entirety does enable me to offer a provisional hypothesis. While it is probable that many cues combine to suggest to the person that he is dying or has died, in my judgment, the most *significant* are the sudden termination of bodily sensations (including, most importantly, the cessation of pain) and the onset of feelings of peace and well-being. When the individual realizes as well that his mind is "still alive," these features collectively tend to trigger the thoughts: I am dying, or, This is death. In my opinion, the external cues, such as seeing one's apparently "lifeless" body or hearing a physician's doubtful pronouncement, are not necessarily as potent or compelling as is that concatenation of internal indicators I have described.

Needless to say, further research is needed to clarify this issue, but it already seems established that the perception of dying or death is still another characteristic feature of the core experience.

Cognitive Processes

In conjunction with the out-of-body stage of the core experience, I mentioned that a number of people reported a sense of detachment characterized their state of mind while close to death. It is possible, however, to be more precise in describing the quality of the cognitive processes which operate during the time of decision. Respondents who commented on this matter (the issue was not raised systematically in our interviews) tended to claim that their thinking processes were clear and sharp—and governed by rational, rather than emotional, considerations. This generalization seems to hold both for people who found themselves out-of-body and for those who had no such impression:

> I could think very clearly, even though I was considered dead [laughs]. *(33)*

> *(What were your feelings and sensations?)* Total relaxation. Complete calm. It was more like a logical decision. I wanted to remain because my children were very small. And there was no anxiety. Cool, calm. *(And logical?)* Logical, yes. This was very definite. *(26)*

> *(How would you describe how your mind was working while in this state?)* Very cognitive. Really, very rational. Very determined. *(62)*

> *(So the thing that is very hard to describe is the fact that you were very alert mentally?) Extremely* alert [with feeling]. *(68)*

> *(Why do you feel you came back? Why did you choose to come back?)* I don't know. I think it's because I had two little children. And I felt that they needed me—more than "up there?" And I think that going up there meant *my* peace and joy, but it meant misery for my children. And I think *even then* I was *thinking* of these things, weighing things. I wasn't feeling any *pain* or *sorrow* or anything, but I was thinking *calmly* and *rationally*—making a decision, a rational decision, a logical decision—*without emotions involved.* Do you know what I mean? Being a mother, she's ruled mostly by emotions. Being *human,* you're ruled mostly by emotions. I didn't make that decision *emotionally.* I made it *logically.* And the choice, both choices were—I mean, I wasn't afraid to die so *that* choice

would have been just as easy for me. But the choice was made *logically*. And I'm sure it was *mine*. Because I was *thinking* logically. Do you understand what I mean? *(24)*

The gist of these and similar observations implies that during the decision-making phase, not only is there no impairment of one's thinking processes, but, if anything, they appear to be enhanced. The decision to return to life seems typically to be made during a state of heightened mental clarity dominated by a (subjective) sense of logic, detachment, and rationality.

Sensory Processes

Sensory processes reported during the core experience seem to parallel the quality of the thinking processes. Although there are certainly exceptions to this generalization, sensory processes when an individual comes close to death seem best described by the word *clarity*. Just as the mind is lucid, one's sensory acuity tends to be sharp and precise. This is especially so when the individual finds himself out of his body.

There are, of course, limits. For example, with only one doubtful exception, olfactory and gustatory sensations are entirely absent. Bodily sensations, as we have already seen, are also lacking. What remain, obviously, are vision and hearing. These are the senses that appear to continue functioning, at least for a time, during the core experience, though even these, as we shall see, may drop out entirely. Finally, a number of people said that when they were subjectively close to death or dead, they existed, in effect, as "mind only."

When visual and auditory processes appear to be operative, however, they tend to have certain definite qualities:

I could see very clearly, yeh, yeh. I recognized it [her body] as being me. *(25)*

I heard the voice. It was a masculine voice. The voice was [pause] almost like over a megaphone. Amplified but not echoing. Very clear. *(26)*

My ears were very sensitive at that point. . . . Vision also. *(7)*

I heard everything clearly and distinctly. *(29)*

> Seems like everything was clear. Everything was clear. My hearing was clear because everything was quiet; I felt like I could have heard a pin drop. My sight—everything was clear. I could specifically see myself or anything that I was looking at, although I was mostly looking at myself. *(45)*

Sometimes this heightened sensory awareness was not attributed to any particular sense organ per se:

> It was as if my whole body had eyes and ears. I was just so aware of everything. *(23)*

In a few cases, as the last quote implied, there was no impression of sensory-mediated perception. Instead, the mind alone existed. This state of mind awareness was usually associated with the decision-making phase of the experience:

> It seemed like I was up there in space and just my mind was active. No body feeling, just like my brain was up in space. I had nothing but my mind. Weightless, I had nothing. And it seemed like I was being asked a question, mentally, whether I wanted to live or wanted to die. . . . The thought was being given to me to decide on my own whether I wanted to die or to live. It didn't seem like it was a question from anybody. It was just like it was in my own mind and I took it for granted that someone was giving me my own powers to decide for myself. . . . I saw nothing. *(33)*

> *(When you heard the voice, you heard it as a male voice. Did you actually hear the words, or—)* It was like it was *coming into my mind.* It was like I didn't have any hearing or sight or anything. It was like it was being *projected into my mind.* *(79)*

> At the time I was talking to the person, I felt *peaceful* . . . I had a perfectly clear understanding of *what* was going on, except to *who* I was talking with. . . . It's like trying to explain [pause] oh, God. Can you imagine floating, suspended in midair, touching nothing, yet you're aware of things, but there's nothing there to be aware of. You've got no sense of feel or touch, but you've got *thought.* The mind's working, but there's no body. No vision. No vision, but the mind is working. And capable of thought. *(68)*

The common theme running through these passages is one of heightened sensory awareness and mental clarity. When present, the senses are sharpened; when absent, it is the mind itself that remains sharp. Sensory and thinking processes seem to work together to make the near-death experience vivid, distinct and subjectively real.

The Noise—and the Silence

According to Moody, many near-death survivors report that their experience was heralded by an unpleasant sound—whistling wind or a ringing or buzzing in the ears. Our own data, however, offer only a few corroborative instances of this auditory phenomenon. *Most* of our respondents report that either they can recall no such feature or that they simply cannot comment definitively on this point. Altogether only fourteen people reported remembering any unusual noises or sounds and although this feature was more commonly reported by core experiencers than nonexperiencers (ten to four), the variety of the auditory stimuli mentioned and the uncertainty of many of these recollections make their reports of doubtful significance and validity. My tentative conclusion, then, is that this phenomenon is not likely to be so frequent as Moody's remarks suggest.

Nonetheless, this is *not* to say that it *never* occurs. There are a *few* instances in which a respondent did describe an effect that seems to correspond to Moody's specifications:

> The first thing I remember was a tremendous rushing sound, a tremendous [pause] it's very hard to find the right words to describe [it]. The closest thing that I could *possibly* associate it with is, possibly, the sound of a tornado, a tremendously gushing wind, but almost pulling me, and I was being pulled into a narrow point from a wide area . . . it was very high-pitched; it was almost piercing. *(20)*

> It was, like, dull, like, I don't know. It was like I was in a mist. It was like a swish . . . like mist going by. *(90)*

> I felt like I might have had a buzzing in my ears. It was just a "zzzz." *(29)*

> I think I went through a tunnel. I think I went through a tunnel and it *seems* to me that I heard something like a siren. A siren and something that might have been like a high rustle of trees. High wind of trees. *(71)*

Recall of these auditory impressions was not only rare but also, as these passages demonstrate, sometimes tentative. More often, respondents did not merely claim to remember no unusual sounds; instead, they would say something like, "Quite the contrary; it was very quiet."

> Everything was perfectly quiet, the quietest I've ever heard anything. There wasn't a sound. *(48)*

> . . . everything was quiet; I felt like I could have heard a pin drop. *(45)*

> Silence. Clear silence. It was brilliant . . . but there wasn't any sound. It's brilliant, it's clear and it's sharp. *(23)*

> . . . my pain was gone and it was quiet, but it wasn't a morbid quiet, it was a peaceful quiet. *(3)*

Although few people were perfectly explicit on this point, the implication of many of their accounts seems more consistent with this sense of peaceful silence than with auditory discomfort. Still, the fact is that the replies to the question on unusual noises, when specific, tend to fall into these apparently opposite categories. Why should this be so?

A review of our own data and the relevant literature[2] suggests a possible answer. Out-of-body experiences sometimes seem to be signaled by a ringing or buzzing sound. All the above cases come from respondents who also reported having had an out-of-body episode. Thus, the auditory effect, when it does occur, may be primarily a cue that an out-of-body state is about to occur. Once the out-of-body state, or a further stage of the core experience, is *established* in consciousness, however, sensory cues fall away and a profound inner silence is experienced. According to this hypothesis, it is the *total absence* of bodily-based cues that gives rise to the silence (as well as to the sense of extraordinary peace initiating stage I.) Presumably, those who reported awareness only of the silence were recalling this *later*, body-absent, period of their experience. The data here are far from clearcut, however, and this hypothesis needs to be evaluated through further research.

Sense of Body, Time, and Space

During the core experience, one's awareness of his body and of time and space undergo characteristic alterations. For most respondents, body, time, and space simply disappear—or, to put it another way, they are no longer meaningful constructs. In this respect, what we all take for granted in our ordinary state of consciousness may be nonexistent in the state of consciousness associated with (apparent) imminent death.

This generalization, too, has its limits. Sometimes the constructs of body, time, and space do not so much vanish as become radically transformed. In either event, coming close to death almost always drastically affects one's awareness of these constructs, as Table 8 makes clear.

Table 8

Perceptions of Body, Time, and Space
(Core experiencers only)

Body Sense	*No.*	*%*
Heavy	1	2
Normal	0	0
Light	13	27
None	25	51
(Not asked or indeterminate)	(10)	(20)

Time Sense	*No.*	*%*
Speeded up	1	2
Normal	1	2
Extended	3	6
None	32	65
(Not asked or indeterminate)	(12)	(24)

Space Sense	*No.*	*%*
Distorted	1	2
Normal	3	6
Extended	1	2
Infinite	6	12
None	11	22
(Not asked or indeterminate)	(27)	(55)

If, in interpreting this table, we restrict ourselves to the respondents who gave definite replies, we find that 97.4% of core experiencers felt that their bodies were light or absent; 94.6% found their sense of time either expanded or absent; and 81.8% experienced space as either extended, infinite, or absent. The *modal* response for all three constructs is overwhelmingly "absent."

The individual answers to these questions tend mainly to be terse and uninformative. Since they are usually nothing more than a denial of the meaningfulness of body, time, and space as experiential concepts, there appears to be no particular need to cite representative responses. Nevertheless, if only for the sake of thoroughness and consistency, consider these responses:

> Well, it was like [pause] like I didn't have a body! I was [pause] but it was *me.* Not a body, but *me.* You know what I mean? *(24)*

> *(What about your sense of bodily weight. Bodily feeling?)* Nothing. *(Absent?)* There was nothing there. *(68)*

> I couldn't really see anything. I couldn't see myself there either. It was just like my *mind* was there. And no body. . . . *(You said you felt like you had no body, but did you feel that you were* [separate] *from your body in any way? or separated from it?)* Yeah, I think so. I felt more like just a mind moving. I left my body back on the bed. *(99)*

> *(What was your sense of time like?)* My sense of time was way off. Time didn't mean anything. It seemed like time had no meaning. It was just [pause] well, I don't know how to explain it, even. *(Was your sense of space affected?)* Well, yes, due to the fact that it seemed like I was weightless, you know, and I could project myself wherever I wanted. *(51)*

> *(What was your perception of* [time] *like when you were in this state?)* Very bad. I really have no idea of how long this went on. Sometimes, when I think about it, it seems like it was forever. . . . *(How about your sense of space?)* Oh, it was a very open space I was in. Very open. *(No limits to it?)* Not really. *(7)*

> It was like I lost time. . . . I was like—I could go *anywhere. (You weren't bounded the way you normally are?)* No. I was very free. I could go anywhere, do anything. *(64)*

> This is the interesting part . . . it *has* to be out of time and space. It *must* be, because the context of it is that it is just [pause] it can't be

put *into* a time thing. . . . Okay, I can't explain the actual words, "You really blew it this time, Frank"—I couldn't tell you if this was said *before* that whole movie thing or after it. Because, somehow, even though I feel it was at the end, it could have just as well as been at the beginning. In other words, that statement related to the whole thing, before and after. I can't explain it. *(What was your sense of time during this whole experience?)* You couldn't relate to time. *(71)*

. . . I found myself in a space, in a period of time, I would say, where all space and time was negated. *(49)*

The difficulty most people had in dealing with the concepts of body, time, and space from the perspective of their near-death experience strongly reinforces the impression suggested by other data that the near-death experience represents a *distinctive state of consciousness,* in which many ordinary features of perception and cognition are completely transformed or altogether absent. From the standpoint of transpersonal psychology, this state of consciousness could legitimately be called *transpersonal* since it meets the three criteria required for it: transcendence of one's usual ego boundaries and the concepts of time and space. From the standpoint of recent formulations of brain functioning, the near-death experience seems to represent a "frequency domain" where time and space collapse and everything merely "coexists." These are matters to which we shall return when we consider the interpretative problems raised by near-death experiences.

Feelings of Loneliness

In *Life After Life,* Moody comments that many people described to him transient feelings of loneliness as part of their out-of-body experience near death. Although this matter was raised with only about half of our respondents, only about half a dozen indicated that they experienced any such feelings of loneliness. When such feelings were reported, however, they tended to occur in conjunction with either a sense of "drifting through space" without a body or as part of an out-of-body episode, which is consistent with Moody's observations. Moody does go on to state, though, that these feelings of loneliness are brief and are dispelled when an individual gets farther into the experience and encounters a reassuring presence of some kind. Though our number of relevant instances is obviously very small, we again did find some evidence to support Moody's contention:

> *(Did you feel lonely?)* For a while. *(When did that end?)* When I met my grandfather. *(7)*
> *(When you were in that state where it was a total nothing, you said you were drifting through an emptiness. Can you tell me more about what that was like?)* Okay, that was like, like, [pause] like wandering around and not knowing where you're going. Like, like going to a strange city or a strange area and you're trying to *find* something but you don't know where it's at and you just go up and down the street and [pause] and you're looking around and you can't find anyone to ask directions or something like that. *(So you felt you were sort of psychologically lost?)* Yeh. . . . *(Did you feel lonely, by yourself, at first?)* Yeh, I did. Until the voice came in. *(79)*

On the question of loneliness, then, our findings are consistent with Moody's when such instances are reported, but the incidence of such feelings seems to be considerably less than among Moody's informants. In our sample, at least, most tended to deny that they felt lonely, even at the outset of their experience.

Approaching the Threshold

Moody has stated that a few of his respondents indicated that they felt they approached some kind of a limit or border, such as a body of water, a door, a fence, and so forth, which presumably represents a threshold between life and death. When we asked our respondents, we found that the answers distributed themselves as follows:

Table 9

Responses to Question: Did You Ever Feel You Were Approaching Some Kind of Boundary or Threshold—a Point of No Return? (Core experiencers only)

	No.	%
Yes	13	27
No	21	43
Not sure	6	12
Not asked	9	18

Although about a third responded affirmatively, no one said or implied that this experience was accompanied by an appropriate *visual image* corresponding to those reported by Moody.[3] Instead, as the chapter on the decision-making process makes clear, this threshold phenomenon was usually a cognitive affair—an encounter with a presence, a stock-taking of one's life—rather than an imagistic one.[4] Some people did report a gray or hazy mist, which Moody mentions, but this was quite rare and not necessarily associated with a feeling of transition. Thus, the *visual symbols* demarcating a barrier between life and death were not found here, but the *sense* of approaching that threshold was very much in evidence.

Coming Back

The event that terminates the core experience is the return to one's body and (eventually) to ordinary waking consciousness. In agreement with Moody, we found that most people were not able to recall just how they returned to their bodies. Often, as Chapter Four makes clear, the last feature remembered is the decision or the command to return; the return itself is usually a "blank."

In those few cases in which the man or woman was able to recall something of this process, the descriptions tally perfectly with those of Moody's respondents.

For example, one of the features mentioned by Moody is the return with a "jolt." In this connection, when I asked one of our suicide attempters how he felt when he found himself back in his body, he told me:

> The thing I remember most is a *falling* feeling. Like I was coming down really fast and then *hit.* And then I woke up with a *jolt. (99)*

This was not the only case where a jolting sensation was experienced. In some instances, however, a person would feel more than a jolt:

> I wanted to stay where I was. And then suddenly . . . I could hear my daughter and children and I realized I have to [pause], I *have* to, [pause], I have to come back. . . . [She felt a "horrendous pain"] And the strongest thing was that pain—no words can describe it. It was as though I was seeing many, many lightning and thunder storms all at once. . . . It was as if I were being pulled out of a *tremendous vacuum* and, and just being torn to pieces. *(20)*

Whether one is jolted or wrenched back, one somehow, as Moody says, "reunites with his physical body." But how exactly does one accomplish that return? Since most of our respondents blank out at this point—possibly because reentry into one's body is typically associated with the onset of pain—the details of the reunion are almost always lacking. *Almost* always. Here, Moody provides an intriguing clue. He states that in a few instances his respondents maintained that they returned "through the head." One of our core experiencers—but just one—also hinted, almost in passing, at this same perception:

> *(What were you next aware of?)* Oh. It was being—going back to my body. It was . . . I said, "No, I want to live," but that was looking at my body, yeah, and the next thing was just a [snaps fingers] flash; it *seems* like a flash. And I was back in my body. I wouldn't hesitate to say that I think I [pause] I [pause] I entered my body through my head [questioning intonation]. But I don't know *why* that is. *(71)*

To comment further on this point would entail a digression into the parapsychological literature on out-of-body experiences, which will not be undertaken here. Instead the intent is to call attention to an aspect of the reentry phenomenon that may be worth examining more systematically in future research on near-death experiences.

In any event, once the individual has returned, painfully or otherwise, to his physical body, the core experience is over.

Summary of the Principal Stages and Qualitative Aspects of the Core Experience

In view of the massive amount of data, both quantitative and qualitative, which has been presented in this and preceding chapters, it seems best at this point to sum up the major features of the core near-death experience. In doing so, I will write as though I am dealing with one individual case in which all the major stages and aspects of the experience are encountered. It is important to bear in mind that I am delineating a *composite* near-death experience—one suggested by the totality of my cases but which is only approximated even by my richest ones. This prototypical summary creates the risk of some distortion and idealization of the experience, but it has the advantage of enabling the reader to appreciate how all the facets of the core experience might cohere in a single, complete case. (The experience itself was found represented to a variable degree in 48% of our sample.)

The experience begins with a feeling of easeful peace and a sense of well-being, which soon culminates in a sense of overwhelming joy and happiness. This ecstatic tone, although fluctuating in intensity from case to case, tends to persist as a constant emotional ground as other features of the experience begin to unfold. At this point, the person is aware that he feels no pain nor does he have any other bodily sensations. Everything is quiet. These cues may suggest to him that he is either in the process of dying or has already "died."

He may then be aware of a transitory buzzing or a windlike sound, but, in any event, he finds himself looking down on his physical body, as though he were viewing it from some external vantage point. At this time, he finds that he can see and hear perfectly; indeed, his vision and hearing tend to be more acute than usual. He is aware of the actions and conversations taking place in the physical environment, in relation to which he finds himself in the role of a passive, detached spectator. All this seems very real—even quite natural—to him; it does not seem at all like a dream or an hallucination. His mental state is one of clarity and alertness.

At some point, he may find himself in a state of *dual awareness*. While he continues to be able to perceive the physical scene around him, he may also become aware of "another reality" and feel himself being drawn into it. He drifts or is ushered into a dark void or tunnel and feels as though he is floating through it. Although he may feel lonely for a time, the experience here is predominantly peaceful and serene. All is extremely quiet and the individual is aware only of his mind and of the feeling of floating.

All at once, he becomes sensitive to, but does not see, a presence. The presence, who may be heard to speak or who may instead "merely" induce thoughts into the individual's mind, stimulates him to review his life and asks him to decide whether he wants to live or die. This stock-taking may be facilitated by a rapid and vivid visual playback of episodes from the person's life. At this stage, he has no awareness of time or space, and the concepts themselves are meaningless. Neither is he any longer identified with his body. Only the mind is present and it is weighing—logically and rationally—the alternatives that confront him at this threshold separating life from death: to go further into this experience or to return to earthly life. Usually the individual decides to return on the basis, not of his own preference, but on the perceived needs of his loved ones, whom his death would necessarily leave behind. Once the decision is made, the experience tends to be abruptly terminated.

Sometimes, however, the decisional crisis occurs later or is altogether absent, and the individual undergoes further experiences. He may, for example, continue to float through the dark void toward a magnetic and brilliant golden light, from which emanates feelings of love, warmth, and total acceptance. Or he may enter into a "world of light" and preternatural beauty, to be (temporarily) reunited with deceased loved ones before being told, in effect, that it is not yet his time and that he has to return to life.

In any event, whether the individual chooses or is commanded to return to his earthly body and worldly commitments, he does return. Typically, however, he has no recollection *how* he has effected his "reentry," for at this point he tends to lose all awareness. Very occasionally, however, the individual may remember "returning to his body" with a jolt or an agonizing wrenching sensation. He may even suspect that he reenters "through the head."

Afterward, when he is able to recount his experience, he finds that there are simply no words adequate to convey the feelings and quality of awareness he remembers. He may also be or become reticent to discuss it with others, either because he feels no one will really be able to understand it or because he fears he will be disbelieved or ridiculed.

After reading this prototypic account, the reader may find it instructive to review the version originally given by Moody (see page 22). The parallels, and even the similar phrasings, are striking. I want to emphasize that this similarity in prototypic descriptions does not at all stem from any conscious desire on my part to parrot Moody; *it stems chiefly from the (apparent) extraordinary similarity between his findings and mine.* There are, to be sure, some points of difference, having to do with such facts as what Moody calls the "being of light" and the threshold phenomenon. These differences, and others, will be discussed in the appropriate place. But no one reading this who is already familiar with Moody's work can fail to be impressed with the similarities between the findings of these two studies. Insofar as Moody's overall characterization of the core experience is concerned, our own independent data are almost totally congruent with it.

There remain some further parameters which Moody himself was not in a position to examine systematically, one of which is the relationship between certain preconditions and the core experience.

Six

Does It Matter How One (Nearly) Dies?

Does it make a difference *how* one (nearly) dies? One of the chief reasons for undertaking this investigation was to determine if the core experience was independent of the circumstances and motives that brought about a near-death episode. Obviously, if the core experience is invariant over a range of near-death conditions, one would be led to conclude that it is a very robust phenomenon indeed. If, on the other hand, manner of near-death onset is a significant factor in affecting either the likelihood or the form of the experience, it would help us to specify more precisely the conditions under which the basic phenomenon is likely to occur.

Accordingly, our investigation was designed to compare three distinct modes of near-death onset: illness, accident, and suicide attempt. Altogether, in our sample we had fifty-two illness victims, twenty-six accident victims, and twenty-four people who attempted suicide.

Since this section will deal with various comparisons across these groups, it is necessary at the outset to point out that there were several antecedent factors on which these groups differed. Whether any of these factors can be said to undermine the validity of the coming comparisons is an open question, but the evaluation of the data must certainly take them into account.

Before going further, however, I think it best to warn the reader that this chapter will be rather technical. It is necessary to be so because this is, after all, a scientific investigation. In keeping with my narrative stance—which is to present our work in a way that is accessible to the general public—I have tried to keep jargon and statistics to a minimum here, as elsewhere. However, I owe it to my colleagues to present what follows, and so I advise those who may not care to immerse themselves in analyses and statistics simply to skip to page 115, where I deal with my material in qualitative terms.

To continue, some of the differences referred to above have already been indicated. I have, for example, commented on the differences among these groups in respect to the source of referral and incidence of interview refusal (see pages 27–31). In general, illness victims were secured mostly through medical referrals, while suicide cases were drawn largely through self-referrals. Accident victims tended to fall in between. Accident victims were almost always willing to be interviewed, while suicide-attempt victims tended to refuse to be interviewed or else access to them was denied. Illness cases fell between these extremes. There were also significant differences in the average age at which the near-death episode took place. Table 10 presents these data.

Table 10

Mean Age at Time of Incident by Sex and Condition

	Illness	*Accident*	*Suicide*	
Females	52.14 (29)	38.20 (10)	34.61 (18)	44.16 (57)
Males	54.21 (23)	28.06 (16)	29.00 (6)	41.55 (45)
	53.06 (52)	31.96 (26)	33.21 (24)	43.01 (102)

Respondents whose near-death episode resulted from illness were significantly older at the time than both accident victims and suicide attempters who do not differ from one another. The difference between the illness victims and the others is, on average, about twenty years. There are still other, and possibly more critical, differences among these groups which make unqualified comparisons hazardous, but these factors are best discussed in conjunction with the specific comparisons themselves.

We can begin, however, simply by examining the incidence of core experiences as a function of near-death condition. Table 11A gives the breakdown.

Table 11A

Incidence of Core Experience as a Function of Mode of Near-Death Onset

	Illness	*Accident*	*Suicide*	
Core experiencers	29	11	8	48*
Nonexperiencers	23	15	16	54
	52	26	24	102

$\chi^2 = 3.64$ $p \simeq .06$

*For analyses in this section, one person who had two near-death episodes—one involving an illness-related near-death *experience,* the other, a suicide attempt not associated with any experience—has been placed in the suicide category. This reduces the number of core experiencers available for these analyses from forty-nine to forty-eight.

This table discloses a trend suggesting that the indicence of core experiences is greatest in connection with illnesses, followed by accidents and suicide attempts, in that order. The respective percentages are 56% for illnesses, 42% for accidents, and 33% for suicide attempts. Nevertheless, this trend is only marginally significant ($p \cong .06$).

The data presented in Table 11A, however, conceal a complication that must now be dealt with. Table 11B will reveal that the incidence of core experiences across categories is significantly influenced by the sex of the respondent.

Table 11B

Incidence of Core Experiences as a Function of Mode of Near-Death Onset and Sex of Respondent

	Illness		*Accident*		*Suicide*	
	♀	♂	♀	♂	♀	♂
Core Experiencers	21	8	2	9	4	4
Nonexperiencers	8	15	8	7	14	2

Illness versus Accident/Suicide
(Core experiencers only)

	Illness	Accident/Suicide	
Females	21	6	27
Males	8	13	21
	29	19	

$\chi^2 = 6.21$, p <02

Examination of the upper table demonstrates that women are most likely to have core experiences in conjunction with illness, whereas men's tend to occur in cases of accident or suicide. Thus, 72% of all female illness victims have a near-death experience, but the percentage drops to 21% for the accident and suicide-attempt categories combined. Only 35% of the men, on the other hand, have core experiences in conjunction with illness, but 59% have them when they come close to death through accident and suicide attempt. Various considerations enable a chi-square statistical test of this difference to be performed using the figures shown in the table at the bottom of Table 11B.[1] It is apparent that a significant interaction is obtained: 78% of all core experiences among women occur in connection with illness whereas among men, only 38% of core experiences are illness-induced (p <.02).

Thus, it seems clear that although mode of near-death onset is marginally related to the incidence of the experience, sex of respondent is even more strongly related. Among women, illnesses are likely to be associated with a core experience; accidents and suicide attempts, however, seldom lead to one. Among men, the pattern is just the reverse. This gender-related interaction then, needs very much to be borne in mind when considering the frequency data relating core experiences to manner of near-death onset.

The previous analyses were based on a simple dichotomous measure of the core experience, that is, whether it was present (WCEI ≥6) or absent (WCEI <6). A finer analysis is available, however, when the depth of the experience, as measured by the WCEI, is used as a basis for comparing the three types of near-death onset. It will be of interest to see whether the gender-related interaction holds up with this measure. The data are shown in Table 12.

Table 12

Weighted Core Experience Index Means
by Condition and Sex

	Illness	*Accident*	*Suicide*	
Women	8.83 (29)	3.00 (10)	3.22 (18)	6.04 (57)
Men	3.83 (23)	6.75 (16)	8.67 (6)	5.51 (45)
	6.62 (52)	5.31 (26)	4.58 (24)	

Inspection of the column means suggests the same rank order as before (illness >accident >suicide), but the difference here is not significant (F = 1.13, one way ANOVA).[2] The individual cell means again seem to point to the sex X condition interaction and this time the analysis (an unweighted means ANOVA) supports this impression (F = 6.98, with $2/96$ df, p <.005). The interaction term is, in fact, the only significant effect disclosed by this analysis. Thus, we see that the deepest core experiences for women tend to be associated with illness, whereas for men the deepest experiences tend to occur in connection with accidents and suicide attempts.

The results of this analysis, then, are broadly consistent with those of the cruder, dichotomous one presented earlier. Whether one is discussing incidence or depth of the core experience, both analyses suggest (but do not give strong evidence for) the same rank order of conditions: illness >accident >suicide. In both instances, however, the only statistically impressive effect is linked to the gender-related interaction, which shows the same pattern for both incidence and depth.

On the basis of these two analyses alone, what answer can we legitimately give to the question: does it make a difference how we almost die? So far, it would seem that although core experiences occur in connection with all three types of near-death onset, their *likelihood* and *depth* vary depending on a *combination* of one's sex and the manner of nearly dying. If one is a woman, for example, near-death through illness seems to have a high probability of inducing a core experience, but near-death through accident or suicide attempt offers a much lower chance. Exactly the reverse seems to be true for men, of course. Somehow, esthetically speaking, this doesn't seem a very satisfactory outcome, and it certainly wasn't one I had expected. Obviously, merely because an outcome is either "unesthetic" or puzzling is no reason to dismiss it as a fluke, but it does tend to make one look for other factors. I have already commented that respondents in the three categories differed from one another in a number of respects, but none of the previously cited differences bore any marked similarity to the pattern observed here. There was, however, another factor, so far unmentioned, that could, in principle, possibly account for the interaction effect. This is the *near-death rating*—an estimate of how close each respondent actually came to death. Could it be that the perplexing pattern of differences in near-death *experiences* is, in actuality, a function of differences in near-death *ratings*?

Near-Death Ratings as a Possible Factor

The tape recording of each interviewee in our sample was listened to and rated by at least three, and sometimes five, judges, including myself. At the end of each interview, each judge made an estimate of how close that respondent actually came to death, using the rating scale shown in Table 13. These ratings were based mainly on the statements provided by the respondents themselves, but whenever it was available, information from physicians or other medical personnel, or from spouses or friends, or from that person's medical records was also used in arriving at a final estimate. The arithmetical average of these ratings for any one person was taken to constitute that person's near-death rating.

Table 13

Near-Death Rating Scale

The following scale is used to judge how close the respondent came to dying.

Name of respondent ______________________
Name of rater ______________________

0	1	2	3	4
In no real danger of dying.	Serious illness, accident, etc., but *not clear* if individual would have died if condition persisted.	Serious illness, accident, etc.; *probably* would have died if condition persisted.	Obviously close to death; *would* have died if condition persisted.	Resuscitated; probably was clinically dead.

The reliabilities among raters on this estimate ranged from .69 to .86, with both a mean and median correlation of .78. These correlations were highest for accident victims (r = .89), lowest for suicide attempters (r = .65) and intermediate for illness victims (r = .71). Overall, then, the reliabilities among raters proved high enough to provide presumptively dependable estimates of respondents' closeness to death. The weakest category in this respect—the suicide attempters—afforded the lowest interrater reliabilities because many of our respondents never received any medical attention, a state of affairs that obviously would tend to increase the variability of our estimates.

The mean near-death ratings by condition and sex are presented in Table 14.

Table 14

Mean Near-Death Ratings
by Condition and Sex

	Illness	*Accident*	*Suicide*	
Women	3.13 (29)	2.52 (10)	2.18 (18)	2.72
Men	2.94 (23)	2.66 (16)	2.08 (6)	2.73
	3.05	2.61	2.15	

If one compares the pattern of data in this table with that in Table 12 (the core experience data), one observes a distinctly imperfect correspondence. The most striking consistency is that the "condition near-death" rating means follow the same rank order as do the core experience scores (that is, illness >accident >suicide) and the effect here is statistically significant ($p < .001$). It is also true that the individual cell showing the highest average core experience index, namely women/illness, also receives the highest near-death ratings. At this point, however, the correspondences cease. The *critical* pattern, reflecting a possible gender-related interaction, is obviously altogether absent here, a fact confirmed by the obligatory analysis of variance ($F < 1$). From this analysis, it appears as if the near-death rating factor hypothesis does not stand up. Yet there may be *something* to it after all as shown by the parallelisms in condition means.

At this point, it becomes important to know whether there is any overall correlation between depth of near-death experience (that is, WCEI), on the one hand, and closeness to death (that is, near-death ratings), on the other. This information is furnished by Table 15.

Table 15

Correlations between WCEI and Near-Death Ratings by Sex and Condition

	Illness	*Accident*	*Suicide*	
Women	.48* (29)	.36 (10)	.07 (18)	.48**
Men	.24 (23)	.23 (16)	.33 (6)	.13
	.38*	.28	.11	

*p <.01
**p <.001

Table 15 shows that while the overall correlation is positive and statistically significant, its magnitude is distinctly modest. Similarly, while all the individual cell correlations are positive, only one is impressively significant, namely, that based on female illness victims. That cell, containing the largest number of cases, obviously has a disproportionate impact on the significant marginal correlations to which it contributes. This analysis suggests, then, that with the *exception* of female illlness victims, near-death ratings are neither highly nor significantly correlated with depth of near-death experiences.

As a final check on this possible factor, an analysis of covariance[3] was performed using near-death ratings as the covariant. If this factor were responsible for the original gender-related interaction, this effect should be substantially reduced by the covariance analysis. The outcome, however, was that the interaction remained significant at the same level as before (that is, p <.005).

This last result reinforces the conclusions drawn from the previous analysis presented in this section: Although near-death ratings appear to have a modest relationship to core experiences, they cannot in themselves be said to account for the gender-related interaction in these experiences. Whatever the explanation for this curious effect may be, it is not a simple function of a near-death rating factor. Since it appears to be a genuine finding rather than a statistical dependency, we must leave the matter noted but unresolved for now. We shall, however, be forced to reexamine it when we discuss and interpret our findings later in this book.

Mode of Near-Death Onset by Stages of the Core Experience

Another way to appreciate the quantitative differences in the core experience among the three conditions is to compare the conditions in terms of the five-stage model presented earlier. A graph that enables this comparison to be made is shown in Figure 2. (See p. 114.)

It is evident that the form of the three curves is generally similar across the first three stages of the core experience. After that point, however, there is a sharp divergence, with the illness curve continuing substantially higher through the remaining stages, while the accident and suicide curves decline sharply. In fact, it should be noted that *none* of the suicide attempters is found beyond stage III, a fact to which I will return in the next section. Though the graphical representation of these comparative data may suggest that this intercondition difference in the terminal stages of the core experience is of small magnitude, statistical analysis shows that this is not so. Altogether 36.5% of the illness victims reach either stage IV or V in contrast to only 6% of the accident and suicide groups (combined). This is a highly significant effect ($X^2 = 12.30$ with 1 degree of freedom, $p < .0005$).

This finding, of course, is largely consistent with the data presented earlier in suggesting that the core experience is more pronounced for illness victims than it is for accident victims or suicide attempters, with the latter seemingly having, on the average, the least pronounced experiences. This analysis by stages, however, has the advantage of revealing just where the intercondition differences are greatest, namely, in the latter stages of the experience. And here, unlike the earlier analyses where these differences were at best only marginally significant, illness victims are found to be clearly and highly significantly more in evidence. Indeed, their dominance of these stages approaches exclusivity. Since females are disproportionately represented among illness victims, it might be thought that this effect is due largely to them. Although there is a trend in this direction (45% of the female illness victims reach stage IV or V, compared to only 26% of the men), in this case, it is not significant. Thus the intercondition differences in the later stages of the core experience appear to be—possibly because of the relatively small sample size involved—independent of the sex of the respondent.

Figure 2. Percentage of Respondents Reaching Each Stage of the Core Experience, According to Category of Classification

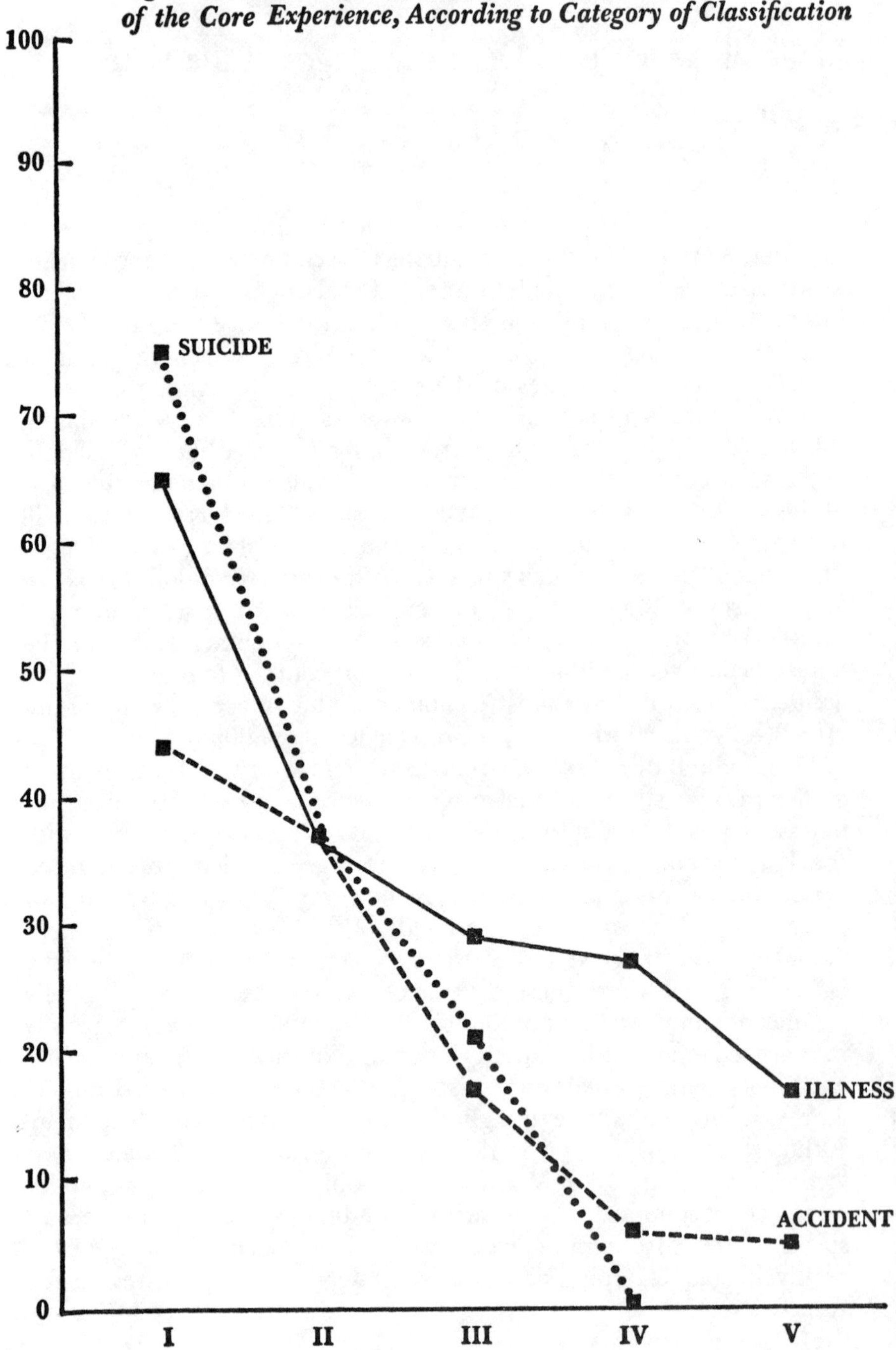

Qualitative Differences Among Conditions

So far I have presented evidence for some important quantitative differences in the incidence and depth of the core experience as a function of how one nearly dies. I have also shown, the last analysis notwithstanding, that the sex of the respondent may interact with the manner of near-death onset to affect the core experience. The graph presented in conjunction with the last analysis, however, suggests as well that there may be noteworthy *qualitative* differences among the conditions—and indeed there are. In this section, I will treat each mode separately in order to bring out these differences more clearly and to set the stage for a final comparison among the three modes of near-death onset.

Illness. All of the features delineated in the prototypical summary of the core experience (see pages 101–103) are to be found in the cases of near-death episodes brought about by illness. As Figure 2 reveals, illness cases represent, on the average, the most complete core experiences, and for this reason I propose to use them as a baseline against which to compare near-death experiences induced by accident or suicide attempt. For the purpose of these comparisons, the prototypical summary may itself be taken as indicative of the qualitative features of the core experience associated with illness. We need to ask, then, in what qualitative ways do experiences triggered by accident or suicide attempt deviate from this standard account?

Accident. Figure 2 has already furnished evidence that the later stages of the core experience tend to be rare (but not absent!) among accident victims. What Figure 2 does not disclose, however, is the *presence* of one feature which appears to be more frequent and more detailed in the experiences of accident victims than it is for either of the other categories. This feature is the *panoramic life review,* already discussed (see page 67). This phenomenon was reported by 55% of the accident victims, compared to only 16% of respondents in the two other categories combined. The small sample sizes involved and the ad hoc nature of the comparison suggests that we interpret this difference ($X^2 = 4.76$, $p < .05$) with considerable tentativeness. Nevertheless, the fact that it is consistent with the little systematic research we have on this point,[4] and the fact that the life review features seemed to be more vivid and extensive when they were triggered by an accidental near-death, incline me to regard it as a facet of the core experience that is *accentuated* by this way of nearly dying. Furthermore, although our sample size here is so small that one cannot legitimately make anything of it, my impression is that near-fatal falls or near-drowning episodes may be even more likely to induce a panoramic life review than are auto accidents. Further research with larger sample sizes in these categories is necessary before this hypothesis can be evaluated.

Something of the detail and vividness of this phenomenon is suggested by several accounts. One of my respondents miraculously survived a fall from an airplane when, at 3,500 feet, his parachute failed to open. In the course of his fall, he had the following experience:

> It's like a picture runs in front of your eyes, like from the time you can remember up to the time, you know, what was happening [that is, the present] . . . it seems like pictures of your life just flow in front of your eyes, the things you used to do when you were small and stuff: stupid things. Like, you see your parents' faces—it was everything. And things that I didn't remember that I did. Things that I couldn't remember now, but I remember two years ago or something. It all came back to me, like it refreshed my mind of everything I used to do when I was little. Like, I used to ask my friends, "Remember this, remember that?" And I say, "Wow, that was a long time ago, I don't even remember that." Everything refreshed my mind of everything. *(Was it a positive feeling?)* It was a nice feeling, it was a real nice feeling. [He then talks about very early childhood memories, when he was four or five years old]. I'll tell you, it was like the bad parts were almost cut out. It was good memories. It was like a picture, it was like a movie camera running across your eyes. In a matter of a second or two. Just boom, boom [snaps his fingers]! It was clear as day, clear as day. Very fast and you can see everything. It was, like, wow, like someone was feeding a computer or something, like putting a computer in your head and programming you, that's what it was like. *(Any sense of sequence?)* It was like starting in the beginning and working its way up to the end, what was happening. Like clockwise, just going clockwise. One right after another. *(70)*

A victim of an automobile accident also experienced this playback phenomenon, but in her case it occurred *after* her accident. Specifically, it took place while she was being operated on, when she thought she was "dead."

> I had a very—it seems as though it was fast—I had a span of my life, just, just everything that happened. Highlights of various very happy points in my life coming up and going backwards [she

> mentions various memories] all fanned in front of me. Very rapidly. Just kind of went past me like a million and one thoughts. [She mentions some: the first time she visited a certain location, her first sports car, and so on] *(Was it like seeing a movie in some way?)* Very fast movie. Just highlights, just certain things. *(Were they mostly positive things?)* Very—everything was positive there. *(How did you relate to these images? Were you involved in them emotionally or were you just a spectator?)* I was a spectator, I was just watching them. *(62)*

Finally, the words of a young man who nearly drowned in a boating accident speak to the same experience:

> . . . it was amazing, I could see in the back of my head an array, just innumerable array of thoughts, memories, things I had dreamt, just in general, thoughts and recollections of the past, just raced in front of me, in less than thirty seconds. All these things about my mother and grandmother and my brothers and these dreams I've had. It felt like this frame, millions of frames, just flashed through. *(What was this like?)* It was thoughts and images of people. And a lot of thoughts just raced [snaps his fingers several times] in split seconds. I had my eyes closed under water, but I could still see these images. *(Was it when you were feeling euphoric that these images and thoughts came to you?)* Exactly, exactly. *(Could you describe these memories in terms of their emotional quality?)* A lot of them were very emotional. [He describes his memory of his mother's death two years before and his recollection of various things that involved them both. He also thought that he might be reunited with his mother. He also thought of his grandmother, to whom he is very close and who was still alive.] I saw her [his grandmother] as not wanting me to die. I saw what my drowning would do to her and I think that was what drove me to always try to resurface. There were thoughts of my brother. Just [pause] silly things—just nitpicking things I thought I'd forgotten. Just [snaps his fingers] kept on racing through. It was like I was going through this memory and, ah, ah, like my whole memory was retaping. I was in reverse. And everything was just backtracking so I could go over it again like a tape recorder. But it wasn't in sequence. *(Like a jumble?)* Yes, yes. *(66)*

Still other accident victims, whose remarks were quoted earlier in other contexts, observed that this phenomenon was "like watching a movie" of one's life which "only seems to take a second" or that it was like a tape that one could selectively edit. There is variation in response to the question of sequence: Some people feel their life is (rapidly) playing in reverse, others say it is roughly chronological, and still others imply that there was no clear sense of sequence. If we remember that the core experience tends to take place in an atemporal context, it is possible to understand these apparent nonuniformities as stemming from the attempt to place a "holographic experience" into a time frame typical of ordinary waking consciousness. What stands out in these accounts is the *tremendous rate* at which these images seem to be processed—experienced as millions of "frames" within seconds. Even allowing for exaggeration, such rates must utterly confound one's sense of time.

These panoramic life reviews represent the one qualitative feature that appears to distinguish accident victims from other near-death survivors, but only in that they may be more common and more vivid in such cases. Just why this phenomenon should be so pronounced among accident victims is a question we shall return to in Chapter Eleven. In all other qualitative respects, the patterning of the core experience in accident victims conforms to the prototypical summary.

Suicide attempt. The most striking feature of suicide-related near-death experiences that sets them apart from the prototypical episode is the total absence of stages IV and V. Among our suicide attempters, no one reported the tunnel phenomenon as such, or saw a brilliant but comforting light, or encountered a presence, or was temporarily reunited with loved ones who had died, or entered into a transcendent world of preternatural beauty. Instead, as Figure 2 makes clear, the suicide-related core experience tends to be truncated, aborted, damped down. It does begin with a feeling of relief or peace and continues with a sense of bodily detachment to the same degree as other categories. But it tends to end, if it gets this far at all, with a feeling of confused drifting in a dark or murky void—a sort of "twilight zone."[5] In any event, our respondents' accounts strongly suggest that the suicide-related near-death experience does not reach completion; instead, it tends simply to fade out *before* the transcendent elements characteristic of the core experience make their appearance. When one also takes into account the fact (see Table 11A, Page 106) that the highest proportion of nonrecall (67%) is found among suicide attempters, it is tempting to conclude that suicide-induced death experiences tend to be different both in form and frequency from those occurring in conjunction with either illness or accident.

Closer examination of this matter, however, will show that such a conclusion is by no means established by the data I have referred to. Instead, I will argue, the interpretation of our suicide-related data has to contend with a number of problematic factors.

At this point, I need only remind the reader that our sample of suicide attempters is by no means comparable to our other respondents, if only on the grounds of self-selection and source of referral. As a group, they also differ from illness and accident victims in a number of additional ways. The effect of each of these differences, singly or combined, would seem to reduce the likelihood of undergoing a complete core experience.

First of all, all but two of our suicide attempters used drugs or drugs and alcohol in their effort to kill themselves. This means that, as a group, their near-death episode was very much more likely to be contaminated by these substances than our other respondents. Since it has already been shown that near-death experiences are negatively correlated with drug-related conditions,[6] it could be that this common mode of suicide attempt either interferes with the unfolding of the core experience or its recall, or both. It has also been suggested[7] that some of the specific drugs often used by our suicide attempters (for example Valium) could induce a state of retrograde amnesia and thus block recall.[8] Consistent with this argument is the fact that the two individuals who attempted suicide in nondrug related ways (either through hanging or drowning) as well as the young man who was accidentally knocked unconscious while on his way to commit suicide by jumping, all had deep experiences. The number of cases here is obviously too small to be more than suggestive, but they are congruent with Rosen's findings, referred to earlier, describing the experiences of individuals who survive suicide leaps. Thus, the totality of evidence (our own and others') and informed medical opinion on this point inclines me to believe that it may be *mainly drug-related* suicide attempts that tend either to lead to aborted core experiences or that interfere with their unfolding or recall. The study of a large sample of nondrug-induced suicide attempts that bring the individual close to death is clearly necessary to clarify this issue.

Even if the mode of suicide attempt proves not to be a significant factor, there are still other intercondition differences that could account for the low incidence of core experiences and the form these experiences take among our suicide attempters. For example, it will be recalled that our near-death ratings indicate that, on the average, suicide attempters had the lowest scores here by a statistically significant margin (see Table 14). Although the correlations between near-death ratings and near-death experiences were not very high (see Table 15), the truncated range of the near-death ratings themselves and the *relative* unreliability of these ratings render unjustified any inclination to dismiss closeness to death as a possible factor. In my judgment, at least, intercondition differences on this variable are *probably* responsible for at least some of the difference between conditions in regard to the frequency and form of the core experience itself.

A third factor of conceivable relevance here has to do with the psychiatric state of our suicide attempters. Though by no means true of everyone in this condition, quite a few of the suicide attempters had obviously suffered or, in some cases, were suffering still from a variety of problems requiring some sort of psychiatric or therapeutic intervention. A fair number of men and women in this category had either received psychiatric help or were in treatment at the time of our interview; still others appeared to be in need of such help. Because no systematic information along these lines was gathered in this study, it is, of course, not possible to make any legitimate comparisons among conditions in this respect. Still, I think I would be remiss if I did not offer my own *opinion* here that, based on my impressionistic observations only, the suicide attempters, as a group, did appear to be substantially more afflicted by psychiatric problems than our other respondents. Such a conclusion, at any rate, would hardly be surprising given the fact of *how* they happened to come close to death. The relevance of this conclusion—if it is valid—is that there has been some evidence offered[9] that the likelihood of having a peak or mystical experience (which I am assuming bears a fairly close relation to the core experience) is correlated with indices of "mental health." If this is so, then perhaps some of the intercondition differences in the core experience can be ascribed to this factor. Again, to settle the point, we need a study specificially designed to gather the necessary information.

For all these reasons, I believe the only conclusion warranted by our interview materials with suicide attempters is that our data are inconclusive. If we could somehow control all of the possibly implicated factors, either through sampling or statistically, it *might be* found that the suicide-related core experience is indistinguishable in its essential features from naturally occuring ones. Certainly none of our data can be taken as precluding this possibility, and transcendent experiences induced by suicide attempts may well yet be found.

At the same time—and I wish to emphasize this point—it must be borne in mind that our data on suicide-related near-death experiences *are* very weak in transcendent elements. For whatever reasons, few suicide attempters can recall any profound experiences when they were close to death and most recall nothing at all. Although *why* this is so cannot be resolved at this point, *the fact itself cannot and should not simply be dismissed for all that.* Despite all the possible factors and qualifications, it may, of course, also be that subsequent research will demonstrate that there is "something different" about the experience of dying when induced by a suicide attempt—at least in some cases. There is even a hint in some of our own data, to be presented in a moment, that suicide victims can expect that their experience on dying will *not* conform to the Moody pattern.

All this is simply to give both sides of the issue a fair treatment. On one hand, we do not yet know whether suicide-related near-death episodes preclude transcendent experiences; on the other hand, just because we cannot take our data at face value here does not mean that the face value interpretation won't one day be upheld.

In any event, merely because the evidence is inconclusive with regard to the invariance or null hypothesis (that is, that the core experience is *not* a function of the mode of near-death onset) should not be taken to mean that we cannot learn from them. The interviews from suicide attempters are, in fact, sometimes as fully absorbing as those from other respondents and are very much worth quoting. In order to acquire a more concrete sense of the qualitative aspects of suicide-related experiences, it will be helpful to present excerpts from two of our most extensive cases. Doing so will also suggest the subtle ways in which the suicide-induced experience *may* prove different from core experiences triggered by illness or accident.

I have already mentioned that suicide attempters seem never to penetrate further than a murky darkness. In one case, a young man who had attempted to hang himself found himself in a completely black space. In an excerpt already quoted (see page 46) he describes seeing himself from a dual perspective: He sees his hanging physical body and he *also* sees himself walking into this black space. This kind of "double" vision is of course unusual, but the entrance into the dark region seems typical of stage III phenomena.

Before losing consciousness, however, something else happened that isn't usual: He heard a voice but it was a *female* voice. And it was from no one in the room.

> While I was tying the noose, I kept hearing a voice. It was a lady's voice, I would say a middle-aged woman's voice, maybe in her forties, but it was kind of low-pitched and it kept saying, "Go ahead, go ahead," telling me, "It's all right, you'll be okay, go ahead." . . . The sound of that voice I can remember perfectly. And it's no one I've ever heard before, at least no one I can remember hearing. It was real soothing. Like I said, it was an older lady. . . . When I heard the voice, it sounded like it was coming from behind me, but it sounded like it was coming out of the back of my head, *not* from in back of me. I looked around to see if anyone was there; no one was there. It was comforting, it was convincing. . . . So I tied the noose and jumped off the chair *(100)*.

Again, we encounter familiar elements, and, again, with a difference. It is, as we know, not rare to hear a voice, but this experience is one of only two in my entire collection of cases in which a voice speaks while the respondent is conscious. Similarly, it is the only instance in which the voice encourages an individual to attempt to kill himself.[10] It also was reported *prior to* the core experience itself. Finally, the voice is identified as a woman. In cases where a gender has been linked to a voice before, it has always been a *male* voice. Context, message, timing, and gender all serve to make this "voice effect" unique in our sample.

Because the number of core experiencers among failed suicides is so small, there is no one case that can be said to be representative of the group as a whole. So rather than quoting brief excerpts from several interviews, I think it will prove most useful to focus on our fullest case. I believe this can be justified on the grounds that if one wishes to examine the qualitative aspects of different modes of nearly dying, then the richest cases can be taken to provide the most instructive basis for a comparative analysis. In making this comparison, however, it must be remembered that, at least among instances of attempted suicide, rich cases are by no means typical.

A young man tried to kill himself by taking an assortment of pills—Librium, Demerol, Valium, Dilantin. As a result of this ingestion, he remained unconscious for four days. He remembers finding himself in a "gray area":

> The only thing that I can remember about this is just *grayness.* Like I was in gray water or something. I couldn't really see anything. I couldn't see myself there, either. It was just like my *mind* was there. And no body.

While he was in this state, he felt good:

> Normally, I'm a very anxious, a very nervous person—a lot of fears and things like that. And during this, all the fear was gone. I had no fear whatsoever. Almost an adventurous feeling. Excitement. *(Did you want to stay in that condition?)* Yeah. It was a very good feeling.

He also was aware of music:

> I also heard music—different music. *(Tell me what it was like.)* It was usually like classical music; I like classical music. It wasn't *exactly* the music I've heard, but it was along that line. *(Do you recall how the music made you feel?)* It made me *relaxed.* The fears went away when I listened to it. Again, the feeling of *hope,* that there's something *better* somewhere else.

He also reported that everything, including the music, sounded "hollow and metallic—echoey" and that these acoustical sensations were associated with the watery grayness. He felt the grayness going *through* him, filling him and this felt good to him. After a while, he became aware of a voice:

> I think [it was] a woman's voice, but [pause] I didn't recognize the voice. *(Do you recall now what she said to you?)* No. I just remember that it was a *soothing* voice. I kind of remember that with the grayness—her voice kind of *calling,* my moving toward it. *(This was a friendly voice, a reassuring voice in some way?)* Yeah. *(. . . and you felt [drawn] to it?)* Yeah. Right. Like that was the place to be.

He tried to get to where the voice was:

> It seemed like I kept trying to *get* to where the voice was, but something was *holding* me back. I *know* I *wanted* to be there; I knew once I was there everything would be fine. I was sure of this. No question about it. But there was still like something holding me back from getting there.

During his experience he had seen images of people he knew. These people somehow seemed to represent the possibility of a good life; they seemed to care. He described this as "like playing back a recording of my life." The issue was joined:

> It felt like the woman's was *stronger.* I wanted to get there but there was just some part of me that wanted to [pause] go back with these images.

And resolved:

> The thing I remember most is a *falling* feeling. Like I was coming down really fast and then *hit.* And then I woke up with a *jolt.*

And afterward:

> When I woke up, the first thing I thought was Oh, God. Thank you. I made it, and I was *extremely* happy. [He had been severely depressed before his suicide attempt.] I was just sitting there *thinking* about it and I felt this—I don't know—*warmth* filling my body. I was very happy, very excited, but then [pause] it was *more* than contented—it was rapture, I guess. But I couldn't explain it to anybody at the time. It was just beyond words. *(99)*

These passages sum up the essential features of his experience. In the course of his interview, he also indicated that although he never clearly saw his physical body on the bed, he did have a sense of bodily detachment and felt he had no weight at all—he was just "pure mind." Neither did he have any sense of time. When he momentarily returned to body consciousness (before drifting back into the grayness), he found the sensory world greatly enhanced—the colors were clearer and more vibrant. The only thing scary about his experience was his fear (which was eventually vanquished) of returning to his body. His experience "in the grayness" was decidedly pleasant and, judging from its immediate aftereffect, very positive and powerful in its emotional impact.

This time we can observe many features in common with the core experience: drifting throught a vast space, feeling good, hearing music and a comforting voice, hearing sounds magnified, seeing a series of flashbacks of one's life, and so forth. But again there are some features that are not commonly found: the environmental vastness is gray (only one other person reported this coloration) rather than dark or black; it has a watery aspect—a unique descriptor among our respondents; it is a *woman's* voice that is heard (the previous case—also suicide-related, obviously—the only other one in the sample where one is reported) rather than a man's. The basic pattern *is* unmistakably similar, and yet there do appear to be some differences. The sheer lack of fully detailed suicide-induced experiences, however, must leave this issue open: There is a *hint* of qualitative difference here *within* the familiar pattern, but more evidence is badly needed before any clarification can be achieved.

Before leaving this case, I want to reiterate one general finding; in my sample, no one who had attempted suicide and who had some recall of the experience reported that it was predominantly unpleasant.[11] The only possible exception is that a few people did describe some unsettling hallucinatory images, but these appear to have been qualitatively different from the feeling-tone of the core experience itself. Certainly, no one felt that he was either in or was on his way to hell. The "worst" perception was a feeling of wandering or drifting in a vast space, but this was a perception that was also reported by respondents who came close to death in other ways. This is not to say that suicide attempts *never* lead to unpleasant experiences, only that there is no strong evidence for this proposition among our cases. Indeed, the affective tone seems to be preponderantly pleasant—at least as much as a limited core experience can afford.

Of course, we are speaking here of *failed* suicide attempts. Our data, obviously, are based solely on the testimony of those who survive the act of self-destruction. But what of those who succeed? Is there any way we can say anything about the experience of those whose suicidal intention is realized?

At first it would appear that there is no way this question can be addressed without entering the world of purported mediums, spiritualists, and clairvoyants, whose allegations about the fate of suicides can obviously not be evaluated scientifically. It turns out, however, that there is another route to this destination, and it is one to which we have access through the accounts of our own respondents.

Just as Moody reports for his interviewees, so some of our respondents who came close to death in ways unrelated to suicide felt that their near-death experiences vouchsafed them certain insights about the probable fate of successful suicides. In most cases, the statements or implications from these respondents seemed to be derived from the "content" of their own experiences rather than from preexisting beliefs or religious views, although this matter is difficult to establish with certainty. Obviously, these assertions cannot be tested any more than can those coming from mediums, but they nevertheless do constitute findings of considerable interest. The fact that—as will be shown—near-death survivors *independently* tend to take very much the same (doubtful) view of the wisdom of suicide seems to me a most significant finding and one that is unlikely to be a coincidence. Again, this is not to imply that near-death survivors have necessarily been privy to a "higher knowledge" regarding suicides; it is to say, however, that their comments on this point, because of their consistency, deserve to be evaluated as part of our effort to determine whether the suicidally induced near-death experience does have certain unique features that differentiate it from the prototypic model.

The woman who had perhaps the deepest experience of all (WCEI = 24) said on this point:

> I know one thing: I think that anyone who tries to commit suicide [pause] that suicide is a devastating thing. *(Why is that?)* Because it's like killing a plant or a flower before it's full-grown or before it's served its purpose. It is not [pause] it is not [pause] not right. Something that is very overt to me is that I know that there are murders and that there are deaths in war and there are accidents and so on, but I think that this is by far a karmic experience. I think that to take one's *own* life, I think that it's very, very [pause] very, very [pause] a terrible thing to do. *(Is this something that you've come to as a result of your experience?)* Yes. Yes. Very, very strongly. *(Not as a result of anything you've read elsewhere?)* No. No. No. *(What do you think a person would experience if he or she tried to commit suicide? And came close to death, as you did?)* I have *no* idea. I mean, the only

thing that I can think and comprehend is that [pause] to try and understand reincarnation. That somehow, instead of evolving, you would regress. *(20)*

A woman who nearly died as a result of an automobile crash and had a deep experience reflected:

> I would never take my life. *(Why not?)* Because if it were self-induced, I don't think I would get the state that I want . . . [it would be] sheer panic and it would be [pause] where I would just die—without any of the effects of peace. *(You mean, it would be like blackness?)* Yes. . . . Right. It would be aloneness, blackness—not cared for. *(So it would be a negative experience, an opposite kind of experience from—)* I think it would be a *fearful* experience. I don't see any goodness in it at all. If it comes about naturally, then it would be okay. *(64)*

These same sentiments were voiced by the woman who, on nearly dying, received paranormal information about her newly delivered baby and felt she had to come back:

> I feel very strongly that it has to be a natural death, in other words, suicide or something that you're going to try to alter it, I would never consider because I think the reaction would be bad. In other words, this feeling that I had that told me I had to come back, had some kind of control over what I was going to do. So I feel that there is something that controls what we do. And if we want to change it in any way, we are not allowed to do that. If I were going to say, "Now I'm going to do it," it wouldn't work. I don't think it would be allowed. I'd fear the consequences, that would be the only fear I'd have. *(Do you think that if someone took his or her own life, would it be the same experience as yours or would it be different?)* It would be very different. That's what I was trying to say. I feel it would not be good; it would be just the opposite. I just have the feeling that they would be punished. *(25)*

Sometimes a feeling of doubt is only vaguely implied rather than clearly articulated, as in the case of a young man who nearly died in an automobile crash:

> Personally, I think at this point that death is an *up* state from our life, that it's a better state. Suicide—I don't know *what* to think about suicide . . . that's a tricky one. I don't know about that. *(71)*

Another idea expressed by some respondents is that even a successful suicide leaves the individual in the same state his suicide was an attempt to end. Another accident victim put it this way:

> When I was twenty, I was put in a mental instiution because I tried to commit suicide. But see, I hadn't got to the place where I am now [at thirty-two]. Two years ago I came to the place where I realized that it's ridiculous to commit suicide because you're just going to have to go through the same kinds of things, the same pain, 'cause that's what brings you to your progression. *(77)*

The same theme—that of the unavoidability of one's destiny—was also sounded by a former suicide victim (who had, incidentally, no core experience):

> I think probably if you commit suicide, you'll probably have the same problems as you do now. If you die a natural death, then everything will be okay. I think if you die a natural death, there's something good waiting for you—I don't know what it is. I also think that to die a natural death you have to accomplish something here, whatever that something is, small or large or whatever. . . . If you kill yourself, you can't accomplish that thing, so, therefore, you're going to be punished. *(87)*

This whole issue of the violation of one's "life plan" through suicide and its potentially negative consequences was summed up dramatically for the young man who hit his head on a rock while intent on making a suicidal leap. He is describing a portion of a conversation (in thought) he had, while unconscious, with what he took to be God.

> . . . then He said, "Do you want to go back?" And He goes, "Finish your life on earth." And I go, "No, I want to die." And He goes, "You are breaking my laws to commit suicide. You'll not be with me in *heaven* if you die." And I say, "What will happen?" And then after this I started coming to. So I don't know what happened after this. So I think that God was trying to tell me that if I commit suicide I'm going to go to hell, you know? So, I'm not going to think about suicide anymore [laughs nervously]. *(79)*

These opinions from near-death survivors, if taken seriously, obviously put the suicidally induced death in a different, more negative, category from those deaths that occur naturally. These respondents suggest that even if the suicidal death experience is not unpleasant, the ultimate consequences will be.

The evidence bearing on the qualitative aspects of suicide-induced near-death experiences is clearly complex, but it leads to a number of interesting conclusions. First, the descriptions from our suicide attempters tend, relative to other categories, to be weakest in core experience elements: No recall is greatest here, and when experiences do occur, they do not penetrate beyond stage III. Second, there are, however, a number of factors that make the suicide attempters noncomparable to other respondents in such a way as to lower the likelihood of the occurrence of core experiences. Third, therefore, the data on qualitive aspects of suicide-related experiences are ambiguous and inconclusive. Fourth, nevertheless, some evidence suggests that certain transcendent features associated with the core experience may occur in suicide attempts, although these features may manifest themselves in distinctive ways. Fifth, when recall exists, the suicide-related death experience tends to be reported as predominantly pleasant. Sixth, the death experiences of a number of nonsuicide attempters (and the opinion of one suicide attempter) all implied that the consequences of a successful suicidal act were likely to be unpleasant.

Can these six conclusions themselves be interpreted to point to a general conclusion? Probably not—our data are simply too fragmentary and contaminated to warrant any single conclusion. However, I want to offer my own opinion here in the hope that it might lead to further research that will eliminate some of the ambiguity surrounding this issue. If the offending factors could be eliminated or sufficiently reduced to provide comparability among conditions, I would speculate that the *initial* stages of the core experience would be invariant across modes of near-death onset. I would also hypothesize, however, that there would come a point when the suicide-induced experience would begin to show a distinctive qualitative difference. This would, according to my view, come during the decision-making phase, when there would be no hint of transcendent glory (for example, the light phenomenon) or of immediate reunion with loved ones. If an individual were to pass *beyond* this stage, either because he was, in some sense, "permitted to" or because his suicide attempt was successful, I am tempted to believe that the admonitions expressed at the end of this section might prove warranted. This aspect of my opinion can, of course, never be evaluated scientifically, but its other components *could* be in an adequately designed study. If such an investigation were undertaken, it might not only be able to resolve some of the empirical issues, but it would also furnish us with a more extensive basis from which to extrapolate the later stages of the core experience when it is induced by suicide.

Summary of Near-Death Experiences as a Function of the Manner of Near-Death

In this chapter, I have presented our findings relating the way in which a person almost dies to his experience of dying. The underlying question here has been whether the core experience is *independent* of the way a person nearly dies.

In general, we found evidence that elements of the core experience were found in all three categories, but that both the incidence and depth of this experience tended to be greatest for illness victims, moderate for accident victims, and weakest for suicide-attempt victims. Analysis of the core experience by stages was also, on the whole, consistent with this rank order. Nevertheless, this main effect was strongly qualified by a gender-related interaction that indicated that core experiences associated with illness occurred disproportionately among women, whereas men were more likely to have had them in conjunction with accidents and suicide attempts. An examination of a possible factor for this interaction effect, namely, closeness to death, proved unavailing, even though it was shown that there was a modest positive overall correlation between near-death ratings and (depth of) near-death experiences. Qualitative analyses of core experiences associated with different modes of near-death onset suggested that there might be some noteworthy intercondition differences. Thus, accident victims appeared somewhat more likely to experience the life review phenomenon than did respondents in the other two conditions, though this effect was not a strong one statistically. Suicide victims were never found to have had experiences beyond stage III, and the experiences they did report tended to depart somewhat from the prototypical pattern, though the number of cases here proved too few to legitimize any conclusions. A speculative, but partially researchable, opinion was offered concerning possible differences between the suicide-induced core experience and those brought about by nonintentional means.

The complexity of our data, together with some of its inconclusiveness, makes any straightforward conclusion difficult to state, but my own reading of the evidence leads me to this tentative formulation: In general, I believe that the *form* of the core experience *is* invariant across modes of near-death onset, but that its *frequency* may well vary as a function of both manner of nearly dying and sex of respondent and their interaction. In short, the experience of dying itself appears to be much the same, no matter how one comes close to death. Some qualifications are also necessary. I believe, and not only on the basis of my own data, that accidental near-deaths are more likely to elicit a panoramic life review than are other modes of nearly dying. I am also inclined to believe that the experience of dying through an ultimately unsuccessful suicide attempt is likely to conform to the basic pattern only until the decision-making phase is reached, at which time it may diverge. More research is needed on this point, however, before *any* conclusion may safely be drawn.[12] Thus, this statement of my beliefs is based more on hunch than on fact. Taken as a whole, however, I believe our data are *broadly* consistent with the claim that the *experience of dying*—that is, the core experience—is largely independent of the means that bring it about.

A question we have still to ask, however, is whether this experience is independent of other antecedent factors that might be assumed to influence it—factors such as a respondent's prior degree of religiousness or his familiarity with other accounts of near-death experiences.

SEVEN
A Search for Correlates

In the last chapter I considered one possible *situational* determinant of the core experience, namely, the means of near-death onset. Here, however, I want to examine the role of several personal factors that could significantly shape the experience. In all, there are four categories of such antecedent variables: (1) demographic characteristics, (2) religious denominational affiliation, (3) religiousness, and (4) prior knowledge of near-death experience research findings.

Demographic characteristics. Is the core experience correlated with any of the usual demographic categories, such as social class, marital status, race, etc.? Table 16 provides the answer.

Table 16

A Demographic Comparison Between Core Experiencers and Nonexperiencers

Social Class Index	*Core Experiencers*		*Nonexperiencers*	
	No.	*%*	*No.*	*%*
1	1	2	1	2
2	11	22	10	21
3	35	71	34	68
4	2	4	8	10
Race				
White	48	98	49	92
Black	1	2	4	8
Marital Status				
Married	23	47	24	45
Single	16	33	16	31
Separated/Divorced	7	14	9	16
Widowed	3	6	4	8
Age at interview	42.12		43.83	
Age at incident	34.06		41.28	

Even a casual inspection of this table is sufficient to reveal that the demographic features are quite similar for core experiencers and nonexperiencers. The only hint of a significant difference is found on the age at incident factor ($t = 2.09$, $p < .05$), which shows that core experiencers tended to be somewhat younger at the time of their near-death episode. It should be noted, however, that this difference is due in part to a couple of extreme cases. Overall, the two groups are notable for their demographic similarity rather than for any disparity.

Religious denominational affiliation. Does religious affiliation relate to the likelihood of having a core experience? The relevant data are presented in Table 17.

Table 17

Religious Denomination Data for Core Experiencers and Nonexperiencers

Religious Denomination	*Core Experiencers*		*Nonexperiencers*	
	No.	*%*	*No.*	*%*
Catholic	17	35	20	38
Protestant	13	27	21	40
None*	15	31	6	11
Other*	2	4	1	2
Agnostic/Atheist	2	4	5	9

*These two categories include at least four Jews.

Again, we see that except for the None category (which was quite heterogeneous), which is larger for core experiencers, denominational affiliation seems unrelated to the likelihood of core experiences. The experience itself is obviously not disproportionately associated with either of the two major divisions of Christian belief nor is it limited to believers.

Religiousness. One of the obvious questions left unanswered by Moody's research had to do with the role of religiousness (as distinct from religious affiliation) as a factor influencing the core experience. Since most people can be assumed to be at least nominally religious, perhaps the crisis of apparent imminent death triggers a set of religious images that represent a *visual* projection of an individual's religious belief system and expectations. If this is so, we might expect that this effect would be more likely or stronger for those who were more religious. In any event, it seems important to determine whether degree of religiousness is in any way correlated with the core experience. In the extreme case, if we were to find that this kind of experience tended to occur predominantly among people with a religious orientation, our interpretation of this phenomenon would be radically affected.

To assess this matter of religiousness, the interviewer asked a series of questions at the end of the interview designed to elicit some information about the respondent's religious beliefs prior to and after his near-death episode. The subject of each specific question and its category of fixed alternatives may be found in Table 18.

Table 18

Religious Beliefs and Preferences Form

Religious	Before	After
Very	____	____
Quite	____	____
Fairly	____	____
Not too	____	____
Not at all	____	____

Belief in God	Before	After
Absolute	____	____
Strong	____	____
Fairly Strong	____	____
Not too Strong	____	____
Not at all	____	____

Life after death	Before	After
Completely convinced	____	____
Strongly convinced	____	____
Tended to believe	____	____
Not sure	____	____
Tended to doubt	____	____
Not at all	____	____

Belief in Heaven	Before	After
Yes	____	____
No	____	____

Belief in Hell	Before	After
Yes	____	____
No	____	____

On the basis of a respondent's answers to these questions, a straightforward *religiousness index* could be calculated as follows: The first two items were scored 0–4, with a score of 4 denoting the strongest religious orientation; the third item was scored 0–5, and the last two 0–1. The scores were then summed for each respondent, with the combined score on the heaven and hell items being multiplied by a factor of two so as to make these two items, taken together, roughly comparable in weight to the remaining three. Thus, the range of possible scores on the religiousness index was 0–17. Since we were interested here in a respondent's religiousness *prior to* his incident, only the answers given to the "before" portion of each question were used to comprise the religiousness index.

To determine the relationship between religiousness and the death experience, it was merely necessary to correlate the religiousness index with the weighted core experience index (WCEI).

This correlation was −.04, demonstrating that there was essentially no relationship between these two factors. In short, how religious one felt himself to be before one's near-death episode (as measured by our religiousness index) was not related to the depth of one's near-death experience.[1]

Two other analyses using religiousness index measures supported this initial finding.

Close inspection of the data suggested that the items dealing with belief in heaven or hell were particularly likely to have been interpreted in heterogeneous ways and thus might be only weakly related to the overall religiousness index. Accordingly, a new index was constructed which eliminated the scores for the heaven and hell items. Using this "purified" religiousness index, the correlation with the WCEI was still negligible: −.01.

Finally, it was necessary to determine whether the likelihood (as distinct from the depth) of a core experience was associated with religiousness. For this purpose, a biserial correlation[2] was calculated between the presence or absence of the core experience and the "purified" religiousness index. This correlation, too, was consistent with the others: −.08.

Thus, the conclusion from these several analyses seems to be that religiousness is *unrelated* either to the likelihood or to the depth of a core experience. Of course, our measure of religiousness is crude and it may be that a more precise and sophisticated index would have evinced some relationship, but I tend to doubt it. My impression during the course of this investigation, and before I came to analyze these data, was that a respondent's religiousness, like other personal and demographic factors, just didn't seem to make much of a difference. It certainly wasn't my judgment that this experience was more likely to be vouchsafed to persons who had been religious all along. Rather, it seems—and this is consistent with what other investigators[3] have found or suggested—that religiousness as such mainly affects the *interpretation* of a near-death experience, not its occurrence. In short, those who are religious seem to be more inclined to give a religious construction to their experience, but they are not necessarily more likely to have one in the first place.

Both our data and my impressions formed in the process of carrying out this study incline me toward the conclusion that religiousness as such plays no determinative role in the core near-death experience. Whether it can be regarded as an *outcome* of passing through the core experience, however, is altogether another question and one we shall come to consider soon in another context.

Prior knowledge of near-death phenomena. Raymond Moody had one advantage in conducting his research on near-death experiences: He did it during a time when few people were knowledgeable about such phenomena. We, however, had to collect ours in the wake not only of Moody's best seller (more than three million copies sold in the United States alone), but also in the aftermath of the publicity surrounding Elisabeth Kübler-Ross and the attention given to near-death phenomena in such popular periodicals as the *The National Enquirer* and *Reader's Digest.* And, as if this weren't bad enough (from a methodological standpoint), during the last few months of our interviewing, a popular pseudodocumentary film, *Beyond and Back,* dealing with near-death experiences, was featured around Connecticut. In view of all the information about near-death experiences that was potentially available to our respondents, one has to wonder to what extent the accounts we were given were influenced or contaminated by prior knowledge of these phenomena.

To assess this factor, we routinely asked each respondent at the end of the interview a series of questions concerned with the degree of his prior (and subsequent) knowledge of near-death experiences. These questions dealt with such matters as books and articles on the subject, television programs or movies concerned with it, conversations with others about such experiences, and so forth. In this way, we were able to evaluate prior knowledge of near-death experiences as a possible contaminant of our findings.

Altogether, we found that twenty-eight respondents, or 28.6% of all respondents questioned about these matters,[4] had some degree of prior knowledge concerning near-death phenomena. Of these persons only a handful had read Moody's books; most had heard about them through reading popular accounts. An additional twenty-five persons, or 25.5%, had learned something about these experiences after their own near-death incident had taken place.

The question of interest to us, however, is whether prior knowledge of near-death experiences is in any way *associated* with the recall of core experience elements. Specifically, are core experiencers overrepresented among those who were already familiar with Moody-type phenomena at the time of their near-death episode? The answer is found in Table 19.

Table 19

Knowledge of Near-Death Experiences

	Core Experiencers	Nonexperiencers	
Some prior knowledge	9	19	28
Subsequent knowledge only	18	7	25
No knowledge	20	25	45
	47	51	98

$X^2 = 9.04$ ($p < .02$)

This table reveals a significant difference between core experiencers and nonexperiencers in prior knowledge, but it is a difference *opposite* to that which a contamination factor would have led us to anticipate. In brief, what this table shows is that among core experiencers, only 19% had prior knowledge of such experiences compared to 37% of nonexperiencers.[5] It would appear, therefore, that prior knowledge of this kind of experience not only does not increase the likelihood of reportage of a core experience, but, if anything, decreases it.[6] *Afterward,* however, core experiencers are more likely to acquire knowledge relating to their own experience (38% to 14%). The percentage of respondents remaining ignorant of these phenomena is about the same for both categories (43% for core experiencers, 49% for nonexperiencers).

Even though core experiencers are definitely not overrepresented among those with prior knowledge of such phenomena, it is still possible that such knowledge would nevertheless influence the reports of those core experiencers who *were* knowledgeable. If this were the case, we might expect, for example, that the knowledgeable core experiencers would have higher WCEI scores. Accordingly, I compared knowledgeable and unknowledgeable core experiencers on this index, classifying them on the basis of any knowledge whatsoever (that is, before or afterward). The means for knowledgeable and unknowledgeable respondents were 11.11 and 10.93 respectively—a nonsignificant difference. This result shows that knowledge of Moody-type phenomena does *not* affect the depth of the core experience reported. Knowledgeable and uninformed respondents recount substantially the same experience.

Clearly, there is no support for the fear that knowledge of near-death experiences significantly influences, distorts, or contaminates the reporting of such incidents. Additional evidence will later support this assertion.

Summary of Findings on Personal Antecedents

The data presented in this chapter can be summarized in one word: negative. The likelihood or depth of a core experience does not seem to be significantly related to standard demographic measures, religious affiliation, religiousness, or prior knowledge of near-death phenomena—except possibly in the last instance, where it may be related negatively. Recalling the last chapter, it may also be noted here that the form of the core experience appears to be largely independent of the manner of nearly dying as well. Thus, the thrust of all the evidence presented in these last two chapters points to one conclusion: At least with respect to the possible antecedents examined here, the core experience appears to be a remarkably *robust* phenomenon, cutting across a variety of situational, individual, and demographic factors. Aside from the sheer physical conditions necessary to induce it, it appears to have no obvious determinants or correlates. Clearly, since systematic work on this question has just begun, it is too early to draw any hard conclusions. It will be interesting, however, to see whether subsequent research is able to establish that there are some antecedent factors that are significantly related to the likelihood or depth of the core experience.

EIGHT

Aftereffects I: Personality and Value Changes

It takes no imagination to conceive that the effects of coming close to death leave a profound impact. Someone who survives a core experience usually reports that the experience was so striking and so singular that the passage of time does nothing to dim its vividness. Nevertheless, such experiences, however dramatic, rarely remain "just" memories; they tend to exert a powerful effect on a person's motivations, values, and conduct. Even those respondents—whom we have so far largely neglected except in passing—who recall nothing while they were close to death, report that afterward their lives were altered in significant and drastic ways by the sheer fact of approaching death. As this and the next chapter will amply demonstrate, however one chooses to interpret near-death phenomena, they are unquestionably real in their effects.

In making this investigation, one of our aims was to document systematically the nature of these changes, which previously had been mainly reported in anecdotal form. We wanted to know whether certain changes could be attributed chiefly to the fact of having come close to death *per se,* quite apart from whether or not a Moody-type experience occurred. And, of course, we wanted to determine whether some changes seemed to depend on having had a certain kind of experience while close to death.

To this end, we asked a series of open-ended questions near the close of our interviews that were concerned with whether the person had noticed any changes in himself that he felt he could trace to his near-death episode. After putting the question in its most general form, we moved on to the following specifics: (1) attitude toward life; (2) religious beliefs; (3) fear of death; and (4) conception of death. In some interviews, but not systematically, we asked about value changes, if any. We also had a series of fixed alternative questions designed to determine whether changes in religious convictions had taken place. Finally, we sought to find out whether individuals had attempted to acquire information about near-death experiences.

Here I will present our findings on the personal and value changes that occur after coming close to death. Then I will move on to discuss changes in religious orientation and attitude toward death. As before, I will offer a combination of quantitative data and interview excerpts to underscore the fact that the consequences of nearly dying are fully as absorbing and provocative as the event itself.

Personal and Value Changes

Men and women who have survived near-death episodes—whether or not they had a core experience at the time—usually report that their brush with death has changed them in some way and, as a rule, has affected them *positively*. The kind of changes described tend to fall into certain specific categories, and on the whole appear to be similar for experiencers and nonexperiencers alike. Table 20 presents a summary of the reported changes that have to do mainly with personal and value orientations. I have grouped these data somewhat arbitrarily into four principal categories: (1) attitude toward life; (2) sense of personal renewal; (3) personality changes; and (4) attitude toward others.

Table 20

Personal and Value Changes for Core Experiencers and Nonexperiencers

	Core Experiencers		*Nonexperiencers*	
Change	*No.*	*%*	*No.*	*%**
Increased appreciation of life	18	37	14	29
Live life to full extent	3	6	4	8
More afraid of life	2	4	2	4
Renewed sense of purpose	12	24	6	12
Sense of rebirth	2	4	2	4
Stronger person	10	20	4	8
More curious	1	2	1	2
More depressed	1	2	1	2
More death-oriented	1	2	1	2
More loving, caring	12	24	10	20
More compassionate	5	10	5	10
More tolerant	4	8	3	6
More patient, understanding	5	10	0	0
Want to help others	4	8	0	0
Miscellaneous	20	41	14	29
Not ascertained	0	0	4	—

*Percentages for nonexperiencers exclude "not ascertained" respondents ents

Several points need to be made concerning the data in Table 20. First, it should be noted that most of the changes reported, as remarked earlier, are positive. This is a particularly noteworthy effect when one remembers that many of these respondents experienced severe pain or psychological dislocation for a long period following their near-death episode. Despite such factors, however, many respondents report that the incident left them with a more positive outlook on life and with stronger feelings of self-worth. Second, the basic pattern of changes is similar for both experiencers and nonexperiencers—parallels outweigh contrasts here, at least for these kinds of changes. Finally, where quantitative differences do occur, they tend to favor core experiencers, but the differences in most cases are suggestive rather than striking. One weak quantitative difference not shown in the table is a tendency for experiencers more often to report multiple changes (more than three changes spontaneously mentioned), but this effect is not significant. ($X^2 = 3.33$, $.05 < p < .10$).

Despite the overall quantitative similarity between experiencers and nonexperiencers reflected in Table 20, it remains my personal conviction that there are some important *qualitative* differences between the two groups that are not obvious from the table. This impression is based mainly on my personal experience in interviewing respondents and on my reactions to hearing the taped interviews of all respondents. I must say emphatically that I have no hard data with which to support this contention, but perhaps by the time the reader finishes this section on aftereffects he may also be able to detect this quality from reviewing the interview excerpts.

For what it is worth, then, I believe that core experiencers are more likely to show a heightened sense of what I can only vaguely call "spiritual awareness" and this quality seems to pervade the other changes that they report. They also seem, more often, to radiate a certain serenity or peace or acceptance of life. The dangers of subjective error in assessing such intangible qualities are very great, indeed, and I do not want to make too much of them here. Yet I think I would be remiss to omit mention of this altogether. Perhaps subsequent research could buttress these impressions by approaching the matter more systematically. In any event, in what follows we must be content to allow the respondents from both categories merely to speak for themselves.

Attitude Toward Life

One common sentiment expressed by near-death survivors was a heightened appreciation of life, especially of the world of nature and of other people.

A female suicide-attempt victim commented:

> [Something] that I don't know quite how to put into words is a greater appreciation of people, things, places, particularly beautiful things and beautiful places and nice things that happen. They seem more vivid; they seem to mean more. . . . I think the whole thing has made me more aware of life and more curious about it. *(82)*

A woman who survived a high fever during which time she felt that God spoke to her said:

> I thoroughly enjoy life. Every day of it. As far as dying, if I were to die tomorrow that wouldn't bother me. But there is more of a thrill to life, each day of living . . . there is an inner feeling that life is terrific, great, fantastic—even on down days. *(26)*

One man who came close to death as a result of contracting cerebral malaria while in Africa, and whose near-death experience did *not* conform as a whole to the Moody pattern, reflected:

> One should consider [being alive] fantastic. [Life] is an absolute miracle. *(49)*

The woman who nearly died of a ruptured appendix said emphatically:

> I'll tell you one thing. I have no fear of letting people know how I feel about them now. The ones I really care about. I used to be very standoffish. I remember two or three years ago [that is, after her near-death experience] telling my brother how much I loved him. You know? And, uh, he was really amazed. It was an unspoken kind of thing that we had. But [I had to] tell him. I let him know. I let him know . . . now, I have a real sense of beauty.

> Before, you'd be out in the summertime, and there'd be things that you'd take for granted. I no longer do that. I sit now and I [pause] watch just nature. Natural things. You know, beauty. *(30)*

A woman who was nearly killed by an automobile explosion but who had no recall whatever for any experience at the time or afterward told me:

> My priorities have definitely changed. [After the accident] my parents arrived from Colorado. My father is a very wealthy man and I know that when he got the phone call from my sister saying, "She's not going to make it; the next phone call you get, she'll be dead," my mother reported to me that he smashed his hand through a window or something like that. I just sort of realized that he would have given up his entire amount of money for me to live. Not that I was that overly concerned with money, but it suddenly made me realize that nothing is important unless you have people around you that you love. . . . Now I feel that I *feel* more for people. Just a greater concern for living and how to make people appreciate of their surroundings, or something like that. I just feel that I have a greater appreciation of being here. *(58)*

A woman who had suffered a number of near-death crises owing to an unusual respiratory condition, and who, during one of them, heard a voice, which she took to be God's, assuring her that she would "suffer but the kingdom of heaven will be yours," clearly articulated the view that life is a precious gift:

> Well, I appreciate things more. And I should tell people I love them more than I do. Life is precious. And it is a gift of God. Every day I've got is a gift. *(15)*

A former racing car driver who had a stage V experience following an accident at a track one night, summed it up this way:

> I would say I appreciate life more because I realize that when it's your time to go, they'll let you go, but when it's not your time to go, possibly the Man Upstairs, in my own thinking, let me see what was beyond, but told me I had more work to do here and come back. *(73)*

Finally, let me quote a little more generously from an interview with a respondent who nearly died from a severe automobile crash, and who had a deep core experience while in a coma. Her comments really epitomize the feelings expressed thus far:

> [Afterward] I enjoyed being with the people more. And I enjoyed just the outdoors. Nature. And *trees* budding. I *still* have a thing for spring. And it was where everything started coming alive. And I *enjoyed* it. *(Do you* [still] *feel some of these same feelings?)* Oh, yeah. Spring is my most favorite time of the year. Just to see everything bursting out—it is just beautiful! The green is beautiful. And snow. I love snow. Because I think it's beautiful. . . . And a spring day like today really makes me happy. To see the buds on the trees and the green grass. It really makes me happy. *(Did you always feel like this or was there something that was accentuated because of the experience?)* I think—I think I *noticed* it more [afterward]. I think that before—before, I used to take spring for granted. But I have the feeling that I'm *looking* more and more—and seeing life. It's really nice. *(Do other people pick up on this? Your children?)* Oh, yes. They can't wait for spring. I think I passed this down to them. *(64)*

One corollary to the enhanced appreciation of life and other people is a decreased emphasis on money and material things generally. This view was explicit in the comments of a number of respondents, including some of the individuals just quoted.

From the same woman:

> I value people more. I don't think I value worldly goods that much. *(64)*

A young man who had been involved in a serious automobile accident, which had triggered a deep near-death experience, found that he developed an:

> . . . awareness that something more was going on in life than just the physical part of it. . . . It was just a total awareness of not just the material and how much we can buy—in the way of cars and stuff, or food or anything. There's more than just consuming life. There's a point where you have to *give* to it and that's real important. And there was an awareness at that point that I had to give more of myself *out* of life. That awareness has come to me. *(71)*

The woman quoted earlier who said that she realized how unimportant money was if you didn't have people around to love, went on to elaborate:

> Well, I think I used to be much more concerned with how the restaurant is doing, how well we did in one day, and blah-blah-blah. Now I feel that I *feel* more for people. *(58)*

Finally, the woman who had the highest WCEI score commented in passing:

> And I feel totally different about home, house—material things. They're so unimportant to me. *(This is a change from how you felt before?)* Yes. Yes. *(20)*

Another theme that seems related to an enhanced appreciation of life focuses on an increased appreciation of solitude. In some cases this may be related to the long recovery period following many near-death incidents, but the desire for intervals of quiet reflection seems to persist beyond the recuperation time.

The young man who had an out-of-body experience in conjunction with his fever-induced near-death episode, one of some half-dozen who reported on solitude, told me that where he formerly would habitually seek out the company of his friends, now:

> I enjoy my solitude a lot more, I enjoy being alone. I've learned to respect my time alone and get something out of it. Life is very valuable and yourself, myself, I'm very valuable too. *(45)*

The young man quoted a moment ago who observed that there was more to life than it's physical, materialistic side, also said:

> From that accident, I've become more of a loner person. You know, I used to be at race tracks [he, too, was a former racing car driver] with ten thousand people around me, in the stands and everything. And at this point in my life [a few years later], it's just the total opposite of it in that I spend more time reflecting, walking on beaches, and things of this nature. [He then goes on to describe one typical instance when, while walking on a beach, he was led to some important insights on the impermanence of things and the nature of eternity.] *(71)*

Implicit, if not stated, in many of these accounts are certain individual value changes which the respondent feels can be attributed to the near-death episode itself or its secondary effects. Again and again, allusions to the same values recur: love, compassion, giving and, more rarely, knowledge-seeking. Although the following quotations could be cited with equal usefulness in some of the sections to follow, it is, I think, helpful to introduce them here by way of summing up the essence of the life changes that, to a large extent, underlie the excerpts already given.

I had just asked the previous respondent whether he felt the information disclosed to him during his near-death experience had been "given" to him for a reason. His response was unequivocal:

> Oh, definitely. Definitely. . . . Somehow we have a more important *mission* while we're here. Okay. That's it. We have a more important mission in our lives than just the material end of it in trying just to get material gains. There are more important things. It showed me the spiritual side in that, basically that—it is important, I guess. That's all I can say. That [pause] that [pause] that *love* is important and that *every human being* on the earth is just as equal to each other. They're all the same. It sort of brought that aspect out in my life. I don't know. It's something I wasn't too aware of before. Before I had a lot more prejudice. *(71)*

Another man who had had a profound near-death experience as a result of a diving accident tried to articulate what values deriving from his experience had become important for him to actualize in his own life.

> *Love.* Not necessarily romantic love from a woman or a man. Love. Fulfilling yourself with that love by—by *giving.* As much as by getting. Which are two separate things. And, not really *thinking,* but just in the way of recognizing that—that we're all in the same boat and we all have weaknesses and we all have strengths, and to help is where it's at. Those three things, I'm telling you, are the way of *being* that I spoke about, that I came back here and I gained. The way of being was, like, those three things. *(77)*

Finally, let me quote at length from a woman who had been badly injured in an automobile crash. Although I interviewed her a year and a half after her accident, she was not yet recovered and spoke with difficulty. She had had no conscious Moody-type experience. Indeed, though she had never read Moody's books, what she had heard about such purported experiences had left her feeling extremely skeptical. Shortly after the interview began, she reflected on what her experience had taught her:

> In my opinion, there are two things in life which keep a person going, or, I should say, which are important. To me, they are the most important things. And that is *love* and *knowledge.* And what I

experienced when I was in intensive care, not only once but several times, when I went out of my consciousness, was a closeness of another human being—the love I was treated with from everybody, including the doctors and including the nurses and most of all, my family, my kids, my children. And I think a lot of people who are very religious or so will say they more or less experienced God, whatever God *I* believe in, right? And love was one of the things I felt [when] I was closer to them. I got more of it than others. And I could *give* more of it, too. I felt very much loved and I felt that I loved everybody. I did not only tell one time that I loved my doctor and I still feel that way because they [pause] they gave me life back again. I think that this is worthwhile, to love somebody, because life is the most precious thing. And I think you don't realize that before you actually almost die. . . . [And] the more knowledge you have the better you will understand why certain things have to be this way and why I have—for an example, a friend who was in, well, he was on a dying list, too. And he never believed in doctors, in nurses, or anything like that. And he is *still* ill, and this is over a year now and he's still ill, very ill. And [pause] I think that's very important that you *know* that certain people love you and care for you. You've got to *know* that; that's a little knowledge. You have to know that certain people love you and not only certain people but *most* people love other people. . . . There may be some people, and one hears about it, that they live in hatred, but I think they don't have the knowledge that it is *so important to love* and to understand what life is all about because I think that's the main thing—that's what it's all about. . . .

I asked her if she had felt that way before her accident:

I did, but I did not feel as strong as I do now. The accident, as bad as it was and as much as I suffered and as much as I will probably never be exactly the same as I was before, but mentally I think I grew. I grew a lot. I learned the value of life more than I did before and I gained actually by this experience. It's very important to me. That itself makes life worthwhile for me, to go on and do whatever is in store for me, you know, and to live to the full extent. *(54)*

As we shall see, the feelings, sentiments, and values characteristic of the passages cited in this section dominate and pervade the other aftereffects yet to be described. Indeed, it is important to remember that, like the core experience itself, the various changes reported here and in the following pages are best understood as all of a piece; the separate sections focus on individual aspects of this totality and are justified only on the grounds of narrative convenience, not fidelity to the changes *as experienced.* The sections to follow, then, reflect different angles from which to review the totality of these aftereffects. Consider, first, the sense of renewed purpose that often animates the lives of near-death survivors, and then the insight emphasized in the last passage—the importance of the search for knowledge.

Personal Renewal and the Search for Purpose

Persons who survive a near-death episode sometimes assert that afterward they felt a sense of rebirth:

> I felt like I was a new person. I felt I finally had a sense of direction. *(30)*

> I found it to be like a rebirth, an awakening. *(7)*

> Well, I *realized* then that I had been *given* a second chance. *(24)*

Almost always, however, there is an implied or explicit sense that one has been spared *for a reason*—that one has been given a renewal of life for a purpose. This sense that one's life is meant to fulfill some objective is fairly common, as Table 20 reveals, and is found with or without a conscious sense of rebirth.

The woman I last quoted, who appears to have been clinically dead for nearly three minutes as a result of a heart attack, later amplified her comment on her sense of having been given a second chance:

> I *knew* that I had a second chance at life and that God had given it to me. . . . I think at the time I thought it was because he wanted me to raise my children. As I get older, and I hope a little wiser, I have a feeling that each one of us has a *little* something to do, to pass on, that God wants us to do. It may not even register in our minds and it may even be very insignificant. But it *definitely* is part of what God wants us to do. And I feel that that's what I *have* to do. He gave me my chance, because *I* have to *do* something. *(24)*

Another woman who nearly died during childbirth said:

> I thought of it since it happened that God must have let me go

> back—must have said, "Go back, there's something more for you to do." I was worried about my husband and my son; I wanted to get back to them. *(29)*

Just like the woman first quoted here, however, this respondent, as we shall learn in a moment, also came later to feel that her "life's task" encompassed more than taking care of her family.

The young man who stumbled on a rock while intent on suicide reflected on the possible reasons he was "spared" in this way:

> I keep thinking about my girl friend and my future daughter. And I think my daughter will do something very important. That she'll do something for the world or maybe she'll find a cure for cancer. And if I would have died, I'd have had no daughter! So something very important is coming from my existence. It might not be my generation. But—it might be my *kids. (So you think that you were spared for a reason?)* Yeah. I think there is a *reason* for my being on earth. *(79)*

Sometimes it seems that the sheer improbability of one's having survived a dangerous near-death incident is sufficient reason—albeit subjective—to infer a purpose to one's life. This kind of view is nowhere better exemplified than in the reflections of the respondent who quite miraculously survived a parachute leap from 3,500 feet when his chute failed to open:

> *(Did you think that you were spared in some way?)* Let me ask you that. Let me ask you that. All right, out of all the orange groves that were there, there's a row here of all orange trees, right [diagramming the physical layout of the orchard into which he fell]? Then there's an irrigation ditch with water in it. Then another row of oranges, then *another* row of oranges, then an irrigation ditch, and I mean, this went on for acres and acres of land. Out of all those orange groves and trees and water there was one irrigation ditch that broke down that morning and all the water went out of it and there was only about three or four inches in it and the guy that owns it said that it has never been that low since they dug the irrigation ditch out. Now you take this: I was going to jump out of the door—my instructor told me to—but I said, "No, I want to make one more jump under the wing off to the side." Now, the timing was right. If I jumped where I was supposed to jump, I wouldn't have landed where I did. But, I mean, out of all the ditches and trees and everything that was there, I landed—they measured it—exactly a foot from the top of

> the bank and slid down. If there was water in there, I would have drowned. I dunno, it was as if something just [pause] guided [trails off] . . . I'm just saying, in my opinion, I don't feel it was just luck, really. I feel that someone wanted me around for something. *(70)*

This sense of purpose is usually only vaguely apprehended. Typically, it is in the nature of an inference, rather than a given of the experience. Most (though not all, as case *79,* above, shows) people, when asked what they feel this purpose is, find that they cannot clearly articulate it—it is something to be discovered in the course of seeking it.

Nevertheless, this sense of renewed purpose seems sometimes to manifest itself initially as a motivational force that both energizes a respondent's life and alters its direction. This kind of change is found in both experiencers and nonexperiencers alike. The woman quoted earlier, who nearly died in childbirth, found that her life acquired a very definite aim:

> I have suffered from depression. And there were times when I felt, gee, there wasn't really anything to live for. You know, just very depressed. This [experience] started a whole different life style for me. After this experience, I decided, you know, I'm wasting my life by sitting here feeling sorry for myself and do something. So I went back to school, got my high school diploma and a year ago decided that I was going on to nursing school. . . . And it was really strange because when I was in high school teaching and nursing were the last things I wanted to do. *(Do you attribute these changes to this experience?)* My whole life definitely was—I was going nowhere. Then, all of a sudden, I decided, this was foolish. I've only got this one life and why not do something with it? Which is probably why I decided to go into nursing, because I feel that it is a very rewarding career to help people. I feel a whole lot better about myself. That I am a person who can do something in my life. *(29)*

Sometimes the change, galvanized by a near-death episode, leads a person away from a helping profession in order to concentrate on actualizing his own inner potentials and talents. The young man who nearly died of a high fever observed:

> It [his experience] made me give up a profession I've had for seven years [as a pulmonary technologist]. I think I started putting a little more value after that experience on my own life. At one time I was easily stepped on . . . but all in all I think I'm a little

more concerned about *my* life, what I want to get out of my life, for me, and me alone. Not in a selfish manner, but, I look at that time as being when I died, I was alone, and I had nobody else around me and it was like the same feeling I have now, that what I have to do in my life has gotta be for me, because when everyone else has gone, if all my loved ones leave me, I'm still going to be me myself and there is more in life for me to do. [He then describes some of the new things he's done or has contemplated doing: He has learned how to renovate houses; he has moved away from home; he has started to write a book; he has started a program of physical conditioning; he has embarked on a regular meditational practice; he has made plans to travel, and so forth.] What makes me happy is, if the experience I had was a death, then I should be very happy that I've been given another chance to live and I should be able to live that life to the utmost. *(45)*

When, a few months after my interview with him, I endeavored to reach him by phone, I found that he had left the state and was traveling in California.

Sometimes a near-death episode seems to engender *both* personal growth *and* a career change, as in the case of the following woman, who was badly injured in an automobile accident but who had no core experience:

(Did your coming close to death change you in any way?) Dramatic. Dramatic. That's all I can say. It's like somebody had taken a meat cleaver, a big, fat, strong, sharp meat cleaver. The shit went over there. What's important came *clearly* into focus. It was once I realized what a close call that was, it was really an extremely profound experience, a magnificent growing experience. At the time of the accident, it just happened that I was not in a very good frame of mind—at the time, I didn't care whether I was alive or dead. I just as soon had been dead. I was really, in retrospect, very depressed, unhappy about my life and whatnot. And had thought many times, "Wouldn't it be nice if my car just went off the cliff and that was the end of it?" But never had acted on it. But then when I realized—I guess in the intensive care unit—solely what had happened and how close I'd come, I was very, very glad to be alive. Just enormously glad. . . . Right after the accident, I remember feeling much more alive than I ever had for years. I wanted to live more, I wanted to live. I realized that I had been wasting my life. . . . And it was a real turning point in my life. [She goes on to discuss how she entered into therapy, went back to school and eventually changed her occupation from that of a

secretary to a vocational counselor, a job she finds much more satisfying because of the contact it affords with people.] *(61)*

Occasionally, this increased tendency to live life more fully and purposively is intensified by the conviction (which may be realistic) that one's life could be cut short. The victim of an automobile accident is aware that, because of the injuries she sustained, she may, in fact, not have more than ten years to live:

> It [her near-death episode] changed my philosophy in life. From being a kind of passive person to a more assertive person. It made me look at things differently. . . . I became restless. I wanted to do everything at once. That's the only negative thing. Now I want to travel. It's got to be now. I want to go back to school. [She has, in fact, enrolled in a graduate program.] It's got to be now. I want my doctorate. It's got to be now. I don't have much longer. *(62)*

More rarely, and particularly for people who have had very deep experiences, this sense of purpose manifests itself in still a different way—as a desire to learn more about the significance of the experience and to find a way to live in accord with the values (see page 139) it seems to inculcate or strengthen. Sometimes I had the feeling that this was what a person was *attempting* to say but didn't quite know how to put it. Again, the possibility of overinterpretation here on my part cannot be discounted. Perhaps the clearest statement of this kind of knowledge-seeking came from the woman who had the highest WCEI score:

> . . . I think that my greatest desire is to develop greater cosmic consciousness, greater awareness. And I feel more and more all the time in myself what I call "centering"—being in *here* and being able to look out at things that I used to find disturbing or upsetting or would be concerned about, now are so unimportant. And I feel that I'm being drawn closer to something meaningful. And I have such a *hunger* to teach or to tell someone about it or to make them aware of it. . . . I feel that I'm *going* somewhere. I feel that I'm *reaching* something . . . [and] in the past eight months, I've been meeting people who are asking the same questions I am; it's like I'm being attracted to those with similar vibrations or wavelengths. [She then mentions several books she has sought out to learn more about this subject.] *(20)*

Although it is rarely so intensely felt, this desire for further knowledge of near-death experiences and their implications is found among many survivors, but it is particularly strong for core experiencers. At the same time, the behavior patterns here are not always similar, even among core experiencers, who are sometimes more inclined than others to *avoid* exposing themselves to this kind of knowledge. Table 21 will clarify these apparent inconsistencies. The question here was whether, subsequent to a near-death episode, a respondent either sought out or avoided material dealing with the subject of near-death experiences.

Table 21

Near-Death Experience Information-Seeking or Avoidance Subsequent to a Near-Death Episode

	Core Experiencers	Nonexperiencers	
Subsequent information sought	19	11	30
Subsequent information avoided	9	0	9
All other categories	19	40	59
	47	51	98*

$\chi^2 = 18.48, p < .001$

*Not ascertained for four respondents

What the data seem to suggest is that material on near-death experiences is, motivationally speaking, more important to core experiencers. They, as a group, are more likely *either* to seek out *or* to avoid knowledge of this subject (indeed, avoiders come exclusively from core experiencers). Thus, this information seems more highly charged—positively or negatively—for core experiencers. Nonexperiencers show a much lower level of interest. These differences, incidentally, are independent of the incident-interview interval; they are just as strong for people interviewed within two years of their incident as for those whose near-death episode occurred years earlier.

Confining ourselves to core experiencers, then, we need to ask: What underlies the patterns of knowledge-seeking or knowledge-avoidance? Most knowledge seekers have straightforward and understandable motives, claiming either that they wished to learn more about such experiences (for example, how common they were, how their own experiences compared to others, and so forth) or they were anxious to put to rest any fears that they might have just "imagined it" or that they were "crazy" or "off-the-wall." Almost invariably, people with such motivations found that reliable information on this score (usually Moody's first book or an excerpt from it) answered many of their questions and erased any lingering doubts. For several, reading Moody's book proved, as might be expected, a great relief.

What about avoiders? Although there was one core experiencer who said she was unable to read Moody's book because it bothered her ("It was too close"), this was not the usual reason mentioned. In most cases, where an indication was given, the reason generally had to do with the person's desire to retain his memory of the experience in an undistorted form. Such people didn't wish to read of similar experiences lest their own become somehow contaminated. Such avoidance, then, was a way of remaining maximally faithful to one's own experience. A typical expression of these sentiments was the following:

> *(Did you ever read Moody's book,* [Life After Life]*?)* No. I never read that *on purpose.* I thought that it would bias my—my discussions about my own experience. *(77)*

Thus, it appears that the patterns of information seeking and avoidance are not so contradictory as might have been thought. Instead, they point to a common and high valuation of the experience, about which either more knowledge is sought or knowledge is avoided *in order* to keep one's memory of it intact.

All the material presented in this section suggests that, for many respondents, the near-death episode is a pivotal one in their lives, leading to diverse manifestations of a heightened sense of purpose. Although this sense of purpose is usually vague and seldom articulated clearly, it is nevertheless obvious that coming close to death is in itself often sufficient to jar a person into a mode of life that is richer in experience, stronger in feeling, and deeper in meaning than it had been before. It is difficult to resist the conclusion that nearly dying is a good device for "waking up" to life.

Personality Changes

As Table 20 makes clear, most of the personality changes reported by near-death survivors were positive ones, suggesting that coming close to death may bring about an enhancement of self-esteem. The comments of several people cited in the two preceding sections could easily have been placed here to illustrate such a change. For example, the young man who nearly died of a high fever, after recounting a number of positive changes in his life, concluded, "Myself, I'm very valuable, too." *(45)* Similarly, the woman who decided to go into the nursing profession said, "I feel a whole lot better about myself." *(29)* Or, consider the woman who had no core experience but who was badly injured in an automobile accident. Prior to this incident, she said, she was very depressed and prone to suicidal thoughts. Now:

> I don't have many, or any, of those passive feelings that I wished that I could die. I'm much less afraid. I'm much more able to be close to people. . . . I'm much more comfortable with myself. I'm not as depressed. I'm less anxious. I really was living with a lot of anxiety and depression all the time, struggling to keep my head above water. Very often I felt it was going over my head. I don't feel that way [now]. *(61)*

Often, this change in self-concept is expressed very pithily, without elaboration. A woman who had an illness-related death experience said:

> I think it's enriched me. I think I'm a stronger person. *(28)*

Another woman who had a deep experience declared simply:

> [Afterward] I felt this tremendous confidence in myself, that I could do anything, which was a very good feeling. *(7)*

Sometimes, this increased sense of self-worth leads one to become more assertive. The woman who suffered a cardiac arrest stemming from a flawed tonsillectomy procedure, spoke of her attitude toward her church:

> I'm *not* sure I'm such a *follower* of the church anymore. Like they say, "You *have* to do this; you have to do that." I don't do that. Because *I* have to do what *I* think is right now. I rely more on *my* feelings than on *their* commands. I don't believe in their commands. I do what I have to do—and *no one* will ever say to me, "You're excommunicated," because *no one* can take *my* church away from me because no one's got the power but God. This is what I mean—it has made me believe in myself and what I believe in, what I feel. . . . I've become more of an individual thinker. I'm not a follower. I'm a thinker. *(24)*

In one case the effect was to eliminate all fear of physical danger:

> Of course, you know when I was in the navy, I was in a very dangerous branch of the service [submarine service]. My life was on the line constantly. But when I came out of this [near-death] experience, I figured anything that I live after this has to be gravy. I just wasn't afraid of anything. [He admitted to being afraid during the war.] Afterwards, I became a race driver, I flew airplanes, I've done everything that a person could get killed very easily at. . . . In that time [afterward], I have been shot at, depth charged, bombed, you name it, I've had it—and it never bothered me one bit. I always remained more or less calm because I figured I had it once and they didn't want me then and I don't think they want me this time and that's just the way I feel about it. *(51)*

In rare instances, an enhanced sense of self-esteem seems to be attributable in part not merely to surviving a near-death episode or having a core experience, but to various physical changes that have occurred following the incident. The young man who was knocked unconscious while intent on suicide provides an example:

> When I was younger, I had surgery on my hips and they had been bothering me quite a bit. And now I go jogging and everything and it's quite cleared up. Once in a while, it's sort of like arthritis, on rainy days you have a little bit of pain. But otherwise, it's quite cleared up. And I had ulcers back when I was in the hospital, and I've had hardly any problem at all. Like, if I drink I have problems, but I mean, eating regularly and whatnot I don't have any problems. And when I catch colds now they clear up a lot faster than they used to. I can't attribute this to the experience, but it's only happened *since* then so I don't know what to say. *(79)*

Although most of the personality and self-concept changes reported are positive, there are some exceptions. One such instance comes from a woman who had an out-of-body experience while undergoing an exploratory examination prior to surgery. In the course of this examination her lung was inadvertently punctured, bringing about a near-death crisis.

> I had a definite personality change. Where I did a definite slide downwards. Where death became an increasing preoccupation and multiple suicide attempts took place after that. . . . Going through that [experience] and coming that close to death and seeing that it wasn't necessarily that painful, that I could discount

pain in coming close to dying—it made it [death] more appetizing. *(22)*

Attitude Toward Others

Many people, particularly those who recalled a core experience, felt that their near-death episode definitely altered their relationships with others. In general, they felt that they loved others—strangers as well as friends and relations—more than they did before; that they were more compassionate and empathetic; that they were more tolerant and less judgmental; and that they were more desirous of helping others. Some of these attitudes have already been expressed in various contexts. Here, all that seems necessary to round out the picture is to present a representative sampling of these changes in interpersonal orientation:

It's given me tolerance. It's made me less judgmental. *(28)*

I think I'm a better person. I try to help people more than I ever did before. That might always have been a part of my nature, but now I realize that I *want* to help. *(4)*

I don't know if I've succeeded, but I *try* more to be a caring person. I think I try more to show that I care for people. *(82)*

I think I was more patient [afterward]. I think I am more understanding. I think I have more tolerance. *(6)*

I also feel I am a very compassionate person because I've known great suffering . . . because all of this happened to me. . . . I've had a great opportunity to help other people—people tell me things that they won't talk to their psychiatrist about. It happens to me continually. *(16)*

There was more compassion there [in his relationships with others afterward]. *(71)*

[Afterward] my husband and I had a really good relationship. It just changed me. It made me more open—to a lot of things . . . it kept me really nice, glowing—very open to people, stuff like that. *(64)*

> *Love.* Not necessarily romantic love from a woman or a man. Love. Fulfilling yourself with that love by—by *giving.* As much as by getting. Which are two separate things. And, not really *thinking,* but just in the way of recognizing that—that we're all in the same boat and we all have weaknesses and we all have strengths, and to help is where it's at. *(77)*

> I think I'm becoming much more tolerant, patient. I've always been a very compassionate person, but I think . . . the compassion is deeper . . . it seems to be directed with purpose now. *(20)*

> I love people now . . . I've never had the ability to love before. I have a *great* capacity for listening to people. I think I *accept* people—most of all—*as they are.* I don't give them *my* rules to live by . . . the ability to accept people *as they are* and to *love* them for *what* they are and not for what you *want* them to be, this has all come about—and I think that God has done this for me. And it's made *me* richer. *(24)*

Clearly, the effect of nearly dying on one's interpersonal relations is a powerful one. Perhaps the overall effect can be summed up by saying that near-death survivors become more *unconditionally accepting* of others. Other people are appreciated and loved more for what they are. Indeed, we have here come full circle on these personal changes because this attitude toward others appears to be still another manifestation of the *heightened sense of appreciation of life* with which we began. All life is appreciated more—including other people. As I observed earlier, the changes following near-death are really all of a piece anyway, and the different aspects I have distinguished here need to be understood as holistically organized.

Summary of Personal and Value Changes

As with the prototypical account of the core experience given earlier, it is necessary to bear in mind that this summary of personal and value changes, in aiming for generality, will lack a sense of nuance and particularity, and will obviously not correspond to any one individual case, though it will read like one.

The typical near-death survivor emerges from his experience with a heightened sense of appreciation for life, determined to live life to the fullest. He has a sense of being reborn and a renewed sense of individual purpose in living, even though he cannot articulate just what this purpose is. He is more reflective and seeks to learn more about the implications of his core experience, if he has had one. He feels himself to be a stronger, more self-confident person and adjusts more easily to the vicissitudes of life. The things that he values are love and service to others; material comforts are no longer so important. He becomes more compassionate toward others, more able to accept them unconditionally. He has achieved a sense of what is important in life and strives to live in accordance with his understanding of what matters.

NINE

Aftereffects II: Attitudes Toward Religion and Death

In addition to triggering personal and value changes, coming close to death tends to bring about a changed outlook on some of life's perennial issues, such as religion and death itself. Before exploring these more "philosophic" (rather than strictly personal) reorientations, one striking fact should be noted. Where the personal changes reviewed previously tended to be found for core experiencers and nonexperiencers alike, the reorientations in world views are characteristic chiefly of those who report a core experience.

Religious Changes

Do near-death survivors *become* more religious afterward? We have already seen that prior religiousness is not a *determinant* of the core experience, but we have yet to discover whether it might be an *effect.* The answer we shall come to, after reviewing a considerable body of testimony, is that indeed they do—but only if they have had a core experience on approaching death. The evidence needs to be presented first, of course, and, as always, certain qualifications will have to be made before we are through, but the same outcome will be found to pervade all our results here: Core experiencers tend to become more religious, whereas nonexperiencers tend to show no systematic change. To determine the extent of religious changes, we asked our respondents a series of related questions. One was, Before this experience, how religious a person would you say you were? The respondent was asked to reply in terms of the following categories: very, quite, fairly, not too, not at all. In most cases, we explained that "religious" should not be understood in a narrow sense to mean church-going per se, but rather should be taken to refer to an "inward" sense of religious feeling. After a respondent replied to this question, we then asked him to answer it according to how religious he felt himself to be at the present time. The difference between the two ratings we used to assess change in religiousness and the results of the corresponding statistical analysis are presented in Table 22.

Table 22

Pre- and Post-Religiousness Scores According to Core Experience Status and Sex of Respondent*

	Women	Men	
Core Experiencers	.833 (24)	.710 (19)	.772
Nonexperiencers	.345 (29)	.292 (24)	.318
	.589	.501	

*A positive score means an increase in religiousness.

ANOVA

Source	*SS*	*df*	*ms*	*F*	*p*
Sex	0.25	1			
Experience	5.25	1	5.25	4.65	< .05
S x E	0.00	1			
Error	104.00	92	1.13		

The data here demonstrate that where all categories of respondents show a net increase in religiousness, the effect is substantial, on average, *only* for core experiencers. The analysis of variance confirms this impression: core experiencers show a significantly greater increase on this variable and nonexperiencers show only a negligible rise overall. The effect of the core experience here is obviously independent of sex—the effect is the same for both sexes. Although the level of statistical significance here ($p < .05$) is not terribly strong, subsequent analyses will provide much more compelling evidence, both statistical and qualitative, for the effect noted in Table 22.[1] There was, incidentally, no significant difference on *initial* religiousness between core experiencers and nonexperiencers.

As a part of our formal interview, we also asked (most of) our respondents whether in their own judgment their near-death episode affected their religious feelings in any way. The results of these self-ratings are presented next.

Table 23

Religious Changes: Self-Ratings

Women
Religiousness

	Increased	Remained the Same or Decreased	
Core Experiencers	18	10	28
Nonexperiencers	8	16	24
	26	26	

$\chi^2 = 3.79, p \cong .05$

Men
Religiousness

	Increased	Remained the Same or Decreased	
Core Experiencers	7	13	20
Nonexperiencers	8	10	18
	15	23	

P = ns

The findings here are consistent with those of the first question for women but not for men. Although the probability level is borderline, significantly more women core experiencers stated that their religious feelings increased afterward, compared to nonexperiencers. For men, there was no difference between categories. There are two conceivable reasons for this small discrepancy from the data presented in Table 22. First, since the data here are nonparametric (that is, based on frequencies rather than averages) rather than parametric, as they were in Table 22, it may be that the average *increase* in religiousness for male core experiencers is greater although the *number* who increase is no greater, compared to nonexperiencers. A second possibility is that since there are more missing cases here, the earlier effect is obscured. In any event, however, it may be helpful at this point to mention that further data to be presented will amply support the assertion that the religiousness changes observed for core experiencers are fully as strong for men as for women. Thus, the self-ratings here for men constitute the only slight exception to the general pattern.

So far, we have examined some evidence that core experiencers tend to evince a higher degree of religiousness than nonexperiencers following a near-death incident. It is obvious on reflection, however, that religiousness is a very broad term, capable of a variety of meanings and shadings. Of these nuances we know nothing as yet, and they turn out to be critical to our understanding of just how the religious views of core experiencers tend to be affected by their coming close to death. These changes, as we shall now see, are both subtle and powerful, and the quantitative data we have reviewed to this point do scant justice to either of these dimensional aspects.

Qualitative Changes in Religiousness Among Core Experiencers

Although there are some exceptions to this generalization, increased religiousness among core experiencers does not as a rule take the form of more frequent church attendance or other modes of formal religious observances. Rather, it is that a *heightened inner religious feeling* reveals itself afterward, and this feeling does not seem to require a formal channel of religious ritual in order to express itself; indeed, some people actually assert that organized forms of religious observance tend to interfere with the expression of this inner religious impulse. In general, then, core experiencers tend to state that they feel closer to God afterward rather than closer to their church; they are more prayerful and privately religious than religious in an external, denominational way. In some cases this kind of religious feeling fades after a few months or years, but for most respondents it appears to represent a lasting transformation of their religious orientation.

Several distinctive aspects of this heightened religious feeling together constitute its principal features. A number of respondents mentioned that they became more prayerful afterward and/or felt a greater awareness of God's presence.

> I did find that for a while after the experience I *did* become more religious. I was praying a lot. [Eventually, she ceased to pray so frequently, but she remained more religious than she had been before her near-death experience.] *(7)*

> [Afterward] I never prayed so much in my life. *(6)*

> My faith in there being a power higher and greater that is somehow controlling my life has been heavily reinforced. *(82)*

> I rely a great deal more on God. I know that very definitely He's there. *(26)*

> I have become very religious since this experience. More and more so. I spend a great deal of time in prayer every morning. *(4)*

> Well [afterward], I felt closer to a—a God. Which I had not for years. [Before] I was an agnostic, I didn't know. *(Do you now feel you know?)* I feel much closer that I know. I find myself praying sometimes to [pause] an unknown Force. *(19)*

> It's more or less that there's something in me that I can call on. I almost feel like there's a supreme being in each one of us that we can call on. Whether that's God or not, I don't really know. [She described herself, however, as being much more religious afterward.] *(29)*

> It's kind of strange, after leaving the hospital, it started crossing my mind to go into religion. I don't know. I'll tell you one thing: I find myself praying or maybe thinking of God or a Superior Being more often now than I have in the past. *(45)*

> After the incident I felt like I had more faith, a *lot* more faith than before. [This change lasted only a couple of months, however.] *(99)*

> I've become a *lot* more religious. I pray every night. I've been asking for other visions in my prayers. *(79)*

Another component of the religious attitude of core experiencers has to do with a feeling that organized religion may either be irrelevant to or interfere with the expression of this inward sense of religiousness.

> [Before I was] fairly religious, but in a superficial way. I was more or less caught up in the *ritual* and the *trappings* of religion. And afterwards, for the short period after, I realized that the ritual and all that [pause] really meant nothing. It was the faith and the deep-down *meaning* that was of importance. *(99)*

> It [the experience] gave me a lot of questions, a lot of questions. I began to question the need for church. [She went on to elaborate that she no longer feels the need of a *building* to be religious. A minister told her that she carries a church within her.] [Now] I don't need the church. *(30)*

> I'm *not* such a *follower* of the church anymore. Like they say, "You *have* to do this; you have to do that." I don't do that. Because *I* have to do what *I* think is right now. I rely more on *my* feelings than on *their* commands. I don't believe in their commands. *(24)*

> I've always had difficulty with religions anyway. And, after this experience, as time went on, as this progression was going on, I found that the need to go to communion, confession, go to a place to pray, observe Good Friday, or any of these kinds of things, not only weren't necessary, but they were *blocking* what was really supposed to be happening. So that's why I have no affiliation. *(77)*

Although indifference or even contempt for organized religion is sometimes expressed by core experiencers, it is usually stated within a context that implies an overall religious tolerance for all ways of worship. From this point of view, there is no one religion or religious denomination that is superior or "true"; rather, all religions are expressions of a single truth. It is the smug sectarian quality of some religious groups to which core experiencers tend to object, not to the basics of religious worship itself:

> All of the religions are more or less blending in together now. The little minor points—you don't believe in this saint or this blessing—these things are really very insignificant. *(24)*

> I don't think of religion as *a* religion any more. God is above all religions. God is the religion, so, therefore, the various religions have no effect whatsoever on me. *(28)*

> I'm not really involved in any *one* religion. I think they *all* have something in common. I'm not really an advocate of any one of them in particular. *(99)*

> I believe in the *basics* of *all* religions. They're *all* connected as far as I'm concerned. *(77)*

> I feel welcome in any church. But . . . no one certain church. . . . Each person is judged by his own doings. So there's not any man that's going to walk up to me and tell that, say, the Baptists are going to be the only people who will ever see heaven. *(68)*

> I know that I can go to a Catholic church, an Episcopalian church, a Baptist church, I don't care *where* you go, it's all the same. There's no difference. It's just a different word. *(20)*

Sometimes the sense of the underlying similarity of all religions goes beyond an articulation of a view of all-embracing religious tolerance and is then phrased in terms of something that transcends mundane forms of religious worship. What seems to be implied here is a "cosmic" view of religion for which no theological doctrines are adequate. One respondent who struggled to put this insight into words summed it up this way:

> Yeah—there's—I just can't explain it because I don't know how to explain it in words. But it's just that everything is *infinite* and this has all been going on, in my mind, the universe has been going on forever. I just can't explain it. . . . Somehow we have a more important *mission* while we're here. Okay. That's it. We have a more important mission in our lives than just the material end of it in trying just to get material gains. There are more important things. It showed me the spiritual side in that basically that—it is important, I guess. That's all I can say. That [pause] that [pause] that *love* is important and that *every human being* on the earth is equal to each other. They're all the same. *(71)*

Again, these changes in religious attitude cannot be viewed in isolation from other personal changes triggered by a near-death episode. The increased prominence of an inner sense of God, the weakening or abandonment of outward religious forms, the spirit of religious tolerance and a dim sense of a cosmic religion—all these changes dovetail with a generalized value reorientation that stresses the importance of love and the role of spiritual values in everyday life.

Indeed, my own feeling is that it would be more accurate to claim that experiencers tend to become more *spiritual* rather than religious (in any conventional sense) following their near-death episode. Unfortunately, the term *spiritual* is even vaguer than *religious* and is perhaps of little descriptive value here. Nevertheless, as I have earlier observed, my personal interaction with many core experiencers left me with the impression that a spiritual awakening had definitely occurred in a number of them and that the term *spiritual,* though ambiguous, is nevertheless the most apt to characterize this quality. This impression, of course, is fostered through direct interaction with these respondents and may not be so apparent from the excerpts from their interviews.

It is important to point out here that although an increase in religiousness is the rule among experiencers it is by no means inevitable. A number reported no change in their religious views. None, however, showed a *decline* in religious feeling.

Belief in God

We also asked our respondents about their belief in God, prior to and following their near-death incident. The alternatives we offered them were: absolute, strong, fairly strong, not too strong, and no belief at all. The data from this question are presented in summary form in Table 24.

Table 24

Pre- and Post-Belief in God Scores According to Core Experience Status and Sex of Respondent*

	Women	Men	
Core Experiencers	.654 (26)	.429 (21)	.553
Nonexperiencers	.232 (28)	.136 (22)	.190
	.435	.279	

*A positive score means an increase in strength of belief in God. No significant effects.

Although the trend is the same as before (that is, favoring the core experiencers), the difference between categories does not reach an acceptable level of statistical significance. If one examines the *percentage* of increasers for both categories (47% for core experiencers versus 28% for nonexperiencers), the difference again fails to attain statistical significance ($X^2 = 2.91$ with 1 df; $p < .10$).

This result, however, is not too surprising in light of our qualitative data. Strength of *belief* in God is relatively stable (most respondents indicate no change); it is one's degree of religious *feeling* that tends to increase—at least for core experiencers. Obviously, one's belief as such may remain constant even when one's religious sense quickens. In addition, a number of experiencers, in responding to this question, stated or implied that they found the abstract term *God,* too full of conventional meanings for it to be a reliable reference word for their religious orientation. In other cases, core experiencers implied a qualitative increase in belief without being able to express this change quantitatively. For example, one woman said that whereas before she "thought" her belief was absolute, afterward she was "sure" that it was *(7)*. Another stated: "Well, I always believed that there was *something*. Now, it's not like I believe *more,* now I *live* like there is." *(77)* For these reasons, the failure to obtain a stronger difference between core experiencers and nonexperiencers on this item is, at least post hoc, perhaps understandable.

Only one core experiencer showed a decline in belief in God. This was a woman who had an out-of-body experience while close to death. In her case, however, the reason for this decline seems to stem, not from her core experience itself, but rather from the period afterward, when she was recovering in the hospital:

> *(Did this experience change your religious view in any way?)* Yes, that was another negative factor. *Not my own personal experience* [italics added] because I went in basically an agnostic. But I came out an atheist. . . . What I saw in the hospital [during the time of her recovery] I couldn't understand. I used to talk with the doctors, "How could you believe in God after what you see every day?" I watched someone that I had become good friends with in the hospital—we became such good friends. She used to come in and bring me flowers and just talk to me and she had a brain tumor. And finally when I got to the stage where I could walk, she got bad and she died four days later. And I watched her die. It was my first time watching somebody die. And that was the point when she didn't know my name anymore—and after that, I became so bitter. And then I went to the pediatrics ward and I would see severely burned children that were just so hideous to look at. And I said, "What kind of a God could make people this awful?" I mean, I knew He was punitive, but this was really sadistic. . . .

And there's nothing you can do, and there's cancer and, oh! I used to see that every day . . . and watching them go, and the suffering and the yelling, the pain, the screaming. When you're in a hospital and have nowhere to go, you do a lot of thinking about things like that. *(62)*

Even this powerful indictment of a "sadistic God" (so reminiscent of Ivan's argument in *The Brothers Karamazov* and of the views of many death camp victims) does not, of course, preclude a heightening of this respondent's *spiritual* sensitivity. Indeed, by becoming more aware of life's tragic dimension, she, too, reveals one of the characteristic concerns of core experiencers—compassion for the suffering of others. Thus, while it is true she has become less a believer in God, she has apparently shown the same kind of value change expressed by those whose religiousness has increased. Such an outcome, then, only reinforces the view that changes in religiousness must be understood as part of a large context of value change; it also would seem to support my contention that it may be that core experiences tend to stimulate spiritual awareness rather than religious belief *per se.*

Belief in Life After Death

Still another question had to do with the conviction that there was such a thing as life after death. In this case, we provided six possible categories of response: completely convinced, strongly convinced, tend to believe, not sure, tend to doubt, and no belief at all. As with our other questions, we asked our respondents to answer in terms of their pre- and post-incident beliefs. Table 25 furnishes the data.

Table 25

Pre- and Post-Life-After-Death Scores According to Core Experience Status and Sex of Respondent*

	Women	Men	
Core Experiencers	1.585	2.075	1.798
Nonexperiencers	0.268	0.286	0.276
	0.902	1.159	

*A positive score means an increase in conviction in the belief that there is life after death.

ANOVA

Source	*SS*	*df*	*ms*	*F*	*p*
Sex	1.40	1			
Experience	56.06	1	56.06	25.60	$< .001$
S x E	1.40	1			
Error	199.22	91	2.19		

There is a huge effect here—one of the strongest of the entire investigation. Core experiencers increase on the average 1.8 scale units—from an average position of "not sure" to "strongly convinced"—where nonexperiencers show virtually no change. Comparison of preliminary scores on this item, incidentally, reveals that although experiencers were somewhat less inclined to believe in life after death to start with, compared to nonexperiencers (the means were 2.10 versus 2.73, respectively), they are significantly more inclined to believe in it afterward (3.93 versus 3.03; $t = 3.18$, $p < .01$). Thus, it is not "merely" coming close to death that tends to convince one that there is life after death; it is, apparently, the core experience itself that proves decisive.

The testimony here is unambiguous. A woman who suffered a heart attack said as a result of her experience:

> I believe beyond any question of a doubt that there is something beyond [this life]. *(4)*

A man who was badly injured in a racing car accident said his experience changed his view of death:

> My attitude toward death is that death is not dying; death is being reborn. You're reborn to a new peaceful life that when you die, you'll be able to experience. *(73)*

A man who suffered a cardiac arrest during surgery stated:

> I would say—and not being religious at all—that there must be something after death, which I never believed in before. I always believed that when you were dead, they put you in the ground and you stayed there. But I'm not too sure about that anymore. *(48)*

A man who appears to have died "clinically" during open heart surgery also became convinced in life after death through this experience:

> Well, it [his experience] gave me the idea that I think there's life after death. I believe that now. Before I believed that if you died, you were just dead. But now I really believe that there is some kind of life after death. *(33)*

The woman who had a cardiac arrest when undergoing a tonsillectomy said that prior to her operation:

> I had a doubt. *(How do you feel about it now?)* Oh, I'm positive now. Completely convinced. *(24)*

Finally, a man who nearly died in a diving accident said that before his accident:

> I thought it was all a bunch of baloney. . . . *(how about now—is there life after death?)* Sure. Definitely. *(77)*

As Table 25 implies, comments like these are quite typical of core experiencers. For most, the idea of life after death becomes not merely highly probable, but a veritable certainty. Nonexperiencers, on the other hand, are not only significantly less convinced that life after death is a reality, but remain relatively unaffected by their near-death episode in this regard.

Global Index of Religiousness Changes

As an overall index of change in religiousness, difference (that is, pre and post) scores for the three items having to do with religious feelings, belief in God and belief in life after death were summed for each individual. (These items make up our "purified" religiousness index previously discussed [see pages 133–134] in connection with our data on religiousness as an antecedent of the death experience.) This overall score obviously represents a *composite* index of religious changes and as such is probably more reliable than any one difference score taken by itself. The data, based on this index, are presented in Table 26.

Table 26

Pre- and Post-Global Religiousness Scores According to Core Experience Status and Sex of Respondent*

	Women	Men	
Core Experiencers	2.74	2.76	2.75
Nonexperiencers	0.95	0.80	0.89
	1.79	1.70	

*A positive score means an increase in global religiousness.

ANOVA

Source	*SS*	*df*	*ms*	*F*	*p*
Sex	0.00	1			
Experience	76.10	1	76.10	11.46	$< .005$
S x E	0.22	1			
Error	570.99	86	6.64		

The results prove clear-cut. On this measure of global religiousness, experiencers show a much greater increase following their episode, compared to nonexperiencers ($p < .005$). Furthermore, the means for male and female core experiencers are virtually identical. Although the "life after death" item plainly contributes a disproportionate share of the variance here, the other two items, it will be remembered, did provide data indicative of the same overall effect. Thus, all our religious indicators converge on a single conclusion: Core experiencers become more religious following their near-death episode than do nonexperiencers.

Beliefs in Heaven and Hell

As a final inquiry into our respondents' religious views, we asked them two simple yes/no questions having to do with their belief in heaven and hell. As I noted earlier, these questions ultimately proved *too* simple since they tended to elicit a variety of questions in response such as, What do you mean by heaven (or hell)? Since the interpretation of these terms were quite variable, the interpretation of the data based on them is necessarily hazardous. With this caution in mind, we can, however, examine these data for whatever dim light they may furnish on the question of near-death survivors' religious beliefs.

The first point that needs to be made is that beliefs in heaven and hell tend to be relatively stable: 71% of all respondents showed no change in belief patterns. (Belief in heaven, by the way, was more common than belief in hell—62% to 44%). Nevertheless, core experiencers were significantly more likely to change their beliefs in some way following their incident than were nonexperiencers (41% versus 19%, $p < .05$). The preponderance of changes among core experiencers was in a positive direction, that is, either a postincident belief in heaven or a lack of belief in hell, or both. Seventy-two percent of the directional changes among core experiencers conformed to this pattern. Among nonexperiencers, there were only seven persons altogether who showed a directional change; of these four were positive, three negative. The number of cases were too small here for a statistically significant difference to emerge.

Thus, the data here suggest that although beliefs in heaven and hell are quite stable, core experiencers are more likely to change theirs (in a positive direction) than are nonexperiencers. Nevertheless, the ambiguity of the questions themselves and the small proportions of changers render this conclusion highly tentative.

This section will close with a few representative comments by core experiencers who did demonstrate a postincident change.

A woman who nearly died during surgery was asked:

Interviewer: Before, did you believe in heaven?
Respondent: Yeah.
Interviewer: What about now?
Respondent: Now I definitely do.
Interviewer: What about hell, before?
Respondent: Not really. No.
Interviewer: What about now?
Respondent: I don't believe in it now at all. *(7)*

The woman who nearly died of a cardiac arrest during surgery for a tonsillectomy had this to say:

Interviewer: Heaven, before?
Respondent: I did, but I was *hoping* it was there. Now of course I *know* it's there.
Interviewer: Hell?
Respondent: Yes, I did. I always believed in hell.

Interviewer: Do you believe in it now?
Respondent: Oh, yes.
Interviewer: What is hell?
Respondent: I don't know how to explain it. To me, it's more of life. It's feeling pain, seeing people you love suffer.
Interviewer: So hell is here then.
Respondent: I don't think it's here, but it's like here. It takes place on the other side of life. *(24)*

A number of core experiencers, however, are quite insistent that there was no such "place" as hell. One woman put it this way:

I don't believe there's a hell. I just feel that when your spirit leaves you, it just goes into a spirit world and that's where it remains. *(Do you mean that this spirit world is like heaven?)* Yeah. *(64)*

A man who experienced a presence and who saw scenes from his life, which he viewed "like a movie," summed up his convictions on the existence of hell as follows:

I don't actually believe there's a hell in the sense of fiery pits. Actually, I'll say this and this is what I believe: God is an All-Loving Source and I don't believe He's up there twisting people's fingers. I had the feeling that it was complete comfort and even things I did wrong, on viewing them, weren't wrong. *(71)*

Summary of Religiousness Changes

In general, core experiencers tend to become more religious following their near-death episode, nonexperiencers do not. The way in which postincident religiousness reveals itself among core experiencers is primarily in terms of an inward sense of religion: They feel closer to God, are more prayerful, are less concerned with organized religion and formal rituals, and express a sense of religious tolerance and religious universalism. It isn't clear that their belief in God *per se* grows stronger, although it is clear that their religious *feeling* does. Following their incident, they are significantly more inclined than nonexperiencers to be convinced there is life after death. Their views on heaven and hell, though usually not affected by their experience, tend to become more positive (that is, a stronger belief in heaven or a weaker belief in hell, or both) when change does occur.

All these changes can more aptly be described by the term *spiritual* rather than *religious*. It seems to me that the core experience tends to trigger or intensify one's sense of spiritual awareness, whereas coming close to death, *without* an accompanying core experience, tends to leave religious views and spiritual values largely intact.

Attitude Toward Death

We also asked our respondents whether their coming close to death had had any effect on their attitude toward death. Most respondents replied in terms of their *fear* of death and those who didn't were usually then asked specifically whether their fear of death had been altered through their near-death episode. The responses to this question fell into six main categories and the full data are presented in Table 27.

Table 27

Effects on Fear of Death
According to Core Experience Status

	Core Experiencers			*Nonexperiencers**		
Effect	*No.*	*%*		*No.*	*%*	
Increased it	1	2		5	13	
No change	3	6	20%	4	11	71%
Never afraid	6	12		18	47	
Decreased it	9	18		3	8	
No fear of death	15	31	80%	8	21	29%
Lost all fear	15	31		0	0	

*15 nonexperiencers were coded in an irrelevant category (most of these representing a "not ascertained" status).

It is clear that the patterns of response to this question vary dramatically as a function of core experience status. The extent of this difference can be more easily grasped by examining the following chi-square analysis.

Table 28

Chi-Square Analysis of
Effects of Fear of Death

	Lost it No fear Decreased	Never afraid No change Increased	
Core Experiencers	39	10	49
Nonexperiencers	11	27	38
	50	37	87

$\chi^2 = 20.43, p < .0005$

The data in Table 28 clearly demonstrate that core experiencers, as a group, tend to show a sharp decline in fear where no such pattern is evident for nonexperiencers. Nevertheless, the form of the question itself is such that the resultant data need to be more closely inspected before these findings can be properly interpreted.

The problem arises from the fact that several response categories used here are ambiguous. For example, the "no change" category does not permit a statement of how afraid of death the respondent was (or is); it is conceivable, therefore, that some in this category could well be placed in other categories of Table 27. Similarly, the "never afraid" category could conceivably be classified with the "no fear of death" respondents. And this last category may very well contain some persons who "lost all fear."[2] For these reasons, the placement of individual respondents into certain categories is somewhat arbitrary and often depends on the particular phrase a respondent happens to use. Not only that, but the lumping of several particular categories into one overall classification is itself a bit arbitrary. Besides these matters of response categories and their classification, it must be remembered that fifteen nonexperiencers do not appear in Tables 27 and 28 and we have no way of knowing whether these respondents' data, if we have had them, would have changed the pattern of findings in a significant way.

Nevertheless, despite these methodological and interpretative problems, there remains little doubt that core experiencers, on the whole, show a drastically different pattern of response to this question than do nonexperiencers. For example, the *only* persons—and there were fifteen of them—who testified that they lost all fear of death were found among core experiencers. Indeed, 62% of all core experiencers said that they now had no fear of death whatever, compared to 21% for nonexperiencers. If one examines the patterns of increased or decreased fear, the same result obtains: Among experiencers, there are nine respondents reporting a decline and only one who says that fear has increased; among nonexperiencers, the corresponding figures are three and five, respectively.

Additional data, not fully reflected in Tables 27 and 28, further buttress the sharp differences between groups. The modal response among nonexperiencers was the avowal that they had never been afraid of death, but this was often said very matter-of-factly, and, at least in some cases, the inflection did not impress me with its conviction. The response of core experiencers was, as a rule, very different. They would often comment on this matter *before* I (or other interviewers) had asked them about it (for example, "I'll tell you one thing, doctor: I'm not afraid of death any longer"), and when they addressed themselves to this point, it was often with great emphasis and emotion, as though it was no mere "intellectual conviction," but rather a deeply felt truth. Overall, my subjective impression throughout the course of this investigation was that the loss or decrease in the fear of death among core experiencers was one of the strongest points of difference between them and nonexperiencers.

I believe the reader will come to share this impression if he examines the comments from core experiencers on this point which I have arrayed below in some profusion.

> *(Do you fear death?)* Not at all. *(Did you before?)* Yes, as far as anyone else would. *(26)*

> *(Did this change your attitude toward death?)* Yes, it has. Yes, it has. Because I had a fear—I didn't want to talk about it. A real genuine fear of death. I used to get *preoccupied* with it. I used to get preoccupied with it. . . . I don't have that anymore. I'm not afraid of it. I'm not ready for it right now—I got things to do. But when it comes, I'm not afraid of it. *(30)*

> I can kind of sum it [his experience] up: I'm not afraid of dying anymore. I guess I've made up my mind that this is the way dying is going to be like and, if this is the way it is going to be, then don't be afraid of it or don't be scared because what I experienced was [pause] almost happiness. *(Had you been afraid of dying before?)* Yes. *(45)*

> Well, one thing I most distinctly remember is that it left me, where

I had been terrified by death before, it now left me with a total *lack* of fear of death. *(4)*

Well, I certainly no longer have any fear of death. *(82)*

I'm not afraid of death at all. *(29)*

I have no fear of dying, I don't to this day. I have no fear of it at all. It's as if I've been there and know what it's like and I am not afraid of it. I'm just not, you know. *(16)*

If that is what death is like, then I'm not afraid to go. . . . If that's any way like the hereafter is, then I'm not afraid to go at all. I have absolutely no fear at all. . . . I'm convinced. I think I had just a peek into it. *(10)*

(Has this eliminated your fears of death, then?) Yes, yes, definitely. *(25)*

(Did this experience change you in any way?) I should say it has. I have no fear of death [said with decided emphasis]. *(53)*

I'm not afraid of dying. I'm really not afraid and I used to be scared to death. *(23)*

It's a very peaceful feeling, believe me. That's why I tell people I have no fear of death. I mean, I have no fear of death. *(Because of these experiences?)* Aw, sure. *(38)*

I'm not afraid of death. This is the point I'm at right now. I'm not afraid of death at all. *(71)*

[Before] I looked at death—let's say I was scared of death. Frightened. So much. When I was a child. Now I find it as a beautiful experience. One of peace, calm . . . *(It doesn't sound as though you're afraid of death.)* No. I think death is a necessary part of living. *(This view of death that you have—is this something that changed as a result of this experience?)* Oh, yeah. *(64)*

Basically . . . death is not frightening the way we *think* it's frightening. . . . It can be a very *beautiful* experience. *(70)*

(Are you afraid of death?) No. I'm not afraid of death at all. *(77)*

(Did it [his experience] change your attitude toward death in any way?)

> Yes! I used to be *afraid* of death. Now, it seems like that, you know, it was a little scary at first, the *wandering* aspect, but *talking* to God and the *warmth* I felt when I was with Him, you know—it was really—Oh! I just get the chills thinking about it, it was so GOOD, you know? And I feel that when my time for death comes, that I won't be afraid to go. *(79)*

> *(Would you say that this experience has in any way affected your attitude toward death?)* I'm not *scared* of it. I'm just wondering when [laughs]. *(68)*

> *(Do you fear death?)* Absolutely not! I have no fear of death *at all. (20)*

Perhaps the strongest statement concerning the loss of fear of death was made by the woman who was apparently clinically dead for three minutes from a surgically related cardiac arrest. Both to conclude and to sum up these comments in a single quotation, I shall draw from a portion of her account:

> I was afraid of death. I remember as a young woman when I had my two children, sometimes I'd wake up crying in the middle of the night and my husband would hold me, because it would *hit* me in the middle of the night and . . . [my husband] would just hold me and talk to me and I would get over it. But, I was *always* afraid of death. Which they say is quite common. Well, I faced death those three weeks I was in the hospital. They never knew whether my heart would stop or not. And they told me this [that her heart could stop at any moment] and I knew this and was aware of it, and yet I had *no fear at all.* First time in my life that I was actually *face to face* with death, that I knew that I would close my eyes and not wake up again and I wasn't afraid. Because I remember the *feeling.* I just remember this *absolute beautiful feeling.* . . . And ever since then I've never been afraid of death. *(24)*

These accounts, as I'm sure the reader will agree, offer powerful testimony for the assertion that having a core experience at the point of apparent imminent death provides a potent antidote to the fear of death. Not only that, but the effect of such an experience seems to be permanent and not merely transitory. No such systematic changes, and certainly not the emphatic and emotionally charged statements on this matter, are found for nonexperiencers. Again, it is *having a core experience* itself that appears to be crucial here, not merely the fact of coming close to death.

There is one last issue, however, that needs to be raised here. How do near-death episodes affect suicide attempters' fear of death?

The first point that needs to be made is that well over half the suicide attempters respond to the question on fear of death with the phrase (or a variant of it), "I never was afraid of death." In their case, perhaps their actions suggest that such statements are more than empty bravado. Most others report no change; two report an increase in fear of death. Only three suicide attempters report a decrease.

As we have already observed, most of our suicide attempters recall no experiences or only an aborted one. Nevertheless, it is important to look at those cases where some kind of suicide-related core experience did occur in order to determine whether core experiences induced in this way also result in a decrease in fear of death.

Actually, two of the persons already quoted in this section *(79* and *82)* who were involved in suicide-related near-deaths[3] resulting in deep experiences have indicated that they lost their fear of death through their brush with death. Another suicide attempter who had a deep experience also felt he was no longer afraid to die:

> The way I feel now is, I don't want to die. But I'm not afraid to die now. Before I was afraid to die, well, not really, but I was afraid to die. But now I'm not afraid to die. I feel that I know what it's all about. *(100)*

Several other suicide attempters who had partial experiences said they didn't fear death and never had. But not all, however. A possible exception—it is, at least, a mixed case—to the general effect of the core experience on the fear of death comes from a suicide attempter who had a deep, though somewhat atypical, experience. Whether it is a real exception the reader can judge for himself:

> *Interviewer:* Did this experience have any effect on your attitude toward death? On your fear of death?
>
> *Respondent:* Yeah, when I think about dying, it *bothers* me. Let's see. For some time I haven't had any faith in Christianity. And so that makes it even worse, thinking that you're going to die—because you don't think that you're going to *go* anywhere. Before, I thought that there would be a heaven or something. But *now* I—I don't know—you go into limbo or something like that.
>
> *Interviewer:* You think you go into a state of a sort of—a no place, a nothing?
>
> *Respondent:* Yeah.
>
> *Interviewer:* So in terms of its effect on your attitude toward death,

it's less positive than it was before, less hopeful or something.
Respondent: Yeah.
Interviewer: Would you say that you're more or less afraid of it?
Respondent: [Pause] I'm afraid of it, but not for the same reason. Before, I was afraid of something *unknown.* Now I think I'm afraid of just leaving people behind. I don't have the same fear.
Interviewer: You don't have a fear for yourself personally, but you have a fear for the survivors of your death.
Respondent: Yeah. *(99)*

Another important related issue is whether coming close to death through suicide, particularly when one does have a core experience, acts as a deterrent to further attempts.

Most suicide attempters without any core experience either denied that they would try again to kill themselves or thought it was unlikely; several, however, could conceive of the possibility and several had, in fact, already made multiple attempts. Merely coming close to death through suicide attempt—as we know from other investigations—doesn't necessarily vanquish self-destructive urges.

What about when one has a core experience? Here, the evidence is again mixed. Most of those who had an experience state with varying degrees of emphasis that they would not attempt to kill themselves now:

> I decided that I have to wait. . . . I figure God's going to take me when he's ready and it doesn't appear that He is. . . . If I came that close to dying and didn't, it's 'cause I wasn't supposed to. *(81)*

> *(Has it changed your attitude to suicide?)* Yes, I think suicide is useless. You know, it's nothing to it. It really doesn't do anything for you. . . . The way I feel now is, I don't want to die. *(100)*

> So I think that God was trying to tell me that if I commit suicide I'm going to hell, you know. So I'm not going to think about suicide anymore [nervous laughter]. *(That did it, then?)* Yeah, I think that did the trick about thinking about suicide. *(79)*

On the other hand, one respondent who had a core experience as a result of a faulty preoperative procedure made multiple attempts to kill herself afterward, precisely because death was no longer terrifying:

> . . . coming that close to death and seeing that it wasn't necessarily painful, that I could discount pain in coming close to dying, it became more appetizing. *(22)*

It should be added here, however, that this respondent's suicide-related near-death episode was very "cloudy and vague" compared to her illness-related one and that she suffers from a variety of severe physical and psychological problems.

Thus, the evidence on the deterrent power of suicide-related core experiences is only suggestive. It is perhaps relevant to note here that the three cases where a suicidal intent or act was *not* associated with either drugs or alcohol *(79, 82* and *100)* were the *only* ones where a loss of fear of death was reported.[4]

In general, then, the core experience acts as a powerful reducer of the fear of death in cases involving near-death through illness or accident and *may* have a like effect on suicide-related cases. (More research on the final point is necessary, however, before any firm conclusion can be reached.)

Conception of Death

From all that has been written so far, it is obvious that having a core experience at the point of apparent imminent death must have an effect on one's *conception* of death. Indeed, it can be assumed that changes in attitude toward or fear of death are mediated by a changed understanding of death. In order to inquire into this, toward the end of our interviews, we would usually ask our respondents to tell us, in effect, what death meant to them. The answers, as can be imagined, were quite variable, but we were able to group them into nine major categories as shown in Table 29.

Table 29

Conceptions of Death According to Core Experience Status

Conception	*Core Experiencers* No.	%*	*Nonexperiencers* No.	%
Annihilation, finality	2	4	6	11
Something beyond	17	35	8	15
Transition, new beginning	14	29	8	15
Peace, beauty, bliss	18	37	4	8
Heaven/hell	1	2	1	2
Reincarnation notions	12	24	2	4
Other	2	4	5	9
No idea	7	14	11	21
Not ascertained	1	2	12	23

*Percentages total more than 100 because many respondents gave more than one answer.

As can be seen, core experiencers tend to hold more definite, more positive views on the nature of death than do nonexperiencers. Among core experiencers, the notion is particularly strong that not only does life continue after death, but that it is likely to be very pleasant. Another point of difference between core experiencers and nonexperiencers is the former's greater openness to reincarnation concepts. It is not, however, that core experiencers necessarily come to profess a belief in reincarnation; it is rather that the underlying idea of reincarnation no longer appears altogether implausible. These differences are highlighted in Table 30.

Table 30

Conceptions of Death
—Selected Comparisons—
According to Core Experience Status

	Annihilation, finality	Peace, beauty, bliss	
Core Experiencers	2	18	20
Nonexperiencers	6	4	10
	8	22	

$\chi^2 = 6.16$, $p < .02$

	Reincarnation mentioned	Reincarnation not mentioned	
Core Experiencers	12	36	48
Nonexperiencers	2	39	41
	14	75	

$\chi^2 = 5.32$, $p < .02$

Since both comparisons presented here are completely ad hoc, the results can at best be taken only as suggestive; nevertheless, they do point to some possible dimensions of conceptions of death where core experiencers and nonexperiencers may differ sharply.

The following succinct statements dramatically convey the affective associations death has to core experiencers:

> If there is a life after death, I think it's going to be very beautiful, if the brief experience I had is an example of what it is going to be. *(48)*

> My attitude toward death is that death is not dying; death is being reborn. You're reborn to a new, peaceful life that, when you die, you'll be able to experience. *(73)*

> *(Your idea of death, then?)* Well, it means utterly at peace. *(6)*

(Is it true to say that death does not represent in your mind any feeling of annihilation or finality?) Absolutely! *(What does it represent?)* Peace! *(4)*

These next passages speak of a sense of continuance:

I was wrapped up in the whole conventional belief in death: "Oh, God, what am I going to do when I die? What is going to happen? [Now] I *know* what is going to happen. It's just going to be another life somewhere else. Maybe in a different form, but I'll still have my soul. *(66)*

(What is your understanding of what death is?) With this experience [pause] there is no such thing. To me, it's just a passing phase, to get someplace else. I don't know what the other place is, but I know that it's all right. *(25)*

Something *will* happen. You *will* go *somewhere.* It's not the end. Just like your life is not the end. *(79)*

The next respondents reveal an openness to reincarnation:

[If you die by suicide], you'll die, but you're going to come back as another creature somewhere else and start all over again and you're going to have the same problems sooner or later. *(100)*

Interviewer: What do you think happens at death?
Respondent: You leave your physical body and you're transformed into your spiritual body. I think that's right.
Interviewer: Have you any idea what happens after that?
Respondent: I would say that we go to a school of learning of some type where we're just—it's just like we walk out of this one class and we're going into this other thing and—just a *very intense learning process.* Then I would just guess a place of comfort and from there either to being reborn again to go on to something else that there is out there that I don't know about.
Interviewer: Is reincarnation an idea that makes sense to you?
Respondent: I think that people are born again if they *choose* to or if they have something that has to be worked out.
Interviewer: Just like you were having a choice at the point where you could have—
Respondent: Right. My actual feeling at that point was that if I didn't [choose to come back], I'd have to start all over again. *(71)*

In concluding this discussion of conceptions of death—and at the same time this entire segment presenting the basic findings of our study of near-death experiences—perhaps it is fitting to give the final words here to the woman who, according to the WCEI, had the most profound experience of anyone:

Interviewer: What do you understand death to be?

Respondent: [Long pause] I really believe that death is just part of a continuous cycle. I think when you are born, consciousness is enveloped with a body. And you grow and you develop and you learn. And I believe that you try to attain—whether you are aware of it or not—you develop a greater awareness of higher consciousness. I feel that with each death, it's like taking off an old coat and putting on another one to grow further and further in consciousness until you become one with God, or with Creation, or with whatever it is. Whatever this great thing is.

Interviewer: So death is just a change in the cycle?

Respondent: Yes. Yes, it's a continual thing. I think of it as just a cycle. Not an end *at all.* Not an end at all. I know that whenever I have another grandchild, I look at him and think, Could you be papa? Could you be mama? *Who* could you be? [She laughs.] And it's very exciting! Very exciting. *(20)*

Summary

Religious changes. Core experiencers, as a group, became more religious after their experience; the religiousness of nonexperiencers remained about the same. The increased religious feeling on the part of the core experiencers involved a sense of being closer to God, feeling more prayerful, taking less interest in formal religious services, but expressing greater tolerance for various forms of religious expression and endorsing an attitude of religious universalism. These changes might be regarded as representing a heightened spiritual awareness rather than religiousness. Although a global index of religiousness demonstrated that core experiencers were significantly more religious afterward than nonexperiencers, the strongest difference here was based on a conviction in life after death: Core experiencers showed a large increase in belief in life after death; nonexperiencers showed a negligible change.

Attitude toward death. Although the data here were marked by some interpretative problems, they seem to show that the effect of a core experience is to significantly reduce or eliminate one's fear of death. Nonexperiencers tended to state that they never feared death in the first place, but there was no strong evidence suggesting that merely coming close to death in itself had much of an impact on fear of death. The suicide-related core experience also seemed to reduce a respondent's fear of death (and possibly the inclination to kill oneself), but the number of relevant cases was too few to draw any definite conclusion.

Conception of death. While both core experiencers and nonexperiencers tended to express belief in some form of an afterlife, core experiencers were both more definite and positive about it. Core experiencers' conceptions of death were more likely than nonexperiencers' to emphasize the peace and beauty of death and to reflect a greater openness toward a reincarnation view of life after death.

TEN

The Principal Findings and Some Comparisons

Now that all the findings from this investigation have been fully presented, we are ready to consider what they have to tell us. This task will occupy us for the next several chapters and will begin here with a comparison of our results with those described elsewhere in the medical and professional literature. In making this comparison, I will, of course, be particularly concerned with evaluating the extent to which our own data support Moody's prior findings. In the following chapters, after considering various explanations that have been proposed, I will offer my own provisional interpretation of the core experience based on a recent scientific model of consciousness that is capable of handling transcendental experience. I will also attempt to explain various specific features of the core experience, using some concepts that may or may not prove scientifically testable. My *preference* will be to articulate a scientific framework for the understanding of near-death phenomena, but I will not be reticent to *speculate* about possibilities currently outside the accepted paradigm of science if contemporary scientific theorizing about states of consciousness seems inadequate. Finally, in light of whatever understanding of near-death phenomena I can provide, I want to conclude by considering the significance of these experiences and by assessing what implications, if any, they may have for what has traditionally been called "the survival problem," that is, whether one's personality, or some aspect of it, can be said to survive bodily death.

The Form of the Core Experience

Juxtaposing two quotations from Moody's first book furnishes us with his challenge:

> All I ask is for anyone who disbelieves what he reads here to poke around a bit for himself.[1] . . . it has been my experience that anyone who makes diligent and sympathetic inquiries . . . about the occurrence of such experiences will soon have his doubts dispelled.[2]

Although I myself did not really doubt Moody's findings or his integrity, I can at least aver that our own findings offer an impressive degree of independent corroboration for his. And while we have somewhat different conceptions of how these near-death phenomena are organized, as I will make clear, there is no substantive disagreement over the form of the core experience itself. I myself have no doubt that Moody and I have had the *same* phenomenon described to us by our respective respondents.

Not only that, but since the publication of Moody's original work, we have had further independent confirmations of his prototypic description of the core experience by other medical and scientific researchers.[3] Aspects of these investigations will be considered later, but for now it is sufficient to note that there has already accumulated an impressive array of findings generally supportive of Moody's original publication (as well as the findings publicly reported by Kübler-Ross). At this point there seems to be little doubt about the authenticity and reliability of the phenomenon.

This much noted, there are still some minor differences in findings and interpretation between Moody and myself which do require comment.

Perhaps the most obvious of these has to do with what Moody calls "a being of light." According to his prototypical description:

> . . . a loving, warm spirit of a kind he has never encountered before—a being of light—appears before him. This being asks him a question, non-verbally, to make him evaluate his life and helps him along by showing him a panoramic, instantaneous playback of the major events of his life.[4]

The experiences described here are, of course, already familiar to us from the abundant interview excerpts presented earlier—with one exception: None of my respondents ever reported *seeing* "a being of light." True, many did perceive a light and most described it as a warm, loving and comforting light; and many also described an undeniable sense of a "presence." Yet, no respondent ever explicitly wedded these two phenomena into "a being of light" and none ever used that term to characterize his experience.

What are we to make of this discrepancy?

In my judgment, not much. First of all, other researchers besides Moody have reported this phenomenon,[5] so it doesn't rest on the word of a lone investigator. Second, the same *elements* comprising the "being of light" seem to be present in our study also; they just didn't quite come together in the way that some of Moody's respondents described. Third, it may be that the "being of light" phenomenon tends to occur mainly in cases of rather extended clinical death experiences,[6] of which my own study had no such certified instances. Finally, even if the last speculation proves unfounded, it may still be that, though authentic, this is a *rare* phenomenon. If, say, it tends to occur in fewer than 5% of core experiences, it is patently conceivable that merely through sampling error no such instance turned up among my respondents. Indeed, as I have already mentioned, several of the phenomena cited by Moody in his prototypic description appeared to be quite infrequent (for example, hearing a noise, feelings of loneliness, sensing a "second" body, traveling through a "tunnel," approaching a border, and so forth) and it is perfectly reasonable, it seems to me, to conjecture that the "being of light" feature is also rarely instanced. This, at any rate, is my own provisional conclusion and the research of others will likely soon afford us a better basis for evaluating. In the meantime, I do not consider this discrepancy a serious one.

Another set of minor differences between Moody's findings and my own have to do with what appear to be, in the main, *differences in incidence* of various near-death phenomena. Since Moody's work is descriptive but not statistical, however, it is impossible to determine whether the low incidence in our reports of the Moody features just reviewed represents a real discrepancy. Since our investigation does not provide a sound sampling basis for inferring the incidence of these phenomena in the population of near-death survivors, further, more comprehensive, parametric research will have to be undertaken to settle this question. My own conclusion, therefore, is that where there is little doubt that these features do sometimes occur in conjunction with near-death episodes, how *often* they occur cannot now be estimated with any real accuracy. As with "the being of light," however, it may be that extended clinical death cases may provide a greater abundance of these elements.

The relative rarity of these features was, in fact, one of the reasons that lead me to propose a conception of the core experience cast in terms of *stages* rather than *elements per se,* as Moody's description would have it. Although these stages do not always unfold in the strict sequence in which I have arranged them, they do appear to accord reasonably well with the chain of events described in Moody's prototypic account. Since we also found that their relative incidence over the entire sample decreased systematically with increasing depth of the core experience, as shown in Figure 1 (see page 40) we can say that this "logical" ordering has a measure of empirical support from our own data.

While I believe that this framework represents an improvement over Moody's "element-conception" approach, it is not without its drawbacks. Any scheme that seems to impose a "logical" temporal ordering on the core experience does a certain violence to it, because, as we have seen, the experience itself tends to occur in connection with a state of consciousness in which time is not a meaningful construct. To speak of stages, then, contradicts the nature of the experience itself. A wholly different paradigm is therefore required to deal adequately with this problem to which we shall return in Chapter Twelve, when we take up the structure of one such possible paradigm. In the meantime, we have to regard the notion of "dividing" the core experience into "stages" as a matter of convenience for narrative purposes and not a strict experiental reality.

Finally, there is one more empirical point that results in a conceptual disagreement between Moody's prototypical account and our interpretation. Moody's description suggests that the near-death experiencer encounters both the "spirits" of loved ones and "the being of light":

> . . . soon other things begin to happen. Others come to meet and to help him. He glimpses the spirits of relatives and friends who have already died, and a loving warm spirit of a kind he has never encountered before—a being of light—appears before him.[7]

Our own evidence, however, indicates that this kind of conjunction between "ordinary spirits" and what I have called a "presence"[8] rarely, if ever, happens. Instead, the accounts of our respondents imply that this tends to be an either/or feature of the experience: Either one sees relatives *or* one encounters a presence, but not both. Furthermore, the qualifications from the last paragraph notwithstanding, the presence phenomenon appears to come "earlier" in the experience and to obviate the "functional need" for spirits. This last statement, however, requires some explanation.

Recall that when a presence is encountered or a voice heard, the respondent usually feels it is up to him to *choose* whether to return to life. And when this choice is offered or seems necessary, the man or woman, sometimes with reluctance, elects to live. This decision usually terminates his experience at that point. Spirits, on the other hand, are glimpsed and heard almost invariably by respondents who never felt the sense of a presence and who, therefore, experienced no urgency to choose. The spirits, however, usually tell the individual, in effect, that he *must* "go back," that "his time" hasn't come yet, thus effectively usurping the power of choice. It is almost as though the individual has "inadvertently" trespassed into a "region" which he is not yet qualified to enter and the spirits, rather like gatekeepers, must usher him out. However one may choose to interpret this phenomenally real event, spirits seem to perform, in these cases, a "fail-safe" function: If the presence doesn't manifest itself or if the individual doesn't himself choose to return to life, the spirits tend to appear to send him back. This "functional" interpretation implies that there should be no *need* for both a presence *and* spirits in a given instance, and that, of course, is consistent with our data. It is in this respect, then, that our understanding of the near-death experience is at variance with Moody's.

Having reviewed some minor points of difference—both empirical and conceptual—with Moody's findings, it would perhaps be well to conclude this section with a reminder of my opening observation: On the whole, Moody's depiction of the near-death experience seems to accord very well indeed with the composite account that I have constructed from the interviews with our own respondents.

The Incidence of the Core Experience

One of the questions to which the present study was addressed was concerned with the relative frequency of core experiences. Although Moody states in *Reflections on Life After Life* that he has talked to many near-death survivors who had no recall, he gives no approximate figures. Of course, since his interviewees are highly self-selected, even if Moody did provide statistical information of this kind it would be impossible to interpret for purposes of parametric estimation.

In the present study, which was plagued with sampling problems of its own, our core experience incidence level was 48% overall and 39% for all medical or hospital referrals. Since our data also suggest that core experience incidence may vary as a function of manner of near-death, our sample values themselves are obviously difficult to interpret. Even if they are reasonably representative of the "true" parameter value, a different study with a different "mix" of near-death survivors could easily arrive at a substantially different incidence level. In addition, since we used a specific criterion (based on the WCEI) for determining the presence and depth of a core experience, studies using different or unspecified criteria could also reach very different conclusions regarding the incidence rate. From our study alone, all that one can apparently conclude is that in a somewhat haphazard collection of near-death cases, the core experience is *not rare.*

Fortunately, however, the present study is not the only one on which to base these estimates. Concurrently with our study, Sabom and Kreutziger were independently conducting a very similar investigation, using a format not unlike our own. Sabom has since continued this investigation on his own and has kindly shared his preliminary findings with me. Before presenting them, it is necessary for me to report that, as a cardiologist, Sabom has interviewed mostly cardiac arrest patients (they constitute approximately 70% of his sample of 107 patients). Most of the remainder were illness-related, comatose patients. Twenty-nine were referred to him because they related an experience. The figures I shall report are based on what Sabom calls his "prospective" patients, namely, those who were "known only to have had an episode of unconsciousness and near-death prior to interview."

To insure comparability, Sabom analyzed his data using the WCEI and he also adopted the same criterion as I had used for assessing the presence of a core experience (that is, WCEI ≥ 6). Arrived at in this way, the core experience incidence level for Sabom's seventy-eight prospective patients was 42%, a figure very close to our value of 39% for our fifty-nine hospital- or medically-referred interviewees.

Thus, two independent studies can be said to have found an incidence rate of about 40% for the core experience if one restricts oneself to what Sabom called "prospective patients." Both studies also found abundant cases in which the core experience occurred in others. The impressive agreement between these studies bolsters our confidence that this phenomenon may be fairly common in an unselected sample of near-death survivors. More systematic studies are obviously necessary to address the matter more definitively, but Sabom's work and our own combine to suggest that other investigators should have no difficulty in finding many experiencers among samples of near-death survivors on which to base these estimates.[9]

Hell and Judgment

There is one point of correspondence with Moody's data that requires some commentary: the *absence* of any hellish experiences. According to Moody's most recent publication,

> . . . it remains true that in the mass of material I have collected no one has ever described to me a state like the archetypal hell.[10]

His failure to obtain any such accounts was duplicated in the present investigation, as I have noted earlier. Although people sometimes reported feeling scared or confused near the beginning of their experience, none felt that they either were on their way to hell or that they had "fallen into" it. On the contrary, as I have repeatedly emphasized, both the affective tone and the visionary aspects of the near-death experience tend to be predominantly and highly positive. Even in suicide-related cases, no one described a mainly unpleasant or hellish experience.

What about other studies? Sabom has also reported a complete failure to obtain any cases suggestive of a hellish experience. In the cross-cultural work of Osis and Haraldsson, which dealt with deathbed visionary experiences in the United States and India, of 112 cases of "afterlife visions" only one was indicative of a "hell." Even here, however, the authors are inclined, on the basis of information they had about this person, to interpret this "vision" in psychodynamic terms. Consistent with our own data from respondents who reached stage V, Osis and Haraldsson found the afterlife vision to consist of stereotypic "heavenly" scenes of surpassing beauty. Other accounts, both scientific and anecdotal, of documented or purported near-death experiences suggest that hellish experiences are extremely rare.[11]

Nevertheless, as Moody himself remarks, "nothing [that he found] precludes the possibility of a hell" and the few cases that have been reported, even though they represent only a tiny fraction of all near-death experiences, cannot be dismissed entirely out of hand.

Indeed, recently a cardiologist, Dr. Maurice Rawlings, has contended that on the basis of his own examination of near-death cases, hellish experiences may be a good deal more common than previous research had indicated.[12] While he has found numerous examples of the classic positive near-death experience, he has also alleged that as many as *half* the cases he has uncovered have had hellish elements.[13] Since his claims are dramatically different from our own findings as well as from those of a number of other investigators, his work deserves a careful assessment.

Rawlings argues that his discovery of many "hellish" cases derives from the minimal time gap between the near-death episode itself and the gathering of information about it. As a cardiologist whose specialty is resuscitation, Rawlings is often able to be present at the scene of a near-death episode so that he is in a position to *observe* as well as to interview the patient immediately afterward. He states that at least one of his patients exclaimed at the time of a series of cardiac arrests that "he was in hell," but that afterward he had *no memory* of this experience! Instead, the patient related only positive elements of his experience, such as being out of his body and encountering deceased relatives in "a gorge full of beautiful colors." This apparently selective recall suggested to Rawlings that perhaps *many* persons might *repress* hellish aspects of near-death experiences. If so, this would help to explain the discrepancy between his findings and those of others. Since most researchers (including myself) tend to interview near-death survivors some time after their episode, the processes of repression and selective recall would already have operated to bias favorably the respondent's account.

Rawlings's thesis, though plausible, suffers, however, from a number of weaknesses, both conceptual and methodological.

In the first place, legitimate questions can be raised concerning the data base on which Rawlings's argument is built. From his account, it is far from clear just how many people he himself has actually interviewed who have had hellish near-death experiences. Like Moody, Rawlings presents no statistics and relies on selected case histories he has assembled from a variety of sources.[14] He is also vague about just how many cases his conclusions actually rest on. In my judgment, his evidence by itself is too amorphous to evaluate.

A second factor may be more worrisome. A reading of Rawlings's book shows that it is not really an objective survey of near-death experiences but is essentially a proselytizing Christian tract. Rawlings himself, through his study of near-death experiences, has become a "born again" Christian, and his book is unabashedly written from that point of view. His interest is, in part, to convince the reader that near-death experiences provide empirical support for a Christian conception of both heaven *and* hell and that to experience the former and avoid the latter it is necessary to follow Jesus. This is obviously an issue that is outside the scope of science, but Rawlings does not even pretend he is writing a scientific book. Indeed, he has told me that he can no longer "be impartial."[15] However that may be, Rawlings's evangelizing use of his near-death material plainly is a potential source of bias that must be borne in mind when assessing his work.

Third, there is no direct evidence to support Rawlings's "repression" theory. Rawlings claims that the reason hellish near-death experiences have been so rarely reported is that the usual interview-incident interval is long enough to allow repression to occur. "If," he says, "patients could be *immediately* interviewed, I believe researchers would find bad experiences to be as frequent as good ones."[16] There are several reasons, however, to question the validity of this.

One fact that tends to undermine Rawlings's claim is that both Moody[17] and Sabom[18] have told me that they *have* occasionally interviewed patients directly after a cardiac arrest (Sabom, like Rawlings, is himself a cardiologist), but have never been told of a hellish experience. A second fact that tends to cast doubt on Rawlings's claim is the experience of persons who take powerful psychedelics, such as mescaline or LSD.[19] Experiences triggered by these psychedelic agents sometimes include extremely frightening hellish visions, but such scenes are usually recalled vividly afterward rather than being repressed. Since there appear to be some notable similarities between near-death experiences and some LSD induced states,[20] the lack of immediate repression of frightening features of such "drug trips" would not seem to be in accord with Rawlings's hypothesis. A third point relates to Rawlings's implicit assumption that if repression does occur, it would tend to cause "selective forgetting" of negative aspects of one's near-death experience. That this is not necessarily the case was shown by some of my own data. In at least two instances of which I am aware, patients were reported by witnesses to have apparently glimpsed beautiful visions at the time of their near-death episodes (as evinced by these patients' remarks and gestures), yet they had no recall of such visions when interviewed later. Thus, no "repression" in the traditional Freudian sense seems to have operated here. Such evidence, scanty as it is, inclines me to believe that unreported near-death experiences are not necessarily likely to be unpleasant, as Rawlings implies.

Finally, though it is true that some near-death survivors state that various aspects of their experience were frightening, such features appear to have been, in the main, *hallucinatory visions,* which were *qualitatively discriminable* from the core experience itself. For example, one woman *(20)* recounted a disturbing "dream" about Mephistopheles in which various orgiastic rites took place. She said she "dreamed that Mephistopheles had somehow taken me captive and was trying to scare the hell out of me." Yet this same woman denied emphatically that this "dream" was anything like her death experience: "That [the latter] was very different; really, no comparison. No comparison at all. . . . The [other] was part of an hallucination or dream or whatever one goes through when they are regaining consciousness." Thus, it may be that at least some of Rawlings's cases involve experiences that are, in fact, different in *quality* as well as content from the core experience itself.

In view of all the questions one can raise about Rawlings's data and his interpretations of them, I believe that a fair judgment of his thesis at this stage of our knowledge of near-death phenomena is: *not proven.*

Notice that I did not say *false,* because I am very far from believing that hellish near-death experiences *never* or *cannot* occur. In my opinion, the weight of *all* the evidence suggests that they do, in fact, take place, but probably far more rarely than Rawlings alleges. In short, though I believe the value of Rawlings's work is seriously vitiated by the deficiencies I have listed, I do not think it is legitimate to dismiss all his case history material. Indeed, I am myself persuaded there is something to Rawlings's contention, even though I am equally convinced that he has probably exaggerated its magnitude.

If we admit that hellish near-death experiences may occur, even if they are not frequent, we obviously need to account for such a possibility in our theoretical interpretation of near-death phenomena. Accordingly, I will shortly propose a theoretical formulation that can both subsume hellish experiences (as well as the core experience) and explain their relatively infrequent incidence. At this point, however, our interest is primarily comparative rather than interpretative, and on that basis all we need say here is that hellish near-death experiences appear very rarely in the literature and, in that connection, our investigation is consistent with the bulk of other findings.

We turn now to a related issue: Is there a sense of judgment when one undergoes a near-death episode?

The testimony most relevant to this question comes from those who underwent what I called a "decisional crisis," particularly those who reported a panoramic life review in conjunction with that phase of their core experience. It was their common testimony that, if a judgment was passed, it was one *they* made of *themselves.* Even when someone was aware of a presence or voice and interpreted it as a "being" external to himself, there was no sense of being judged by it. Instead, love, comfort, and acceptance tended to be felt; *that* was the emotional context in which a self-assessment was often made.

Even when no external presence was felt, there was still no sense of judgment other than self-judgment. The following comments from a suicide attempter were typical:

> The only thing I felt *judged* by would be *myself.* Like in the very beginning, when I thought about these things, all these terrible things, then I thought about the good things, then it felt like I'd just run through my life and I'd think of all the stupid things . . . all the mistakes I've made. I think the judging was mainly myself judging myself. *(99)*

Clearly, the drift of our findings here are perfectly congruent with those originally reported by Moody and with the implications he later ascribed to them. A sense of (external) judgment is not a typical feature of the core experience, but a self-assessment is frequently made when one comes close to death.

Antecedents of the Death Experience

Since very little other research has been addressed to this issue, we shall be limited here to a sketchy comparison of our findings with those reported by other investigators. Where appropriate, provisional interpretations of our own data will be offered so that future research may be directed to them.

The underlying question here, of course, was whether or not the near-death experience is uniform over different modes of nearly dying. The answer to this question—within the very considerable methodological and empirical limits of this investigation—was what might be described as a whispered, hesitant, and provisional endorsement of the invariance hypothesis. As will be recalled, it appeared that the *form* of the experience was constant, though its *frequency* varied according to mode of near-death onset. It hardly needs saying that a larger scale and more rigorously conducted investigation is necessary to establish this tentative generalization.

The limits of the invariance hypothesis were, however, severely strained by three findings in particular, which now need to be discussed: (1) the disproportionate occurrence of the life-review phenomenon in conjunction with accidental near-deaths; (2) the aborted core experience in conjunction with suicide attempts; and (3) the gender-related interaction in incidence and depth of the death experience.

The Life Review in Accidental Near-Deaths

Although the life-review phenomenon occurred for about a quarter of our experiencers, I earlier noted that it was statistically more common in accident victims (where it was found in over half the cases) than among people in other categories. This was not a strong difference, on the basis of the raw figures involved, but, in light of other research, it is a suggestive one and needs to be lingered over for a moment.

Albert Heim, a nineteenth-century Swiss geology professor and inveterate mountain climber, who himself several times experienced near-fatal falls, was apparently the first person to interview many who had come close to death through accidents of various kinds, including warfare. He was particularly interested in accidental falls, however, and in a translation of his work provided by Noyes and Kletti, Heim states that "in many [such] cases, there followed a review of the individual's entire past."[21]

Following up on Heim's initial findings, Noyes and Kletti obtained information from 205 respondents concerning 215 life-threatening incidents. They found that, overall, 29% of their sample reported the panoramic life-review phenomenon. Although, ironically, this effect occurred in only 9% of their sample who nearly died from falling (thus apparently disagreeing with Heim's findings), the percentage of positive instances was quite high in conjunction with both near-drownings (43%) and auto accidents (33%). From the breakdown given by Noyes and Kletti, however, it is unfortunately impossible to determine whether the panoramic life-review phenomenon was, in fact, *more* common in these latter two modes of accidental near-death than in illness-related episodes, but it appears that this could possibly have been the case.

The form of these experiences, incidentally, appears to be identical with those described in this book, including an intimation of a flash-forward, as well as flashback effect.

Obviously, neither Heim's original investigation nor Noyes and Kletti's more recent study does more than hint at the possibility, suggested by our own findings, that accidental near-deaths may be more likely to generate a panoramic life review. If further research does not uphold this relationship, of course, there is "nothing special" that needs to be accounted for—in the sense that no one condition of near-death onset is differentially associated with this phenomenon.[22]

Suppose, however, that accidental near-deaths are more likely to stimulate a life review. Why should this be so?

My own hunch is that one determinant of this effect would be the *suddenness* or *unexpectedness* of the near-death crisis. Many illnesses, obviously, have a long period of onset before bringing the individual to the threshold of death. Suicide attempts are also usually premeditated, at least to a degree. Accidents, however, by definition, are those events that catch the individual unprepared. Such a condition, when the prospect of death suddenly flashes like a lightning bolt of inevitability, might well unleash the life-review effect as a means of *condensing* one's experience into the shortest possible time frame. Subjective time may lengthen tremendously but clock time is, apparently, preciously short. If a core experience is to occur, events need to be compressed in the most drastic way and the life review does exactly that. Just *how* it does it is a question we shall take up later.

This line of thinking implies that it is not the accidental nature of the near-death incident itself that is crucial, but the *suddenness* and *unexpectedness* of the event. It follows, therefore, that in illnesses that occur without warning (for example, a cardiac arrest) or in cases of impulsive suicide attempts, one would expect to find a fairly high incidence of the life review. Obviously, such an interpretation need not remain speculative; it can easily be tested by well-designed research.

Finally, it should be added that this hypothesis specifies only one possible determinant of the life-review phenomenon. Doubtless, there are other factors that may play a part in facilitating it. Noyes and Kletti themselves consider still other possibilities, but we shall not detail them here.

The Suicide-Related Near-Death Experience

We have already considered at great length the complex and ultimately inconclusive data on the experiences of failed suicides. The basic finding here, which suggests a possible departure from the invariance hypothesis, has to do with the fact that suicide attempters seem not to progress beyond stage III. Thus, their death experiences appear to be aborted or truncated, compared to other categories of near-death survivors. In addition, the testimony of several experiencers converges on the belief that successful suicides would *not* experience positive transcendental states. A review of all this evidence left us in doubt whether the suicide-related experience represented a true deviation from the modal death experience.

Other data bearing on this question have been hard to obtain, but the work of a San Francisco psychiatrist, David Rosen, is directly relevant here. He was able to interview six of the eight survivors of suicide leaps from the Golden Gate Bridge and one of the two people who survived a jump from the Oakland–San Francisco Bay Bridge. What Rosen found, in brief, proves quite instructive. A number of these suicide attempters did indeed report elements consistent with the core experience and also were found to show aftereffects similar to those characteristic of our experiencers. Interestingly, one phenomenon they did *not* report was the life review, a finding in keeping with our own hypothesis.

Although Rosen's sample is highly selective and very small, his findings imply support for the invariance hypothesis. Recall that the clearest suicide-related cases consistent with the death experience from the present study were those (few) that did not entail the use of drugs or drugs and alcohol. Rosen's data, coupled with our own, suggest that *drug-free* suicide attempters may well have deep core experiences—certainly in comparison to those who attempt to kill themselves by overdoses of one sort or another. *This conclusion, however, is by no means established* and further research along these lines is urgently needed if the invariance hypothesis is to be established. Such cases are also particularly germane to Rawlings's thesis. Indeed, in my opinion, of all the unanswered questions concerning near-death phenomena, the experience of failed suicides still seems to be the most pressing, on both practical and theoretical grounds.[23]

The Gender-Related Interaction

The last threat to the invariance hypothesis is comprised by the unexpected finding that women are disproportionately likely to have a near-death experience in connection with illness, where men tend to have theirs as a result of accident or suicide attempt. As will be recalled, this difference was a statistically strong one.

No other investigation, to my knowledge, has systematically examined this set of variables in relation to the core experience, and no explanation was readily available from an analysis of our own data. Furthermore, I confess that I cannot think of any explanation that intuitively strikes me as plausible.

Accordingly, though it is probably unbecoming to do so—since it is obviously an easy out—I prefer to abandon the search for an explanation for this relationship until it is replicated in further research. My own inclination is to regard it as a kind of sampling error, (that is, an alpha error) in the absence of any cogent interpretation for this unanticipated effect. This is an unsatisfactory state of affairs, to be sure, but I am prepared to put up with it until I have reason to change my mind.

To conclude this section, it seems fair to say that although much more research needs to be done on the invariance hypothesis, the evidence from our own investigation as well as that from other work leads decisively to the affirmation that the core experience is a highly *robust* phenomenon. That is, across a variety of conditions, it tends to manifest itself in very much the same form. I have not, of course, demonstrated that the experience is itself *strictly* invariant across different ways of near-death onset, but I believe that its basic similarities have proved much more evident than its differences. In sum, it appears that the experience of dying is *essentially* the same, regardless of how that experience is brought about.

Correlates of the Core Experience

Of the various possible correlates of the death experience, the one of greatest potential theoretical significance is religiousness. In the introduction I stated that one of my concerns in undertaking this investigation was to determine the role of an individual's religious belief system in shaping his near-death experience. If religiousness was highly correlated with the likelihood or depth of the near-death experience, that would suggest that the "religious ambiance" of that experience might have its roots in the individual's religious belief system. The crisis of apparent imminent death, then, would merely serve to trigger a visual projection of images consistent with an individual's expectations about the afterlife.

This possible interpretation of the core experience, however, found no empirical support whatever from our data. As will be recalled, neither the likelihood nor the depth of the core experience was related to various measures of individual religiousness. That is to say, religious people were no more likely to report phenomena indicative of the core experience than were the nonreligious. What about the findings of other researchers on this issue?

In the investigation most similar to our own—Sabom's—the findings were virtually identical. Among the seventy-eight prospective patients, those reporting a core experience had a mean religiousness index of 2.1; this index for those not reporting a core experience was 2.4. The difference was not significant. Although Sabom's index was based primarily on frequency of church attendance rather than inward feelings of religiousness, his findings are obviously consistent with ours in suggesting that religiousness per se is not a determinant of the death experience.

Sabom's work, however, is not the only evidence leading to this conclusion. Osis and Haraldsson's cross-cultural study of deathbed visions also affords data consistent with the small role of religiousness and religious beliefs in shaping the core experience:

> Belief [in life after death] did not significanly change the frequency of experiences of beauty and peace and the frequency of images of another world. Apparently, the belief in life after death changes very little of the afterlife images themselves, but rules the religious emotions and sharply increases positive valuation of death.
>
> Patients' personal involvement in religion did not affect the subject matter of visions at all. Deeply involved patients saw gardens, gates, and heaven no more often than those of lesser or no involvement. Experiences of great beauty and peace were also independent of the degree of patients' involvement in religion.[24]

In short, religiousness as such does not appear to affect either the likelihood or content of the core experience; but, as Osis and Haraldsson suggest, it probably does play a role in shaping the *interpretation* the individual gives to that experience. This accords with my own view, based on our own interview data, that an individual's religious belief system is more likely to serve a filtering function *after,* rather than before, the near-death experience. For many persons, the experience *is* a religious experience, but its *content* appears to be independent of one's prior religiousness.

As was the case with religiousness itself, so also were various standard demographic factors unrelated to the incidence or depth of the core experience. Sabom has also reported that the same demographic factors we assessed were completely unrelated to near-death experiences in his own investigation. Much the same picture, by and large, is drawn by Osis and Haraldsson, with the provision that their study is demographically much more complex because of its cross-cultural character. Even Heim stated that his findings were independent of the educational level of his respondents.

No one to my knowledge has yet published an investigation charting the *personal* correlates of near-death experiences, so that we cannot as yet say whether these experiences are systematically related to any individual difference variables, such as level of ego strength or repressive or denial tendencies.

This is not to say, of course, that such relationships will not one day be uncovered, but thus far the seeming independence of the core experience of situational demographic factors as well as individual religious belief systems again suggests its robustness. Still, we do know that not everyone who comes close to death reports a core experience, and the question therefore lingers: Why do some people have the experience and others not?

I once put this question to Raymond Moody, who has perhaps interviewed more near-death survivors than anyone else, with the exception of Kübler-Ross. I distinctly remember his pithy answer: "Ken, I haven't got a clue!"[25]

It remains to be seen whether further research will offer any.

There was, in fact, only one factor found in this investigation that did seem to relate, albeit in a puzzling way, to the core experience: People who had already been familiar with the findings of near-death research at the time of their crisis were *less* likely to report an experience. This was a strong effect statistically ($p < .02$) with nearly twice as many nonexperiencers having heard of Moody-type experiences as experiencers (37% versus 19%). These data clearly show that prior knowledge of this kind of experience was not a contaminant in this study, but what is curious, of course, is why there should be a difference in the *opposite* direction from the one that had been methodologically feared. That is, why should people knowledgeable about the Moody-type experience be less likely to have one?

One might be tempted to regard this as a "fluke" difference except for one additional fact that has recently come to light: Sabom has found the same paradoxical effect in his research. In his case, this difference was also highly significant ($p < .01$). That two independent investigations should furnish evidence for the same apparent "knowledge-inhibiting" effect is certainly striking, though how it is to be interpreted remains a mystery. If this finding is to be taken seriously, it is almost as though vicarious knowledge of this phenomenon is functionally equivalent to the direct experience itself. Such a conclusion, of course, seems extremely far-fetched, but the matter must remain tantalizingly unresolved until further research offers some clarity.

Aftereffects of the Near-Death Experience

Most of the research that has dealt anecdotally with near-death experiences has suggested that their aftereffects are profoundly transforming, particularly in regard to the loss of the fear of death. In the present investigation, both through the interview transcripts and through our statistical findings, abundant evidence has been offered to support the contention that surviving a near-death episode does indeed lead to profound personal changes for many. It is, furthermore, one of the specific contributions of this investigation to disclose which of these changes are apparently dependent on the core experience itself and which are a function of a near-death episode. In this section, we shall be largely concerned with the former category, though since these changes are all of a piece, the entire cluster reported by experiencers must be considered.

Why does the experiencer show the particular *pattern* of changes that we have earlier reviewed? First of all, it is necessary to remember that these changes are mediated by the individual's *interpretation* of his experience and that for him the experience is, above all, *real.* Second, it is for many an experience with definite spiritual or religious overtones. Third, the experience is usually interpreted to mean that there is a life after death *and* that it is a joyous, pain-free life. Fourth, one has apparently been given "a second chance" to live. Fifth, all these impressions have been transmitted in a way so as to make them extremely vivid, compelling, and subjectively authentic. Is it really surprising then, that experiencers resume life by living it more fully, loving more openly, and fearing death less, if at all? Is it surprising that their life seems more grounded in a sense of purpose and is more consciously shaped by the spiritual values of love, compassion, and acceptance? If the implications of the core experience are regarded as *true* by those who have undergone the experience itself, then one would expect, I think, precisely these kind of changes.

A person who has survived a death experience has been, to a variable degree, "spiritualized" and his postincident life is a continuing testimony to the profundity of the event that has marked him. Although it is true that not all the changes last and that many other factors have contributed to them, nevertheless, what is impressive is the power of the core experience to compel positive change. Its effect seems to be to reorganize the person's life around a new "center," which affords direction, purpose, and energy. Indeed, this effect has been described to me by one respondent as akin to "receiving a seed." And so, the experience must not be regarded as merely a "beautiful but frozen memory," but rather it is, for many, a continuing, active force that seeks to manifest itself in life-affirming ways. In this sense, it may certainly be likened to a religious conversion and, I think, most—but not all—our experiencers would not take exception to that expression as long as it was not defined too narrowly.

If we now turn to the question of how well some of the specific changes reported by our experiencers have been corroborated by other researchers, we can, once again, profitably examine Sabom's investigation point by point for each of the three major changes associated with the death experience: (1) increase in conviction of belief in life after death; (2) loss of fear of death; and (3) increase in religiousness.

Increase in conviction of belief in life after death. Our finding was that experiencers showed a dramatic postincident increase in this belief, where nonexperiencers showed virtually none ($p < .001$). Sabom's (1978) results were identical ($p < .001$).

Loss of fear of death. Our findings, despite some methodological ambiguities, strongly suggested a marked decrease for experiencers, where nonexperiencers tended to show no systematic change ($p < .0005$). Again, Sabom's findings revealed the same effect ($p < .001$) and, in his case, were methodologically clean. In addition, he has gone on to show[26] that this effect persists for up to two years after the respondent's near-death crisis (this was the time limit for his follow-up measure).

Increase in religiousness. Our study demonstrated that experiencers tend to increase in religiousness ($p < .05$ to $p < .005$ for different measures). Sabom summarizes his findings here as follows: "Because of the near-death experience, many patients expressed a new or renewed fervor in religious activity, which was not observed in non-experiencers."[27] Again, the responses of our two samples of experiencers seem similar.

Perhaps this is the place to call attention to the remarkable overall similarity between Sabom's findings and our own. Not only in this section but throughout this discussion the various parallels between our independently conceived and executed studies will have been evident to the attentive reader. Whether in regard to the death experience itself, its correlates, or its aftereffects, it is as though we are referring to a *common* sample. This set of similarities is all the more remarkable when one takes into account that we each began our research with opposite biases[28] yet found the same thing. Again, the *robustness* and reliability of the core experience is underlined by these comments.

Altogether, the material from my own investigation and the corroborative evidence from Sabom's work dealing with the aftereffects of the core experience combine to produce a fairly clear image of this aspect of near-death phenomena. Neither the changes themselves nor their underlying dynamics are particularly puzzling or problematical. They are, to be sure, dramatic and striking in many cases, but they represent, on the whole, one of the few features of near-death experiences that do not confound our attempts to understand them.

We come now to the task that we have so long postponed: How to interpret the core experience itself. This is obviously the *key* question on whose answer the final assessment of this extraordinary phenomenon may hinge. The underlying question, of course, has really been with us from the start: Does the core experience have more than a *subjective* validity? And whatever the answer to this question may be, how, if at all, can we *explain* this singular experience?

Eleven

Some Possible Interpretations of the Near-Death Experience

The interpretative issue now rises before us like an indomitable peak and the question becomes: Will the near-death experience yield its secrets to a scientific explanation? Up to this point, the near-death experience has been surrounded by mystery and tinged with numinous qualities, but need it remain so? We need to know whether the theories of science can provide us with a satisfactory interpretation of the phenomena of dying. If they can, and the near-death experience is susceptible to a naturalistic explanation, we will have to view this extraordinary patterning of events as little more than the result of understandable psychological or neurological mechanisms set off by the apparent onset of death. To be sure, even if this proves the case, the *aftereffects* will remain authentic—the near-death survivor's behavior and attitude changes *are* real, whatever the ultimate explanation of the experience itself may be. On the other hand, if scientific explanations are not convincing, we may find ourselves driven to one of two alternatives: (1) to enlarge our concepts of science so as to subsume this phenomenon or (2) to employ another framework in an attempt to understand what the near-death experience represents.

In either event, the *meaning* of the core experience is critically dependent on the interpretation we are justified in giving it.

Obviously, there are a number of *categories* of explanations that are potentially relevant here. Psychological, pharmacological, physiological, parapsychological, and religious interpretations have all been suggested as possibilities. And these perspectives are not necessarily mutually exclusive. For example, a psychological explanation may actually be dependent on a specific physiological condition, say, cerebral anoxia (or insufficient oxygen to the brain). These explanations would, then, reflect different but compatible explanatory *levels*. Another complication is that not all these potential explanations are susceptible to disproof. Some parapsychological and, presumably, all religious explanations cannot be evaluated by scientific methods. That being so, my approach will be to give preference to verifiable scientific explanations in this discussion. Only if *all* such explanations seem inadequate are we justified, I believe, in entertaining interpretative possibilities presently outside the scope of science.

Let us begin, therefore, with several explanations that seek to understand the core experience as a reflection of psychological conditions assumed to be present at the point of (apparent) death.

Psychological Explanations

Depersonalization

Noyes and Kletti have been prominent (but not alone) in advancing a "depersonalization" interpretation to explain reactions to the perception of impending death. Studying mostly accidental near-deaths, they have proposed that the prospect of death initiates a defensive psychological reaction, which serves to allow a person to cope with highly stressful, life-threatening situations. From this perspective, the phenomena associated with the prospect of impending death, such as a sense of peace and well-being, feelings of bodily detachment, a panoramic life review, and mystical transcendence are all to be understood as ego-defensive maneuvers to insulate the individual from the harsh realities of imminent annihilation by providing a cocoon of compensatory fantasies and feelings. In other words, the perception of death results not in physical ejection from one's body, but in *psychological detachment* from one's (apparent) fate. In this respect, their interpretation is obviously patterned after Freud.[1] However, aspects of the experience (for example, the panoramic life review, to the understanding of which Noyes and Kletti have made a significant contribution), are given a neurological underpinning *as well as* a psychodynamic rendering.

Despite its surface plausibility, there are several difficulties with Noyes and Kletti's position that argue for its rejection.

First of all, the classic description of depersonalization they quote differs, as the authors themselves admit, in many ways from the psychological state of near-death survivors. In order to force the near-death experience into the procrustean bed of depersonalization, they have to make numerous ad hoc assumptions for which there is little support. Both Osis and Haraldsson and Sabom have for these, and other reasons, found Noyes and Kletti's thesis either unconvincing or irrelevant.

Second, the depersonalization interpretation is completely unable to handle one rare, but extremely significant, aspect of near-death experiences: the perception of a deceased relative whom the dying person does not know is dead. Several such cases were reported and documented by early psychical researchers[2] and, more recently, Kübler-Ross has mentioned further episodes of this kind.[3] After my own investigation was completed, I heard of such a case myself. A woman respondent informed me that her father, as he lay dying, saw a vision of two of his brothers, one of whom had been dead for years while the other had died only two days previously—a fact unknown to her dying father. The father, however, decided to "return" when he heard his (living) wife call to him and only afterward learned of his brother's recent demise. If near-death experiences are merely elaborate denial reactions, it is hard to see how they could provide the basis for such extraordinary accurate perceptions.

Finally, Noyes and Kletti fail to consider that where stress may indeed trigger a defensive reaction to begin with, the transcendental realities that appear to an individual confronted with death may represent a higher dimension of consciousness and not just a symbolic fantasy rooted in denial. In this respect, Noyes and Kletti seem to fall prey to the well-known tendency of orthodox psychoanalysis toward facile reductionism. In this respect, it might be more important to listen carefully to the testimony of near-death survivors than to follow the predilections of Freud.

For these reasons, the psychoanalytic attempt to explain away near-death experiences as depersonalization seems both forced and inadequate.

Wishful Thinking

A milder version of the depersonalization thesis is the assumption, considered (and rejected) by Moody that near-death experiences are a product of wishful thinking. Since near-death experiences tend to be not merely positive but exceedingly pleasant, it might seem that they would derive from the desire to turn the finality of death into a death-defying "peaceful journey."

Again, this position does not seem to stand up to scrutiny—and for some of the same reasons I rejected the depersonalization view. For example, it, too, would be unable to explain instances where a deceased relative whose death was not known to the near-death survivor was seen.

Moreover, as Kübler-Ross has pointed out, this view would imply that small children who are dying would ordinarily fantasize their parents—the human beings who would be most significant to ones so young.[4] Yet, she reports, they *never* do—unless one or both are dead. Instead, they appear to see *other* relatives or religious figures.

The wishful-thinking hypothesis also has difficulty in dealing with cases where a near-death survivor encounters a relative whom she never knew in life, such as *(7)*, reported in this study. Such a perception could hardly be ascribed to wish fulfillment.

Still other factors are incompatible with the wishful-thinking hypothesis. For one, the *consistent patterning* of the core experience across different people is itself evidence against the hypothesis. Presumably, people *differ* in their wishes in regard to a hoped-for afterlife, yet the sequence of experiences they go through on coming close to death is remarkably alike. It is also noteworthy that the experiences of nonbelievers and suicide attempters also tend, on the whole, to conform to the general patterning of the core experience—yet one would imagine they would wish for the cessation of consciousness.

In sum, the wishful-thinking explanation appears to be . . . wishful thinking!

Psychological Expectations

If the wish isn't father to near-death visions, perhaps it is the thought—in the form of expectations of one's imminent death or of an afterlife.

Expectational determinants, however, seem not to bear any systematic relationship to near-death experiences.

Osis and Haraldsson for example, found that a number of people who expected to live—and were given excellent prognoses by their physicians—nevertheless had powerful near-death visions after which they died.

In regard to expectations of the afterlife based on religious teachings, Moody observed in his original study that ". . . many people have stressed how unlike their experiences were to what they had been led to expect in the course of their religious training."[5] No one, he said, referred to conventional images of heaven or hell in relating their experiences; indeed, no one in his sample (or mine) described anything like an archetypal hell, even though one may suppose that at least a few of our respondents might have feared "going there" when they died.

It should also be noted that since Sabom and I both found that core experiences are independent of religiousness, it can hardly be contended that religious-based expectations shape near-death experiences (although they do influence individual interpretations given them). Thus, religious-minded men and women are no more likely to have core experiences than are the religiously indifferent.

Finally, if expectations tended to structure near-death experiences, one would suppose that those already familiar with Moody-type experiences at the time of their own near-death episodes would be more likely to report such experiences. Instead, as the reader will recall, the *reverse* was true: Uninformed respondents described proportionately more core experiences.

We can conclude, therefore, that psychological expectations also fail to provide an explanatory foundation for near-death experiences.

Dreams or Hallucinations

We have previously considered whether near-death experiences have the quality of either dreams or hallucinations, and concluded that they do not. Instead, according to the testimony of survivors, these experiences were perceived as "real." This characteristic has been noted by other researchers as well,[6] and Moody himself is also very definite on the matter:

> [my informants] report what they underwent as they came near death, not as dreams, but as events which happened to them. They almost invariably assure me in the course of their narratives that their experiences were not dreams, but rather were definitely, emphatically real.[7]

In addition, both Sabom and I have found that our respondents who reported both hallucinations and a core experience could clearly distinguish between them.

Although our data here are limited to self-reports, the testimony is extremely consistent: Core experiences do not seem like a dream or an hallucination—either at the time of their occurrence or afterward.

Thus, the effort to explain (away) the core experience by reference to such psychological concepts as depersonalization, wishful thinking, prior expectations, dreams, and hallucinations has proved unsuccessful. The explanation will have to be sought elsewhere.

Pharmacological Explanations

Anesthetics

Moody has noted that occasionally the use of anesthetics is associated with phenomena that bear some similarity to the core experience. Can anesthetics alone, then, trigger the core experience, independent of the near-death state? Theoretically, this could occur if the administration of anesthetics brought about an elevation of carbon dioxide, a condition known to be capable of triggering visionary experiences.

First, though anesthetics vary, properly administered they have no specific effect on carbon dioxide levels.[8] Furthermore, in cases of cardiac arrests during surgery, the anesthetic is shut off and the patient is given oxygen instead.

Second, there is some evidence that anesthetics may actually interfere with the occurrence of near-death experiences. For example, Moody relates a case of a woman who "died" twice. The first time she did not have an experience, the lack of which *she* attributed to her anesthesized state. In the second instance, where no drugs were involved, Moody reports that she had a complex experience. This observation is also consistent with Miller's findings that the typical anesthesized patient has no recall of any kind afterward.[9]

Third, where—in an atypical case—some experience *is* described, Moody contends that the experience usually deviates in obvious ways from the core experience pattern.[10]

Finally—and most telling—not only in my study, but also in Moody's and in Sabom's, some of our respondents who described core experiences were never given any anesthetics whatever and, in some cases, did not even receive any medical treatment. Obviously, if the effect is sometimes observed in the absence of the putative cause (that is, anesthetics), that cause is not a sufficient one.

Therefore, we conclude that although anesthetics may not preclude phenomena associated with near-death experiences, such experiences cannot be explained by them.

Other Drugs

If anesthetics are not responsible for inducing the core experience, what about other drugs?

From what has already been noted, it is clear that in many instances no drugs of *any* kind were either used by or given to respondents who related core experiences. Indeed, there are a number of reasons to think that many drugs might actually interfere with, rather than facilitate, the occurrence or the recall of a core experience.

First, both Moody and Sabom have pointed out that the effects associated with drug usage in medical settings are *variable,* where the core experience itself, as we know, tends to adhere to a common format. For example, Sabom cites an instance where a core experiencer could clearly distinguish his near-death episode from a delusional hallucination stemming from the use of a medical narcotic. In this case, the near-death experience was described as "being clearer, not distorted, more 'real', and associated with a calm and peace not previously encountered."[11]

Second, in the present study, we have already noted that suicide attempters represented the category of respondents with the highest incidence of nonrecall (67%). This fact is relevant here because all but two of our suicide attempters used drugs or a combination of drugs and alcohol in an attempt to kill themselves. These drugs obviously did nothing to facilitate recall and probably induced instead a state of retrograde amnesia. Indeed, the few suicide-related cases where the deepest experiences were found tended to be those in which no drugs were used.

Finally, Osis and Haraldsson went to considerable trouble to determine the relationship between various medical factors and aspects of the near-death experience. Although their cross-cultural research was focused on mood changes and visionary (stage V) experiences occurring at the point of death, their findings are completely consistent with the thrust of this section: Drug-related conditions were associated with an *impairment* of the near-death experience. In fact, they found that fully 80% of both terminally ill and recovered patients had a visionary experience that definitely could *not* be ascribed to medication; most of these were under no medication whatever at the time of their episode. I will elaborate on these important findings later. For now, however, it will suffice to reiterate: Pharmacological factors cannot serve to explain the core experience.[12] Indeed, the evidence suggests that drug usage tends to be negatively associated with the experience.[13]

Physiological and Neurological Explanations

Since as one nears death a state of physiological deterioration sets in, revealing in itself such conditions as blood pressure decreases and interference with or stoppage of cardiac and respiratory functions, it is reasonable to suppose that the depleted physiological state of the individual may in some specific way trigger the core experience. Although there are a variety of theoretical mechanisms and biochemical changes that might be suspected of being involved here, the two that have so far been considered most seriously are temporal lobe seizurelike firing patterns and cerebral anoxia.

Temporal Lobe Involvement

Noyes and Kletti have proposed that some aspects of the core experience (for example, the panoramic life review) might be traceable to seizurelike neural firing patterns in the temporal lobe. Moody and Sabom have also considered this kind of mechanism, however, and both have found it inadequate to explain the *entire range* of near-death phenomena. Although some similarities exist between experiences induced by temporal lobe stimulation or associated with temporal lobe seizures on the one hand, and the core experience on the other, many *differences* between the two are also apparent, as Sabom clearly points out. The evidence at the present time, then, seems clearly to rule out neurological interpretations linking the core experience with abnormal temporal lobe patterns.

Cerebral Anoxia

The most common physiological speculation offered for the core experience suggests that it can be understood as resulting from insufficient oxygen to the brain (or, correlatively, the buildup of carbon dioxide). Since heart rate decreases and respiratory failures would tend to bring about precisely these effects, it is obvious that, at first glance, this is a plausible mechanism.

It is true that the overwhelming majority of our core experiencers were, so far as we know, unconscious or comatose at the time of their experience, though it seems extremely doubtful that *all* these people would, on that account alone, have experienced significant hypoxia. In Moody's investigations, it was possible for him to be even more definitive on this point. He explicitly rejects this interpretation because "... all of the phenomena [of the core experience] ... have been experienced in the course of near-death encounters in which this cutoff of blood flow to the brain never took place"[14] Again, we have a state of affairs where a postulated cause is sometimes absent from instances where the effect has been observed.

Doubt on the cerebral anoxia hypothesis is also cast by Osis and Haraldsson. They were able to demonstrate that visionary aspects of the core experience were often found in nonhallucinating, *conscious* patients whose experience occurred well before the final slide into the coma which typically precedes death. In fact, they state that "the majority of the patients who had these visionary experiences were in a normal, waking state of consciousness."[15] Such data are obviously difficult to interpret from the standpoint of cerebral anoxia.

In addition to empirical evidence that tends to undermine the cerebral anoxia interpretation, there is another argument that can be raised against it. Suppose, for a moment, that anoxia *was* the trigger to the core experience. One would still have to explain just how that condition could bring about all the *specific effects* reported by core experiencers which comprise the experience. And how would the cerebral anoxia theory explain the knowledge that core experiencers sometimes have of the status of a loved one whose death has not been disclosed to them? Examined in this light, the trouble with the anoxia theory is that it tends to be embraced too glibly and leaves most of the *specific* effects of the core experience still unaccounted for.

That at least is the case when this interpretation is used in an effort to explain away the core experience as a physiological by-product. There is, however, another, more subtle version of this theory, which does not involve using it in a *reductionistic* way, and before concluding this section it will be worth considering it.

Grof and Halifax, in drawing the parallels between naturally occurring near-death experiences and psychedelically induced "death" experiences, suggest that the underlying mechanism may be the same: disruption of oxygen transfer on an enzymatic level. In embracing this version of the cerebral anoxia hypothesis, they are still unable, of course, to rebut the empirical objections suggested by Moody's and Osis and Haraldsson's work, but their views are of interest to us because of a conceptual twist they give. According to them, the oxygen-deficient condition of the individual induces an *altered state of consciousness,* which, in turn, activates "unconscious matrices" (possibly associated with archaic parts of the brain) containing the "elements" that comprise the core experience. In other words, Grof and Halifax are suggesting that at the moment of actual or psychologically imminent death, a "stored program" (the phrase is my own) is released, which tends to unfold and to be experienced as the coherent unity I have labeled the core experience. It is imperative to note, however, that this matrix or program is associated with an *altered state of consciousness* that corresponds to an *alternate reality,* access to which is not normally available in one's ordinary waking state.

Thus, what Grof and Halifax seem to be proposing is that the onset of apparent or psychological death first induces certain critical physiological changes which then permit the individual to "slip into" another reality—a reality that becomes available only through the activation of an unconscious "program."

This is obviously a vastly different conception of the role of cerebral anoxia than the version we have already rejected. Here the alleged physiological changes do not explain away the core experience but merely enable the individual to undergo a transformation of consciousness which sensitizes him to a "new reality." The core experience itself is seen as a perception of that reality and not merely as a by-product of the individual's physiological state.

While this interpretation cannot be reconciled with all the findings so far reported by near-death researchers, the idea of a stored program, released at the point of apparent death, nevertheless, is a provocative one that warrants further attention.

Other Physiological or Neurological Explanations

It is, of course, possible to speculate on other physiological or neurological mechanisms that could play a role in shaping the near-death experience. It has, for example, been suggested that because there are some phenomenological similarities between near-death experiences and those occasioned by sensory isolation procedures[16] the same underlying mechanisms may be involved. This is certainly a reasonable hypothesis since both situations entail a severe reduction of sensory-based input to the brain; in addition, kinesthetic cues are minimal, if not absent. The only problem with this line of thinking, as Moody himself points out, is that there is very little consensus on how to interpret the visions associated with sensory isolation. For this reason, the problem would merely be shifted rather than solved: Instead of having to account for near-death visions, we would now be compelled to explain those occurring under sensory isolation. Even assuming that the visions under the two circumstances are identical—which is doubtful—one would still be left wondering whether such visions reflect the unfolding of a stored program or merely the imagistic representation of basic neurological activities in the brain. Between those alternatives is, of course, precisely where we *now* find ourselves in regard to near-death experiences.

This is not to say that sensory isolation research shouldn't be pursued with the *specific aim* of identifying experiential parallels between visions occurring in that setting and those stemming from near-death episodes. If one could, for example, artificially induce the core experience through sensory deprivation procedures, it might prove possible to gain a much clearer view of its determinants and, conceivably, its underlying neurological mechanisms. It might also turn out that nearly dying and sensory isolation "merely" represent two different but equivalent means of transcending sensory-based reality and entering into other states of consciousness, which would have to be explained in their own right. At this point, it is impossible to decide the issue, and one can only hope that some enterprising researcher will take the hint.

Another neurological possibility relevant to the near-death experience has to do with certain neurotransmitters, notably those called endorphins. These chemicals are associated with certain analgesic effects and a sense of psychological well-being,[17] conditions which, as we know, occur in the initial stages of the core experience. Perhaps coming close to death unleashes increased endorphin production in the brain, thus providing a neurological underpinning for at least the beginning of the core experience. Perhaps. No one, to my knowledge, has investigated this question. Again, we must await further research to see if this possibility represents anything more than an untested, if plausible, speculation.

In general, this is the status of proposed physiological or neurological explanations. Either research has rendered them unlikely or, as with the last two possibilities, the research remains to be done. In the meantime, all we can do is to keep an open mind on the question. Simply because no one has yet found the neurological key to unlock the mysteries of the near-death experience doesn't mean that none exists. Near-death experiences are complex phenomena and the search for a satisfactory neurological explanation, if one is diligently pursued, is likely to be demanding.

In this regard, I would like to advise any neurologically minded researcher interested in investigating this issue of one important constraint: Any adequate neurological explanation would have to be capable of showing how the *entire complex* of phenomena associated with the core experience (that is, the out-of-body state, paranormal knowledge, the tunnel, the golden light, the voice or presence, the appearance of deceased relatives, beautiful vistas, and so forth) would be expected to occur in subjectively authentic fashion as a consequence of specific neurological events triggered by the approach of death. It is not difficult—in fact it is easy—to propose naturalistic interpretations that could conceivably explain some aspect of the core experience. Such explanations, however, sometimes seem merely glib and are usually of the "this-is-nothing-but-an-instance of" variety; rarely do they seem to be seriously considered attempts to come to grips with a very puzzling phenomenon. A neurological interpretation, to be acceptable, should be able to provide a *comprehensive* explanation of *all* the various aspects of the core experience. Indeed, I am tempted to argue that the burden of proof has now shifted to those who wish to explain near-death experiences in this way.

In the meantime, I think it is fair to conclude that physiological or neurological interpretations of near-death experiences are so far inadequate and unacceptable. The definitive physiological or neurological explanation remains to be articulated. Now that the phenomenon itself has been established as a reliable feature of the dying experience, we can only applaud serious scientific research and theorizing in this direction.

While we wait for a plausible interpretation of this kind, we are obviously free to explore other categories of explanations. As we so far have found none of those stemming from the conventional sciences to be arguably adequate, we seem to be driven to consider the less conventional scientific viewpoints. Thus, we find ourselves at the threshold of the scientific study of "impossible" events—parapsychology.

Perhaps those scientists who are used to pondering impossible matters will have the conceptual tools to demystify the "impossible" event with which this book is concerned.

TWELVE

Beyond the Body: A Parapsychological-Holographic Explanation of the Near-Death Experience

As I mentioned in the first chapter, psychical researchers—the forerunners of today's parapsychologists—were among the first scientists to concern themselves with death-related experiences. Although the results of their investigations were never widely accepted by the scientific community, many of their conclusions have been upheld by more recent investigations of near-death experiences, both within and outside the field of contemporary parapsychology. It may profit us, then, to see whether parapsychological concepts can help us understand how the core experience comes about and what mechanisms underlie it.

Before that, however, I want to make a few personal observations concerning both the utility and the drawbacks of the parapsychological perspective.

In my opinion, this perspective offers us the most convincing conceptual framework for understanding the dynamics of the core experience. I say this not as a parapsychologist—for I am not one—but as a psychologist who has spent the last two years sifting through various interpretative possibilities. I will, therefore, want to linger over this approach in order to make the case for its utility as cogent as I can. Of course, I recognize that future research may undermine the value of this kind of interpretation or lead to its abandonment altogether. But, I would submit, at the present rudimentary state of our knowledge, it represents our best hope for getting an exploratory handle on this otherwise enigmatic phenomenon.

That said, it is necessary to be equally frank about the limitations and disadvantages of using the parapsychological perspective in this way. Four problems occur here. First, the empirical foundation underlying this approach is often embarrassingly weak. Although the field of parapsychology was accepted in 1969 as a member in good standing by the American Association for the Advancement of Science, and the methodological sophistication of modern parapsychological research has received high praise by knowledgeable outsiders,[1] much of the early work—to which we must sometimes refer—is often anecdotal in nature and not amenable to direct verification. It is only the impressive *convergence* of parapsychological data—both "hard" and "soft"—that justifies our reference to materials that would otherwise have no place in a book of this kind. In any event, where such questionable data need to be cited, they will be qualified accordingly.

The second point centers on the nature of parapsychological *concepts.* Historically, many of these concepts, such as telepathy, clairvoyance, precognition, psychokinesis, and so on, have simply been unacceptable to the scientific and medical community at large chiefly because they seemingly could not be accommodated within the prevailing scientific paradigm that governs the practice of what the philosopher of science, Thomas Kuhn, calls "normal science."[2] Actually, as the writer Arthur Koestler has pointed out, such concepts are not nearly as mind-boggling as those in modern quantum physics, which even physicists sometimes confess they can't understand.[3] In fact, physicists, and often Nobel laureates at that, have played a leading role in parapsychology from the outset, and the parallels between the two fields have often been noted.[4] This somehow suggests a kind of double standard by which the writings of physicists dealing with such speculative possibilities as quarks and tachyons are treated with respect, where the writings of parapsychologists on out-of-body experiences or reincarnation phenomena go unread or are simply dismissed.

There is evidence, however, that this cavalier attitude toward parapsychology is softening somewhat as scientists themselves become aware of a revised perspective in science, called a paradigm shift,[5] in which the concept of consciousness seems now to be emerging as central to work in many fields (for example, the neurosciences, medicine, physics, and psychology). In the present context, I will have to make a plea similar to that which has traditionally been sounded by parapsychologists themselves: for openness to concepts that remain generally unacceptable to the scientific community. It is my opinion that without such concepts the near-death experience simply cannot be understood. If it is true that a paradigm shift is underway, perhaps now there will be a greater openness to parapsychological concepts and my request will prove unnecessary.[6]

A third problem is perhaps more serious than mere unfamiliarity with or hostility to parapsychological ideas. I am referring here to the difficulty in establishing rigorous scientific procedures for determining the existence and effects of certain parapsychological phenomena. Although some of those I will be discussing have been studied in laboratory settings,[7] such study is not always possible. In many cases, one needs to exploit unusual circumstances or exceptional people in order to examine a given phenomenon at all. Sometimes, in order to investigate a problem, special instrumentation has to be used, the readings from which may be inaccurate, misleading, or subject to various interpretations. And, of course, parapsychological phenomena are notoriously unstable and variable. All these handicaps have contributed to the low esteem in which much parapsychological work has traditionally been held. For the time being, there is not much that we can do but to recognize these limitations as serious ones and to hope that future research, coupled with a paradigm shift, may be able to improve this state of affairs somewhat. I am not going to pretend that those matters can be ignored here. But I will try to document my case as best I can and will suggest some ways in which aspects of my interpretation could be tested. Perhaps if there are a few testable features of this interpretation that can be repeatedly confirmed, it will not be too difficult to suppose that other aspects of the interpretation—which can be checked only indirectly or not at all—might also be true.

Finally, I want to indicate that the parapsychological framework I will employ, though important, is not by itself fully adequate to deal with all the aspects of the core experience that need to be explained. For this reason, I mean to graft a *states-of-consciousness* component onto the body of the parapsychological interpretation I will propose. This component will be based, in large measure, on recent developments in neuroscience and is usually referred to as the *holographic theory* or paradigm.[8] This theory, as I will show, has specific implications for the changes in consciousness that are reported in connection with the core experience, explanations for which are not available using parapsychological concepts alone. Therefore, the explanation I will be advancing will actually involve a hybrid parapsychological-holographic model. In my view, these two components together can furnish an account of virtually every aspect of the core experience to which science is capable of speaking.

In presenting this interpretation, it seems best to start by trying to account for each of the major stages of the experience. Various specific features (for example, the life review) that are not necessarily coordinated to any one stage of the core experience will, however, also be dealt with in the course of this examination. For the purpose of this discussion, I will be condensing the five stages of the experience into three clusters: peace and out-of-the-body components (stages I and II); the tunnel and the light (stages III and IV); and "the world of light" (stage V).

Peace and Out-of-Body Components

I begin with the hypothesis that the first two stages actually represent an out-of-body experience, whether or not the individual is aware of it.

That is, I believe that what happens when an individual is near the point of apparent death is a *real,* and not just a subjective, *separation* of "something"—to be specified shortly—from the physical body. It is this "something" that then perceives the immediate physical environment and then (on subsequent stages of the core experience) goes on to experience events outside of the time-space coordinates of ordinary sensory reality.

What is it that splits off from the physical body at the point of apparent death? For the present, there are two possibilities. One is that it is a person's *consciousness* that has detached itself from his body. The other is that it is actually a *second* body of some kind. This "body" has been called by various terms, but since it is usually described by those who claim to see it as a *replica* of the physical body, let us simply use the term *the double* to refer to this alleged second body. Of course, these two possibilities need not exclude one another: It may be that what happens during a near-death episode is that one's consciousness itself shifts its "locus" from the physical body to the double, or that one's consciousness is contained within the double all along.

At this point, perhaps it is wise not to settle on a particular interpretation of what this hypothesized split actually represents. After we consider the evidence bearing on this matter, we will be in a better position to do so. Nevertheless, for the time being, just to have a way of talking about it, suppose we adopt the convention that it is one's consciousness only that leaves the body during a near-death episode.

If this is so, then all the attributes of stage I fall neatly into place. If consciousness is no longer in the body, the individual is suddenly free of all input from body-based cues; he exists as *disembodied* consciousness or consciousness (temporarily) without a body. When people report feelings of extraordinary peace, lightness, painlessness, quiet, and so forth, it certainly implies that they are free from all bodily based sensations. While such reports hardly prove that one's consciousness has left the body, these are—as we will shortly see—precisely the kinds of self-reports we would expect under such conditions. The fact that core experiencers sometimes claim to be out of their bodies obviously does nothing to lower the probability of this hypothesis.

The implication of this hypothesis, then, is that the feelings associated with stage I of the core experience are dependent on being out of body. They are, in fact, as will be shown, the affective concomitants of the out-of-body condition. To anticipate somewhat, I will argue that the entire range of core experiences actually represents an *extended* out-of-body experience and that all the phenomena associated with dying cohere impressively as soon as one begins to build on this assumption.

So much for the postulated origins of the core experience. We now need to ask: What is the *independent* evidence in support of this hypothesis? Specifically, we need to ask: (1) What are the data suggesting that out-of-body experiences are real events? (2) What are the subjective attributes associated with an out-of-body condition and what are its effects? (3) Has anyone ever seen the alleged double and, if so, under what conditions?

The answers to these questions will serve to lay the empirical foundation for a comprehensive understanding of the core experience.

It is no exaggeration to claim that in the parapsychological literature the evidence for the reality of out-of-body experiences is abundant. Crookall's work[9] alone represents an analysis of thousands of cases collected, albeit somewhat indiscriminately, from all over the world. Celia Green, and English parapsychologist, has reported the results of a survey of some four hundred out-of-body experiences,[10] providing us with a most valuable body of evidence we will be considering shortly. Charles Tart has conducted several laboratory studies of out-of-body experiences[11] and has, in addition, hundreds of cases in his own collection. Osis has also done considerable laboratory work dealing with such experiences[12] and has already reported the results of a new, extensive survey similar to Green's.[13] Much of the well known anecdotal literature on out-of-body experiences as well as most of the scientific studies conducted by parapsychologists through 1974 are described by Herbert Greenhouse,[14] a journalist. Beyond the investigators already mentioned (and this is far from a complete list), our understanding of out-of-body experiences has been deepened by the detailed descriptions of such experiences by individuals who have learned to leave their bodies virtually at will. Among the best known of these accounts are those provided by Robert Monroe, Sylvan Muldoon, and Muldoon and Hereward Carrington, Oliver Fox, Yram, and Vincent Turvey.[15]

Although interpretations of these experiences vary, the many similarities in the reports of those who claim to have been out of their bodies leave little doubt that such episodes represent a distinctive category of human experience. Obviously, I cannot do justice here to the voluminous literature I have cited dealing with such experiences, but I would invite any reader still skeptical or even curious about them to examine it with some care. Doing so will suffice, I think, to convince all but the most diehard materialists of the reality of out-of-body experiences.

If we can take the existence of such experiences as established, we next need to inquire into their attributes and effects. Here Green's work is particularly relevant. Her research evidence unequivocally demonstrates that what her informants (many of whom had their experiences in the absence of any physical trauma) report is *precisely* what our respondents relate in connection with the first two stages of the core experience.

Let me give some specific examples of this unmistakable correspondence.

> One of the most striking and characteristic features of the ecsomatic state [Green's term for what I have called an out-of-body experience] is that of autoscopy—i.e., the subject apparently viewing his own body from the outside.
>
> If the ecsomatic experience takes place indoors, the subject frequently refers to his ecsomatic position as being near the ceiling, e.g., "suspended against the ceiling." Again, the corner of the ceiling is often specified.
>
> Sometimes the subject appears to view his surroundings from a height greater than that of the room in which his physical body is located.
>
> Subjects sometimes report that their sensory acuity is increased in the ecsomatic state, saying that their senses were "heightened" or "enhanced."
>
> Many subjects comment on the "brightness" or "vividness" of colors in the ecsomatic state.
>
> There is rarely any indication that the information about his environment, which is conveyed to the subject by his perceptions in an ecsomatic state, is in any way erroneous. For example, if the subject describes his physical body as having a certain appearance while he is observing it from the outside, his description is in accordance with the observations of independent observers, if any are present.
>
> Subjects usually report that their intellectual faculties were unimpaired in the ecsomatic state; indeed, their reports often suggest a greater than usual degree of mental clarity.
>
> Subjects characteristically report their experiences of the ecsomatic state as being distinguished by sensations of naturalness, completeness, reality, lightness, freedom, vitality, and health.
>
> Nearly one in ten of single subjects [that is, individuals relating a single experience] report feelings of excitement, elation, exaltation, and the like.

> Subjects characteristically emphasize that they were not frightened, worried or anxious; observing, for example: "I looked at myself without concern," "I was not the slightest afraid," or "I certainly was not worried." On the contrary, subjects describe themselves as being calm, relaxed, detached, or indifferent.[16]

Many additional citations could be quoted, but they would only be redundant to the point I am trying to establish: the parallels between Green's description of the ecsomatic state and the initial stages of the core experience. Can there be *any* reasonable doubt that the core experience begins (at least in many instances) with an out-of-body episode?

Not only are the qualities Green describes characteristic of our accounts of the beginnings of the core experience, but some of the aftereffects coincide with those observed for our sample. Although Green apparently didn't investigate this issue, we have it on Tart's authority that

> The effect on a person of having an OOBE [i.e., out-of-body experience] is enormous. In almost all cases, his reaction is approximately, "I no longer believe in survival after death—I *know* my consciousness will survive death because I have *experienced* my consciousness existing outside my physical body."[17]

Consistent with our findings, Tart also observes that

> In almost all reported OOBES, the person is totally convinced that this was a "real" experience, not some sort of dream or hallucination.[18]

If the core experience begins with a process of separation from the physical body, we still need to know just *what* it is that separates. Here we return to the question we set aside earlier: Is there a second body—a double—that splits off at this point, or is it consciousness itself that somehow detaches itself from the physical body? If there is a double, has anyone ever seen it and, if so, under what circumstances? This question can be approached from a dual perspective: that of the "disconnected" individual himself and that of the external witness to the process of separation.

According to Moody, most of his respondents, while subjectively out of their physical body, found themselves to be "in" another body. Typically, however, his interviewees found it difficult, if not impossible, to describe this body. It is, of course, weightless and invisible, but sometimes it seems to have a human shape and is capable of at least visual and auditory perception. Moody remarks that this second body is usually characterized by such terms as a *mist, cloud, vapor, energy pattern,* or the like. He felt that the term that best epitomized its quality was the *spiritual body.*

Kübler-Ross has taken a similar position.[19] According to one report:

> Patients who "died" perceived an immediate separation of a spirit-like self-entity from their bodies. This spirit then became aware of its former body lying in bed.

On the other hand, most of our respondents implied or stated that they were *not* aware of a second body, but rather felt as though it was simply "themselves" or "their mind" that was conscious while out of the body. Our data agree with those of Green, who found that 80% of her subjects reported that they appeared to be a "disembodied consciousness" rather than inhabiting a second body. Nevertheless, she also found some instances where a second body *was* experienced and it is sometimes described as a duplicate or replica of the physical body.

From these several sources, then, about all we can conclude is that the *perception* of a second body—the double—is *sometimes* reported by persons having an out-of-body experience, but it is by no means always the case.

Perhaps the perspective of the witness to another's death will provide us with a clearer picture of what happens at death. Is the double ever seen by observers and, if so, how is it described?

It goes without saying, of course, that if such perceptions were common we should all know about them. A diligent search of the literature, however, is sufficient to establish that glimpses of a second body splitting off from the physical at death have occasionally been reported and that independent accounts reveal a strong overall similarity.

Let me begin with a suggestive instance—one which, admittedly, by itself, is hardly more than a secondhand bit of curious lore from another culture. I have taken this account from Greenhouse, although the original source is to be found in Muldoon and Carrington. According to a nineteenth-century missionary, the Tahitians believe that at death

> . . . the soul [is] drawn out of the body, whence it was borne away, to be slowly and gradually united to the god from whom it had emanated. . . . The Tahitians have concluded that a substance, taking human form, issued from the head of the corpse, because

> among the privileged few who have the blessed gift of clairvoyance, some affirm that, shortly after a human body ceases to breathe, a vapour arises from the head, hovering a little way above it, but attached by a vapoury cord. The substance, it is said, gradually increases in bulk and assumes the form of an inert body. When this has become quite cold, the connecting cord disappears and the dis-entangled soul-form floats away as if borne by invisible carriers.[20]

Is there any reason to regard this belief as anything more than a bit of anthropological exotica? If we can trust Crookall's (and others') investigations of death-bed perceptions, the answer may well be: yes.

In one of Crookall's books,[21] he presents roughly a score of such reports from Western observers, but I will mention only two instances here.

> Estelle Roberts described her husband's transition. "I saw his spirit leave the body. It emerged from his head and gradually molded itself into an exact replica of his earth-body. *It remained suspended about a foot above his body, lying in the same position* i.e., *horizontal, and attached to it by a cord to the head. Then the cord broke and the spirit-form floated away, passing through the wall.*"[22]

The similarity between this description and the Tahitian belief concerning what happens at death is unmistakable. Here is a second, more extended, example of the perception of the formation of a double, as given by Crookall. The account was furnished by a twentieth-century physician, R. B. Hout, who apparently witnessed a number of such occurrences. In this case, he is describing the death of his aunt.

> My attention was called . . . to something immediately above the physical body, suspended in the atmosphere about two feet above the bed. At first I could distinguish nothing more than a vague outline of a hazy, foglike substance. There seemed to be only a mist held there suspended, motionless. But, as I looked, very gradually there grew into my sight a denser, more solid, condensation of this inexplicable vapor. Then I was astonished to see definite outlines presenting themselves, and soon I saw this foglike substance was assuming a human form.
>
> Soon I knew that the body I was seeing resembled that of the physical body of my aunt . . . the astral body [Hout's term] hung suspended horizontally a few feet above the physical counterpart . . . I continued to watch and . . . the Spirit Body [again, Hout's

term] now seemed complete to my sight. I saw the features plainly. They were very similar to the physical face, except that a glow of peace and vigor was expressed instead of age and pain. The eyes were closed as though in tranquil sleep, and a luminosity seemed to radiate from the Spirit Body.

As I watched the suspended Spirit Body, my attention was called, again intuitively, to a silverlike substance that was streaming from the head of the physical body to the head of the spirit "double." Then I saw the connection-cord between the two bodies. As I watched, the thought, "The silver cord!" kept running through my mind. I knew, for the first time, the meaning of it. This "silver cord" was the connecting-link between the physical and the spirit bodies, even as the umbilical cord unites the child to its mother . . .

The cord was attached to each of the bodies at the occipital protuberance immediately at the base of the skull. Just where it met the physical body it spread out, fanlike, and numerous little strands separated and attached separately to the skull base. But other than at the attachments, the cord was round, being perhaps an inch in diameter. The color was a translucent luminous silver radiance. The cord seemed alive with vibrant energy. I could see the pulsations of light stream along the course of it, from the direction of the physical body to the spirit "double." With each pulsation the spirit body became more alive and denser, whereas the physical body became quieter and more nearly lifeless . . . By this time the features were very distinct. The life was all in the astral body . . . the pulsations of the cord had stopped . . . I looked at the various strands of the cord as they spread out, fanlike, at the base of the skull. Each strand snapped . . . the final severance was at hand. A twin process of death and birth was about to ensue . . . the last connecting strand of the silver cord snapped and the spirit body was free.

The spirit body, which had been supine [horizontal] before, now rose . . . The closed eyes opened and a smile broke from the radiant features. She gave a smile of farewell, then vanished from my sight.

The above phenomenon was witnessed by me as an entirely objective reality. The spirit-forms I saw with the aid of my physical eye.[23]

Besides the cases furnished in Crookall's book, there are other, similar, ones described in Sir William Barrett's pioneering book on deathbed visions and further instances are recounted by Greenhouse.

It would be easy to multiply examples of these visions of a second body separating from the physical at death, but it is not likely that additional accounts would measurably increase our understanding of this phenomenon.

What, then, can we say concerning such reports?

First, it must be acknowledged that, despite the basic similarity of these visions and the apparent sincerity and clearheadedness of the witnesses who provide them, their evidential value is very weak. This is an instance of the point I made previously, concerning the anecdotal nature of much of the data collected by psychical researchers, especially the early investigators. Many similar cases are better than a few, of course, but anecdotal data *at best* can only be suggestive.

Second, it appears that these visions tend to be seen chiefly, if not exclusively, by persons with clairvoyant sight, with "astral vision," as it were. Typically, only a single observer (of several) will report such a vision, but occasionally multiple witnesses seem to agree on essential details. If modern researchers were to reinvestigate this deathbed phenomenon, a possible strategy would be to station (with the knowledge and consent of the dying individual, of course) two or more psychics or clairvoyants in the room and ask them each to describe or sketch what they saw as death approached. If there was a correspondence in the perceived timing and formation of a spirit double among the reports of such observers, that would certainly be a valuable, if less than thoroughly convincing, corroboration of the separation hypothesis. There are claims in the literature that the second body has been successfully photographed, but due to the notorious difficulty in establishing photographic proof of paranormal events, this kind of "evidence" is highly suspect. Whether any modern photographic techniques could ever provide convincing documentary evidence for the existence of the double is, in my opinion, an open question.

Third, if, for the moment, we entertain these data seriously—if only for the purpose of hypothesis formation—they could provide us with a possible explanation for the discrepancies in the self-perceptions of a second body. Recall that some people sense or see themselves in a second body, whereas others do not. The clairvoyant visions I have cited, however, all suggest that the formation of a second or duplicate body *takes time,* that it does not appear all at once. If that is so, then it becomes understandable why only some people would feel that they were "in" such a body; presumably those who failed to report such perceptions were at an earlier stage of the dying process, a pre-second body stage, to be exact. Whether this alleged second body is actually an objective reality (albeit in another set of dimensions to which some clairvoyants are presumably sensitive) or is nothing more than what esotericists call a "thought-form" (that is, a mind-created reality in the physical space-time with which we are all familiar) is a question that we must leave unanswered. It may even be that it is not a terribly helpful way of phrasing the alternatives.

The last point that needs to be made here is perhaps the most important one. Not only is there a high level of agreement across independent witnesses concerning the formation of a spirit double at death, but their descriptions accord, on the whole, very neatly with the accounts provided by near-death survivors themselves! That is, both the *external* perspective of the witness and the *direct* testimony of the individual close to death converge on what is occurring during the *initial* stages of death: There is a splitting-off process that takes place during which one's center of self-awareness is freed from the constraints of the physical body.

Nevertheless, there is one difference of degree we should note between these two perspectives: The outside observer usually provides a more *detailed* description of these death-related events. The second body is clearly observed forming; the connecting cord is not only perceived but is usually reported to be pulsating; the cord seems to snap or be severed at the point of physical death; and so on.

Obviously, from the data presented earlier in this book, such detailed perceptions are *not* typical in the accounts of near-death survivors. Perhaps it is understandable that someone caught up in this extraordinary process would not be as sensitive to some of these detailed features as would someone observing it from the outside. In addition, since some of these alleged phenomena occur at the point of death, not all of our *near*-death survivors would have got far enough into the experience to be able to observe them. Nevertheless, one can still ask whether there are *any* cases in the literature on near-death experiences where such precise details are recounted.

Although there may well be other accounts with which I am not familiar, I was able to locate only one. Fortunately, it is a well-documented case, though not a recent one, and it was thoroughly investigated by two of the leading and most respected early researchers of the British Society for Psychical Research—Richard Hodgson and F.W.H. Myers, whose book *Human Personality and Its Survival of Bodily Death* is a classic.

The case involves a certain A. S. Wiltse, a medical doctor, who nearly died of typhoid fever in 1889. Wiltse obtained sworn depositions from the witnesses, including his own physician, concerning his medical condition and the actions that took place during his coma. In reading his testimony, the accounts I have just finished relating—especially the one provided by Dr. Hout—should be borne carefully in mind. In presenting this case, I am drawing on a summary provided by Moss.

> Feeling a sense of drowsiness come over me, I straightened my stiffened legs, got my arms over my breast, and soon sank into utter unconsciousness.
>
> I passed about four hours in all without pulse or perceptible heart beat as I am informed by Dr. S. H. Raynes, who was the only physician present. [During that time] I came again into a state of conscious existence and discovered that I was still in the body, but the body and I had no longer any interests in common.
>
> With all the interest of a physician, I beheld the wonders of my bodily anatomy, intimately interwoven with which, even tissue for tissue, was I, the living soul of that dead body. By some power, apparently not my own, the Ego was rocked to and fro, laterally, as a cradle is rocked, by which process its connection with the tissues of the body was broken up. . . . I felt and heard, it seemed, the snapping of innumerable small cords. When this was accomplished, I began slowly to retreat from the feet, toward the head. . . . As I emerged from the head, I floated up and down and laterally like a soap bubble attached to the bowl of a pipe until at last I broke loose from the body and fell lightly to the floor, where I slowly rose and expanded into the full stature of a man. I seemed to be translucent, of a bluish cast and perfectly naked. . . . As I turned, my left elbow came in contact with the arm of one of two gentlemen, who were standing at the door. To my surprise, his arm passed through mine without apparent resistance, the severed parts closing again without pain, as air re-unites. I looked quickly up at his face to see if he had noticed the contact, but he gave no sign—only stood and gazed toward the couch I had just left. I directed my gaze in the direction of his, and saw my own dead body. It was lying just as I had taken so much pains to place it. . . .
>
> Without previous thought and without apparent effort on my part, my eyes opened. Realizing that I was in the body, in astonishment and disappointment, I exclaimed: "What in the world has happened to me? Must I die again?"[24]

The detailed correspondences of Wiltse's description with the accounts given earlier are obvious and remarkable. Perhaps the parallels are so marked in his case because of the apparent extraordinary length of his clinical death. In any event, such cases, though rare, strongly support the observations provided by clairvoyant witnesses to deathbed scenes, as well as enlarge our knowledge of the details of the splitting process.

Although the evidence I have already presented—from both the external and the internal perspective—argues strongly for some kind of separation hypothesis, it may be worthwhile to consider briefly one additional class of observations bearing on the initial stages of the core experience.

I have so far scrupulously avoided drawing on esoteric writings on death (of which there is, needless to say, an unwelcome overabundance). Esoteric writers often have interesting ideas to offer, of course, but since they are usually presented *ex cathedra,* one is usually left in an intellectual quandary over how to evaluate them. Since they are generally untestable anyway, such ideas usually are of little value for scientific inquiry.

Nevertheless, I want to relax my standards here just for a moment in order to consider a few passages from a little book called *The Transition Called Death.* It was originally published in 1943 and was written by Charles Hampton, a man about whom I know nothing except that from the contents of his book I infer that he was both a priest and a clairvoyant. His book is written in the usual authoritative style common among esotericists.

The reason I wish to cite it here, however, is because what Hampton claims happens at death accords astonishingly well with the empirical evidence I have just finished presenting. Consider, for example, this passage concerning the silver cord at the moment of death:

> As the rest of the body becomes negative and dead, the heart and brain become more alive because all of the forces of the body are now concentrated in the upper part of it. When a dying person says: "Everything is becoming clear; my mind is more lucid than it has ever been," we may know that the transition is taking place. The head becomes intensely brilliant; it is like a golden bowl. All this time the silver cord also becomes more alive; etheric matter flows over it like a rapidly moving fluorescent light, but imperceptibly extracting the life force more and more, somewhat as a suction. Where the silver cord joins the main nerve ganglia it consists of thousands of very fine threads. As the life forces flow back into the higher world, those threads begin to break.[25]

Later on, he has these comments to make on the [etheric] double:

> During earth life the etheric double is coterminous with the nervous system as well as enveloping it. In outline, in form and feature, it is a replica or double of the physical body in matter finer and more tenuous than the finest gaseous substance, yet it is still physical matter. . . . The etheric double disintegrates or dematerializes once it is abandoned. It never was intended to be a vehicle of consciousness. Its function was to convey vitality to the

> body through the nervous system. . . . Its appearance is that of a bluish-white mist. . . . Death means that the etheric double is disunited from the nervous system, but the double is no more to be preserved than the physical is; it is part of the physical and will disintegrate. Immediately on awakening in the astral world the etheric matter fades out like mist.[26]

What to make of these uncanny parallels is hard to say. It certainly sounds as though Hampton was basing himself on our case material—or material like it. The extent of which his pronouncements are actually rooted in his own direct clairvoyant perceptions, however, is unfortunately never made clear. Despite his old-fashioned terminology and didactic style—elements not likely to endear him to the scientifically minded—Hampton's observations obviously express at least one esotericist position congruent with the empirical data on the separation hypothesis.

Conclusion

In making my case for an out-of-body interpretation for the initial stages of the core experience, I have argued that there is abundant empirical evidence pointing to the reality of out-of-body experiences; that such experiences conform to the descriptions given by our near-death experiencers; and that there is highly suggestive evidence that death involves the separation of a second body—a double—from the physical body. I want to reiterate here that this interpretation is subject to all the weaknesses associated with the parapsychological approach and should be evaluated in that light.

There is one implication in this separation hypothesis that needs to be brought out. Some readers may think that I have tried to sneak in the concept of the soul through the back door, even though I have steadfastly avoided this term. Certainly, talking about "something" leaving the body at death sounds suspiciously like soul-talk even if another expression is used. For my part, it might be well to remember that the root meaning of psychology—my own field—is "the study of the soul" or psyche, even though this is *not* a definition one tends to find in the textbooks. Osis and Haraldsson are even more insistent on this point when, in speaking of psychology, they observe "it is time to consider the concept of 'soul' if empirical facts demand it." Clearly, their opinion is that the facts *do* demand it. Moody seems to take a similar position.[27]

My preference, however, is to continue to eschew the word *soul* on the grounds that it is entirely too religiously tinged to be helpful in scientific work. In this respect, I find myself totally in accord with Tart's views, which are stated with admirable concision:

> . . . *soul* is not simply a descriptive term but one that has all sorts of explicit and implicit connotations for us because of our culture's religious beliefs. Even though a person may have had no formal religious training or may have consciously rejected his early training, such an emotionally potent concept as soul can have strong effects on us on a subconscious level. Since a prime requirement of scientific investigation is precise description and clear communication, a word like *soul* is difficult to deal with scientifically because of the deep, hidden reactions it may evoke in the human practitioners of science.[28]

Instead, I would content myself with saying that out-of-body experiences provide us with an empirical referent for the possible origin of the concept of soul. As such, I favor restricting its use to religious contexts. On the basis of the separation hypothesis, however, I do endorse the proposition that consciousness (with or without a second body) may function independently of the physical body.

Finally, there is the so-far-neglected issue of the "mechanisms" underlying the separation of consciousness (or the double) from the physical body. An answer to this question could only take us into the wilds of esoteric speculation, where I have no wish to roam. Even the assumption of a connecting cord of energy that breaks at death does not get us very far. What exactly is this cord? Of what is it composed? How does it function? Is there only one such cord? These and similar questions present a thicket of problems that I wish to sidestep with a polite, "No, thank you." Other explanations I have heard proposed, for example, that out-of-body experiences are triggered by the excitation of a subtle biological energy, usually called kundalini,[29] are similarly speculative and unverifiable at the present time. For me, it is sufficient to postulate that a separation can take place. Just *how* it occurs is a problem I must leave to scientists more imaginative and daring than I.

To account now for the later developments of the core experience we will have to go beyond the approach of parapsychology and employ a different but compatible framework, based, in part, on an emerging paradigm in contemporary scientific thought: holographic theory.

The Tunnel and the Light

We are now at the stage of the core experience where the individual's consciousness is assumed to have split off from his physical body and is continuing to function independently of it (possibly now having its locus in the double). And it is here that events far more puzzling than the out-of-body experience itself begin to take place. For an individual now becomes aware of traveling through a dark tunnel or void toward a brilliant golden light. Part of this experience may also entail an encounter with a "presence" or the hearing of a "voice," at which time one comes to take stock of his life in an effort to decide whether one should live or die. Part of this assessment—which is sometimes consciously linked with the presence or voice—may involve a rapid, almost instantaneous life review.

How may we understand what these extraordinary phenomena represent?

My own interpretation rests on the assumption that these experiences reflect psychological events associated with a shift in *levels of consciousness*. The intermediate stages of the core experience can be understood as initiating a transition from a state of consciousness rooted in "this-world" sensory impressions to one that is sensitive to the realities of another dimension of existence. When consciousness begins to function independent of the physical body, it becomes capable of awareness of another dimension—let us, for ease of reference, simply call it for now a fourth dimension. Most of us, most of the time, function in the three-dimensional world of ordinary sensory reality. According to the interpretation I am offering, this reality is grounded in a *body-based* consciousness. When one quits the body—either at death or voluntarily, as some individuals have learned to do—one's consciousness is then free to explore the fourth-dimensional world. This means, as we will see, that the elements of the core experience with which we are here concerned are *not* unique to near-death states but are potentially available to *anyone* who learns to operate his consciousness independent of the physical body. *Any* trigger that brings about this release may induce such experiences. It happens that coming close to death, for reasons that are obvious, is a reliable trigger effecting this release of consciousness. But to repeat: *Anything* that sets consciousness free from the body's sensory-based three-dimensional reality is capable of bringing about an awareness of the fourth dimension. There are numerous accounts of these experiences by individuals who have entered into this realm—without dying.[30]

It may strike some readers that I have rather abruptly abandoned my scientific orientation to embrace a vague mystical conception of the core experience. This is not so, however. These aspects of the core experience can be interpreted in scientific terms if one uses some of the postulates of holographic theory, which will be presented shortly. In fact, the exciting thing about this approach, which had its origins in both the neurosciences and physics, is that it offers a means to make good theoretical sense of the mystical world view. Many writers have, in fact, already contended that science and mysticism meet in holographic theory and can be seen to represent two divergent "methodological" paths leading to a common vision of the nature of the universe.[31] If these writers prove correct, holographic theory may turn out to be one of the most significant intellectual developments in the history of modern thought, because, through it, a profound synthesis of knowledge may be achieved. This is its promise, but, of course, it is entirely too soon to determine whether this promise will be realized.

In the meantime, however, we can make use of this approach to develop an interpretative framework for the understanding of the core experience.

Although holographic theory can be exceedingly complex and technical, it is possible to present a simplified version of it for our purposes here and then apply it to the core experience.

Holography is actually a method of photography—photography without a lens. In holography, the wave field of light scattered by an object—say, an orange—is recorded on a plate as an interference pattern. The idea of an interference pattern can be illustrated by imagining that one drops three pebbles simultaneously into a shallow pan of water. The resultant waves will crisscross one another. If one were then to quick-freeze the surface ripples, one would have a record of the interference pattern made by the waves. When the interference pattern is then illuminated by a laser beam, the orange reappears as a three-dimensional image. This image is a hologram.

The photographic plate itself is a jumbled pattern of swirls. These swirls—the interference pattern—store the information, however, and release it in response to a coherent light source (the laser beam).

One of the most extraordinary properties of the interference pattern is that any part of it contains information about the whole. That means that if one broke off a portion of the pattern storing information about the orange and illuminated *only* that portion, an image of the *entire* orange would appear.

What is the relevance of holography to an understanding of the states of consciousness presumably involved in near-death experiences? Just this: It has been proposed by Karl Pribram, the well-known neurosurgeon and holographic theorist, that the brain itself functions holographically by mathematically analyzing interference wave patterns so that images of objects are seen.[32] "Primary reality" itself is said to be composed of frequencies only. Different cells of the brain respond to different frequencies, and the brain functions like a *frequency analyzer,* breaking down complex patterns of frequencies into their components. These frequencies are then converted into our familiar object world by a process analogous to the illumination of an interference pattern by a laser beam. Thus, in Marilyn Ferguson's explication of Pribram's theory:

> Our brains mathematically construct "concrete" reality by interpreting frequencies from another dimension, a realm of meaningful, pattern primary reality that transcends time and space.[33]

There is apparently a fair amount of empirical support for the theory, although it remains controversial. It has proved helpful in illuminating long-standing problems in psychology, such as how memory is distributed in the brain. Consideration of this aspect of the theory, however, would take us off the track we need to follow.

To make the connection between near-death experiences and holographic theory, we must emphasize the properties of what Pribram calls the *frequency domain*—the primary reality composed of frequencies only. Of this realm Pribram has said:

> The frequency domain deals with density of occurrences only; time and space are collapsed. Ordinary boundaries of space and time, such as locations of any sort, disappear . . . in a sense, everything is happening all at once, synchronously. But one can read out what is happening into a variety of co-ordinates of which space and time are the most helpful in bringing us into the ordinary domain of appearances.[34]

From this statement it is only a short step to the implications of direct relevance to us. Pribram, who, from his own statements, appears not to have had any mystical experiences himself, nevertheless has observed:

> As a way of looking at consciousness, holographic theory is much closer to mystical and Eastern philosophy. It will take a while for people to become comfortable with an order of reality other than the world of appearances. But it seems to me that some of the

> mystical experiences people have described for millenia begin to make some scientific sense. *They bespeak the possibility of tapping into that order of reality* [that is, holographic reality] *that is* behind *the world of appearances.* . . . Spiritual insights fit the descriptions of this domain. They're made perfectly plausible by the invention of the hologram.[35]

Indeed, parapsychologists and students of mysticism have not been slow to discern the implications of Pribram's holographic theory for their respective domains of interest. If one assumes that paranormal events (such as telepathy or synchronicity—meaningful patterns of "coincidence" without apparent causal connections) or mystical experiences are manifestations of a holographic reality—where, remember, time and space are collapsed and where, therefore, causality can have no meaning—then a great deal that was formerly puzzling or paradoxical in these domains falls neatly into place, as we will see.

By now, the direction I am taking here will be evident, but let me spell it out clearly. I assume that the core experience *is* a type of mystical experience that ushers one into the holographic domain. In this *state of consciousness,* there is a *new order* of *reality* that one becomes sensitive to—a frequency domain—as time and space lose their conventional meaning. The act of dying, then, involves a gradual *shift* of consciousness from the ordinary world of appearances to a holographic reality of pure frequencies. In this new reality, however, consciousness still functions holographically (without a brain, I must assume) to interpret these frequencies in object terms. Indeed, as Pribram himself has argued—and he is not alone in this—the universe itself seems to be organized holographically.

Access to this holographic reality becomes *experientially* available when one's consciousness is freed from its dependence on the physical body. So long as one remains tied to the body and to its sensory modalities, holographic reality *at best* can only be an intellectual construct. When one comes close to death, one experiences it directly. That is why core experiencers (and mystics generally) speak about their visions with such certitude and conviction, while those who haven't experienced this realm for themselves are left feeling skeptical or even indifferent.

Such, at least, is my general interpretation of the core experience.

At this point, it becomes necessary to see whether this holographic conception can help us to make sense of any of the *specific* aspects of the core experience of concern to us here. While this may not always be the case, where holographic theory seems relevant I will try to indicate just how it is. In any event, from this point onward, it will be useful to bear the holographic perspective in mind.

Now, we must return to the specific phenomena of the core experience mentioned at the outset of this section. Let us begin with the sense of *moving through a dark tunnel or dark void.*

There are, of course, many possible interpretations of this effect. They range from assumptions that it reflects decreased blood flow or impaired respiration to speculations that tunnel "perceptions" actually represent the flow of the "vital force" through the connecting cord. Between these purely physiological and unverifiable esoteric interpretations, however, is a psychological one that has recently been suggested to me. Since it tends to square with my states of consciousness interpretation, I will offer it here.

According to Itzhak Bentov, another prominent holographic theorist and consciousness researcher, the tunnel effect

> Is a psychological phenomenon whereby the consciousness experiences "motion" from one "level" to the other. It is the process of adjustment of the consciousness from one plane of reality to another. It is usually felt as movement. This is so only for people . . . for whom this is new. For people who are used to going into the astral or higher levels, this tunnel phenomenon does not happen anymore.[36]

Thus, what Bentov appears to be saying is that the tunnel or darkness is an intermediate or transitional zone occurring between levels of consciousness. It is as though one's awareness is "shifting gears" from ordinary waking consciousness to a direct perception of the frequency domain. The gap in *time* while this shift is being effected is experienced as movement through (a dark) *space.* What is actually "moving," however, is awareness itself—or mind without a body—and what it is moving "through" is the gateway to holographic, or four-dimensional, consciousness. This is why Bentov can imply that when this shift becomes habitual it occurs instantaneously. Tunnel effects, then, are merely the mind's experience of transitions through states of consciousness.[37]

Another argument in support of a psychological interpretation of the tunnel phenomenon is based on occasional reports one can find in the literature where people claim to be aware of "others" in the tunnel. To illustrate this, let me simply relate an anecdote recently told me by Raymond Moody.[38] After one of Moody's talks, a woman approached him in order to recount her own near-death experience. Part of it involved her moving through the tunnel toward the brilliant golden light. What was unusual in her case, however, is that as she was moving through the tunnel, she saw a friend of hers coming back! As they drew nearer, somehow the friend conveyed the thought to her that he had been "sent back." Later, according to what Moody was told, it developed that her friend had actually suffered a cardiac arrest at the approximate time of the woman's own experience. At this writing, Moody is attempting to verify the details of this case and to find out whether the friend himself had any awareness of the woman informant in the tunnel. In any event, if authenticated, this is certainly a provocative, and, to my knowledge, unique case.

Finally, the tunnel effect is not restricted by any means to near-death circumstances. This phenomenon has been reported in out-of-body episodes not associated with death, where a transition in consciousness was subjectively taking place.[39] Such occurrences are again consistent with a psychological interpretation of the kind that I am advancing and also reinforce the point made earlier that aspects of the core experience may occur whenever consciousness can be detached from the body.

The next phenomenon that manifests itself is, of course, *the brilliant golden light,* which is sometimes seen at the end of the tunnel and at other times appears independent of a tunnel experience. Sometimes, as we have noted, people report that it envelops them rather than being seen as though at a distance.

What is this light? In my own view, it represents *two* distinct, but related, phenomena.

One interpretation is that it represents the "light" associated with the state of consciousness one enters after death. At this level of consciousness—where we are no longer constrained by the sensory systems of the physical body—we are presumably sensitive to a higher range of frequencies, which appear to us as light of extraordinary brilliance and unearthly beauty. In many traditions, this is spoken of as the light of the "astral" world or plane, and it is said that, for most people, this is the realm to which one "goes" after death. Of course, there is no way of providing acceptable scientific evidence for such statements, but it is perhaps at least noteworthy that virtually every description that purports to convey a sense of "the next world" depicts "a world of light." This is true not only for ancient esoteric traditions,[40] but is also found in the accounts of accomplished individual mystics, both historical[41] and contemporary.[42] Not only that, but the extensive popular literature on "life after death" is replete with descriptions from a great diversity of sources which accord with this conception of an astral realm. None of this material, however voluminous, would be evidential in the courts of science, but it still seems reasonable to ask: Could they *all* be in error?

In my own opinion, the idea of an astral reality—or call it whatever else you will—to which we may become sensitive at the point of death is not an outlandish notion, even if it can never be established scientifically. In any event, my own provisional conclusion is that one interpretation of the light phenomenon reported by our respondents is that it represents a glimpse of this astral reality.

In this context, it might also be recalled that holographic theory also postulates a primary reality defined as a "frequency domain." One can wonder whether one *level* of this frequency domain might correspond to what has traditionally been called the "astral plane."

I said before that, in my judgment, the perception of the brilliant golden light actually represents *two* separate but related phenomena. If "astral light"—as a range of frequencies to which we are sensitive in a fourth dimension, or holographic reality—is one aspect of the light effect, we still need to know what the other is.

And at this point, we must enter boldly, if with considerable trepidation, into the heart of the interpretative mystery of near-death experiences. What we will find there, however, will not so much resolve the mystery as it will enlarge our sense of it.

Moody spoke of a "being of light," and though none of our respondents used this phrase some seemed to be aware of a "presence" (or "voice") in association with the light. Often, but not always, this presence is identified with God. However this may be, I want to consider what the light represents when it is conjoined with the sense of a presence or with an unrecognized voice.

Here we must, I think, make a speculative leap. I submit that this presence/voice is actually—oneself! It is not merely a projection of one's personality, however, but one's *total self,* or what in some traditions is called the *higher self.* In this view, the individual personality is but a split-off fragment of the total self with which it is reunited at the point of death. During ordinary life, the individual personality functions in a seemingly autonomous way, as though it were a separate entity. In fact, however, it is invisibly tied to the larger self structure of which it is a part. An analogy would be that the individual personality is like a child who, when grown up, completely forgets his mother and then fails to recognize her when they later meet.

What has this to do with the light? The answer is—or so I would say—that this higher self is so awesome, so overwhelming, so loving, and unconditionally accepting (like an all-forgiving mother) and so *foreign* to one's individualized consciousness that one perceives it as *separate* from oneself, as unmistakably *other.* It manifests itself as a brilliant golden light, but it is actually *oneself,* in a higher form, that one is seeing. It is as though the individual, being thoroughly identified with his own limited personality, asks: "What is that beautiful light over there?" never conceiving for a moment that anything so magnificent could possibly be himself in his complete—and, we need to add here, divine—manifestation. The golden light is actually a reflection of one's own inherent divine nature and symbolizes the higher self. The light one sees, then, is one's own.

The higher self, furthermore, has total knowledge of the individual personality, both past and future. That is why, when it is experienced as a voice, it seems to be an "all-knowing" one (to use the phrase of one respondent).[43] That is why it can initiate a life review and, in addition, provide a preview of an individual's life events. At this level, information is stored holographically and is experienced holographically—simultaneously or nearly so. In fact, the life review *is* a holographic phenomenon par excellence; I have even heard a couple of individuals, who knew about holograms, characterize their life reviews in this way. In Pribram's words, in holographic consciousness, "everything is happening at all once, synchronously."[44]

From this perspective, it is easy to understand why so many interpret this kind of experience as "a conversation with God" or simply "being with God" and, in a sense, they are right. If one can accept the idea of a higher self, it is not difficult to assume that that self—as well as the individual himself—is actually an aspect of God, or the Creator, or any such term with which one feels comfortable. Since most people are used to thinking dualistically of God as somehow "up there" while they remain "down here," they can be expected to interpret their experience with their higher self as a direct encounter with God. The idea of "God" is, after all, more familiar to most people than is the notion of a higher self.

This is perhaps not the appropriate context to get deeply into this issue, but readers familiar with various spiritual traditions will know that the point of many spiritual disciplines, such as meditation and prayer, is precisely to cultivate an awareness of one's higher self in order to align one's individual personality with it. It is believed that in this way one can live more fully in accordance with the total being of which one's personality is but an expression. In this light, one might argue that the onset of apparent death may trigger this kind of awareness directly and involuntarily. It is interesting to observe that, as we have previously seen, such experiences tend to bring about "a spiritualization of consciousness" in some near-death survivors, similar to that expressed in the lives of those who are already consciously following some kind of "spiritual" path. Thus, one may speculate that the near-death experience may represent, at least for some, a *sudden* means of awakening to a higher spiritual reality. This kind of interpretation, however, lies outside what science itself can establish.

There is one further feature of the core experience that we must consider in connection with the higher-self interpretation I have advanced: the decisional crisis. If the higher self does indeed have total knowledge of the individual personality, both past and future, that knowledge must include the "programmed" time of death for the personality. Thus, when an individual is told that he is being "sent back" or that "his time has not yet come," this presumably reflects the "life program" of that person's life.[45] The "spirits" who sometimes give these injunctions also seem to have access to this information.[46] It will be recalled, however, that the majority of individuals who report that a decision was made about their fate feel that *they* made it themselves—that they were given a *choice.* In such instances, we must either assume that the "life program" of an individual is modifiable after all—at least in certain states of consciousness—or that the higher self knows all along what choice the individual himself will make. At this level, we can only speculate whether the sense of choice individuals feel they have is real or illusory. For my part, I would like to believe that it is real, but it is difficult to see how we could ever know this.

There are *hints,* however, in the literature on near-death experiences. Moody, for example, cites an extensive case in which a man first learned from a voice that he was to die, only to be allowed to live after all. This is how the man in question described this aspect of his experience. Before this, he had been very worried about the welfare of his adopted nephew:

> And again I felt this presence, but I didn't see any light this time, and thoughts or words came to me, just as before, and he said, "Jack, why are you crying? I thought you would be pleased to be with me." I thought. "Yes, I am. I want to go very much." And the voice said, "Then why are crying?" I said, "We've had some trouble with our nephew, you know, and I'm afraid my wife won't know how to raise him. I'm trying to put into words [he was in the midst of writing a letter when the presence manifested itself] how I feel, and what I want her to try to do for him. I'm concerned, too, because I feel that maybe my presence could have settled him down some."
>
> Then the thoughts came to me, from this presence, "Since you are asking for someone else, and thinking of others, not Jack, I will grant you what you want. You will live until you see your nephew become a man."[47]

Such a case makes it appear that the "life plan" can indeed be altered but that it may be the higher self that must consent to the change.

In considering such matters, perhaps it is best not to try to be too definitive concerning what the "rules" are! As always, the reader is free to ponder this material and arrive at his own conclusions.

I have been so far assuming, of course, that the higher-order entity which seems to be in charge of things is actually the individual's higher self, but there are certainly other interpretations. Here, however, I want to consider one possible alternative. Just as the concept of the double (the second body) may suggest to the religious-minded the idea of the soul, so the concept of the presence may appear to some to represent the idea of the "guardian angel." Before one dismisses this notion as a fancy worthy only of Sunday school classes, let me refer to a portion of a near-death experience that suggests that we should not be too quick to reject it after all.

John Lilly, a scientist best known for his research with dolphins, relates a powerful near-death experience in his autobiographical work, *The Center of the Cyclone.* In the course of his experience, he became aware of two "sources of radiance, of love, of warmth." These conveyed to Lilly a series of "comforting, reverential, awesome thoughts" and instructed him in a number of spiritual matters. Lilly's entire experience is far too complex to condense here, but at its end, these beings identify themselves:

> They say they are my guardians, that they have been with me before at critical times and that in fact *they are with me always,* but I am not usually in a state to perceive them. I am in a state to perceive them when I am close to the death of the body.[48] (My italics.)

Lilly's account certainly squares with a common understanding of the concept of "guardian angel," and other near-death testimony is consistent with this interpretation. Despite such instances, however, I am not convinced that the concept of guardians or guardian angels cannot be reconciled with that of the higher self. In fact, at this point I am inclined to believe that such guardians themselves represent an *aspect* of the higher self and not "entities," which are somehow separate and independent of it. Furthermore, a closer examination of Lilly's own account affords some evidence for this more inclusive interpretation.

Recall, first of all, that the guardians conveyed to Lilly that they were with him always. Then consider carefully these additional excerpts from Lilly's description:

> Their magnificent deep powerful love overwhelms me to a certain extent, but I finally accept it. As they move closer, I find less and less of me and more and more of them in my being. They stop at a critical distance and say to me that at this time I have developed only to the point where I can stand their presence at this particular distance. If they came any closer, they would overwhelm me, and I would lose myself as a cognitive entity, merging

> with them. They further say that I separated them into two, because that is my way of perceiving them, but that in reality they are one in the space in which I found myself. They say that I insist on still being an individual, forcing a projection onto them, as if they were two. They further communicate to me that if I go back to my body as I developed further, I eventually would perceive the oneness of them and of me, and of many others.[49]

It seems to me that the whole thrust of this paragraph is consistent with the assumption that these guardians actually represent an aspect of the total self of which Lilly's personality is only a part. He finds that they threaten to overwhelm his very (individual) essence; that he is in danger of "merging with them"; that they are not two, but one essence, together with Lilly; that they tell him that he still insists on being an individual; and so on. To me, this sounds as though it is really the higher self speaking and that is is *perceived* by Lilly in the form of two guardians.

In view of Lilly's early religious training, this makes sense. He was reared a Catholic and says that as a child he was strongly influenced by his Church's imagery regarding angels, cherubim and seraphim and the like. Since it has already been noted (see footnote 43, page 295) that the higher self tends to speak in an idiom consistent with the respondent's style, it is reasonable to suppose that it may also reveal itself in a form congruent with an individual's early religious training and belief system. This interpretation would also apply to Craig Lundahl's investigations of the near-death experiences among Mormons, where guardian angels are also sometimes mentioned.

I am inclined to conclude, therefore, that the guardian angel interpretation, rather than constituting an alternative to the one based on the concept of the higher self, is actually only an alternative *manifestation* of the latter.

We have now considered most of the major phenomena associated with the tunnel/light stages of the core experience. In my opinion, the holographic perspective provides an interpretative framework that helps to make sense of some of these phenomena, though not all of the concepts I have employed (for example, the higher self) in my explanation derive from holographic ideas. Nevertheless, in evaluating this framework's utility, we must always bear in mind that since *we* are not functioning in a holographic reality right now, we cannot reasonably expect to be in a position to judge definitively the appropriateness of this framework. In this respect, those few people who are *both* conversant with holographic theory and have had a near-death experience would seem to have the best qualifications for assessing the relevance of this kind of interpretation here.

Before turning to the last stage of the core experience, however, it may be helpful to make explicit one further aspect of the core experience that *is* easily understandable in holographic terms. I have in mind the perception of time and space. We have already seen in Chapter Six that the modal near-death experience is one in which the concepts of time and space have no meaning. This is precisely what we should expect if the experience takes place in a holographic state of consciousness, since in that state

> . . . time and space are collapsed. Ordinary boundaries of space and time, such as locations of any sort, disappear. . . .[50]

This is not only the common testimony of our own near-death survivors, but has also been indicated in the near-death narratives of famous scientist-mystics as well.

Lilly's own account, for example, ends with the lines:

> In this state, there is no time, there is an immediate perception of the past, present and future as if on the present moment.[51]

Carl Jung, a psychiatrist noted for his explorations of the deep unconscious, had an extraordinary near-death experience when he was about seventy. In describing it in his autobiographical work, *Memories, Dreams, Reflections,* he comments:

> . . . I can describe the experience only as the ecstasy of a non-temporal state in which present, past and future are one. Everything that happens in time had been brought together into a concrete whole. Nothing was distributed over time, nothing could be measured by temporal concepts. . . . One is interwoven into an indescribable whole yet observes it with complete objectivity.[52]

Later, in discussing the possibility of life after death, Jung goes on to say:

> . . . the psyche at times functions outside of the spatio-temporal law of causality. This indicates that our conceptions of space and time, and therefore of causality also, are incomplete. A complete picture of the world would require the addition of still *another dimension;* only then could the totality of phenomena be given a unified explanation. . . . I have been convinced that at least a part of our psychic existence is characterized by a relativity of space and time. This relativity seems to increase, in proportion to the

distance from [normal] consciousness, to an absolute condition of timelessness and spacelessness.[53]

Clearly Jung is describing a holographic conception of reality and is doing so, as he concedes, partly on the basis of his own near-death experience.

This conception, then, seems to fit the experiences of both gifted students of the inner life and those whose near-death experience was their first conscious encounter with a world beyond time and space. It is on the basis of such correspondences as these that holographic theory seems to me to offer the best hope of providing a scientific underpinning for an understanding of the core experience.

We will see further evidence of its applicability when we examine some of the features associated with the final stage of the experience.

"The World of Light"

The last stage of the core experience seems to fulfill the promise implied by the encounter with the brilliant golden light. Here one appears to move *through* that light and into a "world of light." At this point, the individual perceives a realm of surpassing beauty and splendor and is sometimes aware of the "spirits" of deceased relatives or loved ones.

What is this world?

In holographic terms, it is another frequency domain—a realm of "higher" frequencies. Consciousness continues to function holographically so that it interprets these frequencies in object terms. Thus, another "world of appearances" (just as the physical world, according to holographic theory, is a world of appearances) is constructed. At the same time, this world of appearances is fully "real" (just as our physical world is real); it is just that *reality is relative to one's state of consciousness.*

In esoteric terms, this is the—or one—level of the so-called astral plane. As I have already mentioned, the esoteric literature is replete with descriptions of this world of light.

If one reads the literature that purports to describe this realm or if one simply rereads the accounts of stage V provided by our respondents (or some of Moody's in *Reflections on Life After Life),* one quickly forms the impression that everything in this world is immeasurably enhanced in beauty compared to the things of our physical world. That is why it is often characterized as a world of "higher vibrations."

That such talk isn't mere metaphor was suggested by the comment of one of our respondents *(20)*, who, in attempting to describe the music of this realm, likened it to "a combination of vibrations . . . many vibrations." Of course, music *does* consist of vibrations, but it isn't ordinarily spoken of in that way. Such observations again hint that those near-death survivors who reach this stage are responding directly to a frequency (vibratory) domain of holographic reality.

But in just what sense is this realm a holographic domain? Just where do the landscapes, the flowers, the physical structures, and so forth *come from*? In what sense are they "real"?

I have one speculative answer to these questions to offer—a holographic interpretation of the astral plane. I believe that this is a realm that is created by *interacting thought structures.* These structures or "thought-forms" combine to form patterns, just as interference waves form patterns on a holographic plate. And just as the holographic image appears to be fully real when illuminated by a laser beam, so the images produced by interacting thought-forms appear to be real.

There might appear to be a serious imperfection in this holographic analogy: The pattern produced on the physical holographic plate is, after all, only a meaningless swirl. It only becomes coherent when a coherent beam of light (that is, a laser) is used to illuminate the swirl. What, then, is the equivalent of the laser in the stage V realm?

The logic of my speculation seemingly leads to a single conclusion: It is the mind itself. If the brain functions holographically to give us our picture of physical reality, then the mind must function similarly when the physical brain can no longer do so. Of course, it would be much simpler if one merely assumed, as some brain researchers (for example, Sir John Eccles[54] and Wilder Penfield[55]) appear to have done, that the mind works *through* the brain during physical life but is not reducible to brain function. If the mind *can* be supposed to exist independent of the brain, it could presumably function holographically *without* a brain. If one is not willing to grant this assumption, one would seem forced to postulate a *non-physical* brain of some kind that operates on this "astral" level. At this point, we would have passed over the limit of tolerable speculation. In my view, it is preferable merely to assume that sensorylike impressions at this level are functionally organized in a way similar to sensory impressions of the physical world, that is, holographically.

If we can assume this (leaving the question of the "mechanism" open), then the attributes of stage V would fall neatly into place. Since individual minds "create" this world (out of thoughts and images), this reality reflects, to a degree, the "thought-structures" of individuals used to the world of physical reality. Thus, the "forms" of the stage V world are similar to those of the physical world. *However,* since this is a realm that is also (presumably) composed of minds that are more clearly attuned or accustomed to this higher frequency domain, those minds can shape the impressions of the "newly arrived." The holographic result—an interaction of these thought patterns—thus tends to create a "higher gloss" to the perceived forms of this realm—that is, they are experienced in an enhanced way. One is tempted to say that *what* is seen is, at least at first, largely determined by preexisting schemata of near-death survivors, but that *how* (finely or beautifully) it appears is influenced primarily by minds used to that frequency domain.

The gist of this speculative holographic interpretation, then, is that "the world of light" is indeed a mind-created world fashioned of interacting (or interfering) thought patterns. Nevertheless, that world is fully as real-seeming as is our physical world.[56] Presumably—and this is an admitted and obvious extrapolation—as one becomes increasingly accustomed to this holographic domain and to "how it works," the correspondences between the physical world and this realm grow increasingly tenuous. Eventually one would suppose that an individual's consciousness would become anchored in the four-dimensional reality of the holographic domain and the familiar structures of our world would be radically changed there in ways we can only surmise.

The holographic interpretation can obviously also be used to account for the perception of "spirit-forms," a common feature of stage V experiences and deathbed visions. Just as object-forms are, theoretically, from a holographic point of view, a function of interacting mind patterns, so, too, are encounters with "persons" in "spirit bodies." Such "entities" are, then, the product of interacting minds attuned to a holographic domain in which thought alone fashions reality. The fact that communication between the near-death survivor and the "spirit-form" is usually said to be telepathic in nature again points to a world of existence where thought is king. From this angle, one can easily see that the manifestations in this high order of reality could easily transcend the forms of our sensory world. As individuals whose consciousnesses are rooted in the natural world, we can only speculate on the levels of mind that may be able to influence perceptions in the frequency domain associated with stage V experiences.

Before concluding our discussion of this domain, we must return to an issue we raised but did not resolve earlier: the matter of hell.

Stage V experiences, as we have seen, are almost always described in terms of paradisical imagery; the individual appears to enter a world of incomparable delight. Yet, in discussing Rawlings's work, we saw evidence that near-death survivors sometimes have hellish experiences. The bulk of the evidence plus the methodological shortcomings and tendentiousness of Rawlings's research led us to conclude that such experiences are probably very much rarer than Rawlings himself claims, but that they sometimes do occur.

The question is how to account for them.

Rawlings's own interpretation is that hellish experiences simply reflect a lack of a personal commitment to Christ. In this respect they serve as a warning of the ultimate consequences of failing to make such a commitment.

Without wishing to get entangled in theological issues, I must confess that I find this interpretation too simplistically doctrinaire for my taste. But quite apart from my personal opinion, even some of Rawlings's own evidence fails to square with his interpretation. For example, Rawlings cites the case of one man, described as "a staunch Christian, the founder of a Sunday school, and a lifelong supporter of the church,"[57] who had multiple near-death experiences, the first of which was hellish while the remaining two conformed to the Moody pattern. That kind of variation is not explicable on the basis of Rawlings's interpretation. Neither is the fact that, according to Osis and Haraldsson's cross-cultural research, Hindus have very much the same kind of paradisical (or stage V) deathbed visions as do Christians.

My own interpretation, naturally, is quite different. Rawlings is not the only investigator to find evidence of an occasional near-death experiential sequence that begins unpleasantly and ends well. Robert Crookall has also described this sequence (sometimes, however, in connection with out-of-body experiences only) and so has Moody. In addition, Ritchie has recounted a detailed personal example of this kind.[58] The sequence, in fact, when it is reported, *always* seems to be from "bad to good." My interpretation of hellish near-death experiences is predicated on this particular sequence.

In my view, what is happening in these cases is that the individual is "passing through" a lower frequency domain (although he may occasionally—temporarily—"get stuck" there). This domain is also a holographic reality and is organized in precisely the same way as the paradisical realm we have already considered. The principal difference is in the nature of the minds that are interacting to create this reality.

Even if this kind of interpretation is correct, however, there would still seem to be a problem. Why is this domain so rarely reported compared to the paradisical realm? One proposal has it that the tunnel phenomenon serves as a shield to protect the individual from an awareness of this domain.[59] It will be recalled that the tunnel effect itself was interpreted as representing a *shift in consciousness* from one level to another. Functionally, this state of affairs can be compared to a traveler riding a subway *underneath* the slums of a city: the subway tunnel prevents him ever being directly *aware* of his surroundings although the slums are there. Instead, like the typical near-death survivor, he begins his trip in darkness and emerges into the light.

That this is no mere fanciful analogy is suggested by one of Moody's cases. One woman, who was believed to be "dead" for fifteen minutes, reported that during one stage of her experience she became aware of what Moody calls a "realm of bewildered spirits." In describing this realm she says that:

> . . . what I saw was after I left the physical hospital. As I said, I felt I rose upward and it was in between, it was *before* I actually entered this tunnel . . . and before I entered the spiritual world where there is so much brilliant sunshine [that I saw these bewildered spirits].[60]

In my opinion, then, the near-death survivor is usually kept from having a direct awareness of this realm, just as, for perhaps different reasons, he usually has no recall for his "return trip." Hell may exist as a "lower frequency domain," but most near-death survivors never seem to encounter it and, if they do, only a tiny fraction seem to "get stranded" there. What may happen *after* the initial stages of death—something this research cannot speak to—remains an open question.

Conclusions

So much for the interpretation of the core experience. Since I have taken up so much space in presenting my parapsychological-holographic formulation, I will make only a few brief comments here before concluding this chapter.

First of all, by no means do I want to leave the impression that I feel that I have totally "explained" the core experience in a theoretically satisfactory way. There are many loose threads still lying about, as any perceptive reader undoubtedly will have noticed. For example, the whole question of whether the core experience is really in the nature of a "stored program" that is released at the point of death (or perhaps in other ways), as Grof and Halifax have proposed, was never resolved. The relevance of the possible neurological basis of near-death experiences is likewise still largely an uncharted territory. I can only hope that my discussion of such issues and my own interpretation will motivate other researchers to probe these matters more deeply.

Of course, it is at this point an unanswerable question whether the mysteries of the near-death experience can ever be fully understood through scientific investigation alone. Such experiences may well have an infrangible or nonphysical quality that will prevent us from providing a truly comprehensive scientific accounting of them. Try as we may (and I believe, should) to articulate such an understanding, it may finally prove to be the case that science can take us only so far in shaping that understanding.

These observations bring us, finally, to the role of religious and spiritual concepts in the interpretative matrix of the near-death experience. It is obvious that my own interpretation, though I tried to keep it grounded in scientific theory and research, occasionally was forced to stray into the spiritual realm. I confess that I did so with considerable intellectual reluctance, but also with a sense that it would have been intellectually cowardly to *avoid* doing so. In my opinion—and I could be wrong—there is simply no way to deal with the interpretative problems raised by these experiences without confronting the spiritual realm. Indeed, Pribram himself says, in a passage already quoted, that:

> Spiritual insights fit the description of this [holographic] domain. They're made perfectly plausible by the invention of the hologram.[61]

In my view, not only plausible but *necessary*. In the paradigm shift (which I have previously alluded to) that seems to be leading to a recognition of the primary role of consciousness, the world of modern physics and the spiritual world seem to reflect a *single* reality. If this is true, no scientific account of *any* phenomenon can be complete without taking its spiritual aspect into account.

This position, of course, is hardly new. It has been espoused in one form or another, not only by mystics, but by large numbers of influential scientists and intellectuals as well. I could list many names of well-known men and women to buttress this point, but instead let me conclude simply by quoting the most eminent scientist of our century. To me, his attitude suggests not only the proper spirit in which to approach the study of near-death experiences but also its likely effect on the world view of those who do explore them.

Perhaps it is ironically fitting that Albert Einstein himself did not believe in life after death, but his words nevertheless speak to the emotions kindled by familiarity—either direct or vicarious—with the near-death experience itself:

> The most beautiful thing we can experience is the mysterious. It is the source of all true art and science. He to whom this emotion is a stranger, who can no longer pause to wonder and stand rapt in awe, is as good as dead: his eyes are closed. This insight into the mystery of life, coupled though it be with fear, has also given rise

to religion. To know what is impenetrable to us really exists, manifesting itself as the highest wisdom and the most radiant beauty which our dull faculties can comprehend only in their most primitive forms—this knowledge, this feeling, is at the center of true religiousness.[62]

THIRTEEN

Implications and Applications of Near-Death Experience Research

We have now approached the limit of knowledge of the near-death experience that can be disclosed to us through scientific inquiry alone. We have seen what it is like to die and what happens in the lives of people who somehow manage to survive their encounter with death. We have also examined a variety of theoretical explanations that provide some clues concerning how such near-death experiences might occur in the first place.

But now we reach questions to which science itself is unable to speak: What is the *meaning* of these experiences? What are their implications for our lives? What do they reveal to us about the nature of reality? What is their relevance to religious and spiritual issues? In short, just what—as human beings, not merely scientists or scholars—are we to make of all this?

These are the kinds of questions that most readers of this book will, I am sure, have pondered throughout. However objective and scientific we may strive to be in our work and thinking, we naturally find ourselves dwelling on these matters, especially when we are confronted with experiences that *inherently* trigger such concerns. All of us ultimately must deal with these larger meanings, which form a context for our lives, and with the underlying values that give them direction. And these issues, as the philosopher Huston Smith has pointed out, are precisely what science, as presently constituted, cannot by its nature address.[1] For our answers here we must turn to other sources: religion, philosophy—or ourselves.

Questions such as those I have raised explicitly here admit of no certainties. There are no pat answers to be found and no consensus to be expected. Each of us must quest after these answers individually and arrive at his own conclusions. Scientific data or the pronouncements of scientists may *help* in that search, but, at bottom, it is up to each inquiring individual to achieve his own understanding through extra-scientific means.

Here, of course, our common experience has been our study of near-death experiences and their aftereffects. Each reader, accordingly, will have arrived at *some* kind of assessment of their meaning, even if it is one that is largely intuitive or implicit. Naturally, too, I have my own view—which is important chiefly for myself, not for others. If I choose to share it, it is obviously not because I give it any special weight and certainly not because I think it is compelled by our data, but only because I believe that some readers may genuinely wish to know what I myself make of these materials.

So for the next few pages, I will, in a sense, remove my white lab coat and describe my own beliefs—for what they may be worth. I feel somewhat (but not entirely!) comfortable in doing so now only because I trust that by trying not to obtrude my own opinions earlier, readers of this book will have had the opportunity to arrive at their own views uninfluenced by mine.

One of the first questions I am generally asked, following my talks on near-death experiences, is whether I believe that they are indicative of a "life after death." Usually—still having on my scientific garb—I remind my audiences that what I have studied are *near*-death experiences, not *after*-death experiences. The persons I have talked with have been close to death and, in some cases, may have survived the initial stages of death, but they have not *actually* died. Therefore, one can only extrapolate—if one is so inclined—from these experiences, what, if anything, might occur after death. There is obviously no guarantee either that these experiences will *continue* to unfold in a way consistent with their beginnings or indeed that they will continue at all.

That, I believe, is the correct *scientific* position to take on the significance of these experiences. But my questioners can usually figure that out for themselves, and that answer is not really responsive to the implicit question that I sense behind the words. *That* question is better phrased as: Well, you must have given all this plenty of thought. What do you *personally* make of it? Do *you* think there is life after death?

Here, I no longer have the floor of science to support me and must, therefore, support myself. This time, however, I would like to go beyond a simple statement of my own beliefs by outlining the framework within which they fall.

I *do* believe—but not just on the basis of my own or others' data regarding near-death experiences—that we continue to have a conscious existence after our physical death and that the core experience does represent its beginning, a glimpse of things to come. I am, in fact, convinced—both from my own personal experiences and from my studies as a psychologist—that it is possible to become conscious of "other realities" and that the coming close to death represents one avenue to a higher "frequency domain," or reality, which will be fully accessible to us following what we call death. Let me be clear, however, that it would be exceedingly naive for anyone to believe this on the basis of my say-so (or anyone else's), nor would it be justified to claim that the findings I have presented in this book in any way *prove* this assertion. What I do hope is that the material I have offered here will initiate or contribute to a personal search aimed at the exploration of such issues as "life after death." The "proof" of this matter is, in any case, not something one will find in books.

My own understanding of these near-death experiences leads me to regard them as "teachings." They are, it seems to me, by their nature, *revelatory experiences.* They vouchsafe both to those who undergo them *and* to those who hear about them an intuitive sense of the transcendent aspect of creation. These experiences clearly imply that there is something more, something *beyond* the physical world of the senses, which, in the light of these experiences, now appears to be only the mundane segment of a greater spectrum of reality. In this respect, core experiences are akin to mystical or religious experiences of the kind that William James discusses so brilliantly in his classic lectures on the subject.[2] Anyone who makes the effort to inform himself of the nature and consequences of genuine mystical or religious experiences will soon become convinced that the core experience is itself a member of this larger family.

Why do such experiences occur? Surely, no one can say with any certainty, but I have one speculative answer to offer, though I admit it may sound not only fanciful but downright playful. I have come to believe that the universe (if I may put it in this fashion) has many ways of "getting its message across." In a sense, it wants us to "wake up," to become aware of the cosmic dimensions of the drama of which we are all a part. Near-death experiences represent one of its devices for waking us up to this higher reality. The "message"—for the experiencing individual at least—is usually so clear, potent, and undeniable that it is neither forgotten nor dismissed. Potentially, then, those who have these experiences become "prophets" to the rest of us who have fallen back to sleep or have never been awake. From this point of view, the voices we have heard in this book are those of prophets preaching a religion of universal brotherhood and love and of divine compassion. This, obviously, is no new message; it acquires its significance chiefly from the unusual experiential circumstances that give rise to it—the state of consciousness associated with the onset of apparent death.

Of course, the experiences we have discussed in this book happen, for the most part, to ordinary men and women, who have neither the inclination nor, usually, the charismatic gifts to become religious prophets in any serious, sociological way. Indeed, the typical near-death survivor will disavow any such ambition and will usually say that his religious or spiritual understanding is not one he wishes to impose on others. We have already seen that some of these men and women have been, in fact, reluctant to discuss their experiences at all, much less to broadcast them indiscriminately. Certainly, no "new" religion has yet grown up around these experiences, nor is it easy to see how or why one would; there is nothing new here.

For these reasons, I prefer to think of these experiences as *seed* experiences. The individual to whom a core experience happens is given a *chance* to awake; the seed may or may not take root. If it does, it shows itself by developing the individual's spiritual sensitivity in ways that are obvious to others. As with a mystical experience, a core experience in itself is not *necessarily* transformative. Much depends on how the experience is interpreted and integrated.[3] Nevertheless, the seed experience rarely remains just a treasured memory, like a flower chastely preserved in glass. On the contrary, it appears to be a *dynamic* structure, *like* a seed, in that its nature is to unfold and flower within the individual in such a way as to manifest itself without. It is in this sense that it seems to represent a *potential* for development and self-actualization. In any event, for at least some near-death survivors, it becomes a central motif in their lives, governing the direction of their spiritual development. Such lives—where the seed potential is realized—then become lives lived in accordance with the vision one has had of what we can call Greater Life.

Another question I am often asked is why some people have (or can recall) this experience where others remember nothing on coming close to death. There has not yet been enough research directed to this question for me to give any reliable answers here. Nevertheless, in line with my own personal interpretation, I could perhaps suggest one possibility (although there is, as far as I can see, no way to test it). *If* these experiences occur in order to provide a means of awakening to a "higher reality," then perhaps those who report such experiences somehow "needed" them to provide a catalyst to their own development. If we allow ourselves the dubious luxury of a teleological argument for a moment, it may be worth pointing out that many near-death experiencers appeared to suggest that *following* their experience their lives took on a meaningfulness and direction that was formerly lacking. By the same kind of reasoning, perhaps this is why those who are previously informed about Moody-type experiences are less likely to have them: The universe has already got its message across; the seed of awakening has already been planted in a different way.

I hope it will be understood that I am offering these ideas only as personal speculations and that I myself regard some of them very doubtfully, since they are obviously based on a logic that cannot really be intellectually defended. It is certainly possible to dismiss them totally while accepting the general interpretative framework presented in the last chapter. Still, while we are on the topic of impossible questions, let me consider just one more that is sometimes put to me.

How is it, questioners will ask, that all of a sudden we are hearing so much about these near-death experiences? Haven't people always had these experiences?

In normal contexts, I usually reply that there are a number of factors responsible for this development: the liberating climate for this research provided by Kübler-Ross's work and the thanatological movement generally; improvements in resuscitation technology; the effect of Moody's work in facilitating discussion of these experiences on the part of those who formerly would not have divulged them; and so on. Typically, I also mention selected historical examples of these experiences so that my audiences will know that they are by no means only a phenomenon of modern times.

In *this* context, however, I want to mention a different kind of answer to this question, one that speaks to a different level of meaning and is quite beyond our capacity to evaluate by any formal standards. Again, it is offered only in the spirit of speculative food for thought.

I think everyone realizes that the closing decades of this century already give us grave cause for uneasiness concerning the destiny of the human race on this planet. Predictions of widespread, even global, calamities are plentiful, and though the scenarios differ, all of us have heard enough of them for them to have become real *as possibilities.* Could it be, then, that one reason why the study of death has emerged as one of the dominant concerns of our time is to help us to become globally sensitized to the experience of death precisely because the notion of death on a *planetary scale* now hangs, like the sword of Damocles, over our heads? Could this be the universe's way of "innoculating" us against the fear of death? Even if planetary catastrophes should befall us in the next decades (and of course I am not *predicting* that they will), resulting in deaths on a massive scale, we could never be certain why the thanatological movement arose when it did. But our gloomy global prospects certainly help make our interest in death understandable. The connection between these two developments is, of course, interpretable in many ways (and at several levels), of which my suggestion is merely one speculative possibility.

Now, assuming that the world *is* going to endure for a while after all, I want to turn our attention to quite different matters: new directions in near-death research and the possible applications to be derived from research in this field.

New Directions in Near-Death Research

This investigation and other similar, already-published explorations of near-death phenomena hardly constitute the last word on this important subject. In fact, it is closer to the truth to say that so far research devoted to these experiences has done little more than establish the existence of the core experience. Many questions remain to be answered concerning the factors and effects associated with it before we can say we have any real understanding of it. Accordingly, I would like to take a few moments here to suggest what lines of research seem most worthwhile to pursue, given our present level of knowledge of near-death phenomena.

First, it seems to me, we need more extensive and rigorous studies of near-death experiences in different populations. Perhaps the foremost question to be answered through this research is this: Is the core experience a *universal* phenomenon? Osis and Haraldsson's study, though highly significant in itself, is only a promising beginning in the cross-cultural work on near-death phenomena. We need much more evidence here before we can conclude anything concerning the extent to which the core experience pattern is transcultural. Also falling into this category would be studies of near-death experiences of children, prisoners who have committed serious crimes (for example, murder) and suicide attempters who have not used drugs to kill themselves. The special circumstances of these three groups would contribute significantly to our understanding of the possible limits associated with the core experience. Another interesting group to study, as Moody also pointed out, would be mothers who during or immediately after childbirth may have had a near-death experience. My impression from our study is that many unusual experiences may be found among this population.

Second, there are still a host of questions revolving around the issue of why some people recall this experience while close to death where others do not. As we have seen, it may be that at one level this issue cannot really be addressed through scientific procedures, but at other levels it is clearly amenable to scientific study. At this point, all we know is that demographic variables tend to be unrelated to recall, but there may be individual personality factors that might be predictive. For example, it could be that persons high in defensiveness or repressive tendencies might be less likely to remember such experiences where people gifted with psychic ability or ease of dream recall might be more likely. In any event, studies focusing on such individual characteristics might be able to shed some light on these questions. Of course, it would be provocative if *no* relationship whatsoever between such factors and core experience recall was uncovered! Another aspect of this issue to which further research should be directed is the question of the effect of prior knowledge on recall of a core experience. Both Sabom and I, in our independent investigations, found an unexpected and statistically significant *negative* relationship here. Future research should be geared to determining if this is indeed a consistent relationship and, if it is, how it is to be interpreted.

Third, the study of aftereffects is one richly deserving of further attention. More systematic work needs to be done documenting the changes that can be attributed to the near-death experience itself. In this work, it is also necessary to go beyond the self-report measures used here; perhaps behavior rating scales (to be filled out by family members) or direct observational investigations could be undertaken as a first step in supplementing our knowledge here. Particularly promising would be studies aimed at detecting the development of psychic abilities (which may be enhanced following core experiences) and those concerned with the measurement of belief and attitudinal shifts (for example, openness toward the idea of reincarnation, fear of death, and so forth).

A fourth set of research possibilities centers around direct observational studies of the dying. Too much of our data comes from *ex post facto* accounts and, correspondingly, not enough from on-the-scene witnesses. Such investigations are particularly crucial to assessing such notions as Rawlings's repression hypothesis and the hypothesis that the double separates from the physical body at death. Obviously, such research presents many formidable problems quite apart from the ethical issues involved, which are themselves considerable. Perhaps some public- and private-duty nurses could be enlisted to serve as unobtrusive observers, as could some chaplains. If some of these men and women were also gifted with clairvoyant sight, the possibilities for significant observations would, of course, be that much richer. In any event, some attention can and ought now be given to working out the procedures for such observational studies so as to rebut the criticisms that will stigmatize such work as "ghoulish" or "coldly clinical." Along these lines, I have some suggestions that I will put forward in Appendix IV of this book.

Finally, there is a clear need for neurologically trained investigators to undertake the kinds of studies that will speak to some of the neurological and physiological speculations outlined in Chapter Eleven. So far we have almost nothing *but* speculative possibilities that have been proposed in an offhand way to account for the core experience. Although I myself remain unconvinced that a neurological interpretation will be found that will serve to "explain away" the core experience, nevertheless, I strongly feel that the search for this level of explanation should be intensified by those who feel "the answer" may be found here. No avenue that holds out some hope for insight into this phenomenon should go untraveled—even if it contains the possibility of totally undermining one's prior convictions.

It remains to be seen what course near-death research will actually follow as it develops, but whatever work may be undertaken to enlarge our theoretical understanding of the core experience, it will run concurrently with an allied aspect of this endeavor: application. And this work is already beginning.

Applications

Granted that there is still much to be learned about near-death phenomena, we cannot delay our consideration of how the knowledge we have already gained can best be used in dealing with death and dying. Indeed, as I have just observed, the applications stemming from this research are not just matters of potential; they are, in some cases, already fact.

In my opinion, the applications tend to fall into three rather distinct categories: (1) those aimed at individuals who are close to death, either as a result of illness or psychological inclination (that is, suicidal individuals); (2) those that pertain to individuals who have recently survived a near-death incident; and (3) those directed toward individuals who have not been close to death themselves, but who may be concerned with another's actual or possible death—or their own. In what follows, I will consider each of these categories of application in turn.

Individuals Close to Death

Many people fear death and many fear it unnecessarily. We have seen how having a near-death experience, however, tends to eliminate or drastically reduce that fear of death. If one could transmit, even vicariously, the *effect* of the near-death experience to those who are about to die, could we not expect a reduction of apprehension in these men and women as well?

Sabom and Kreutziger have evidence that just hearing about these experiences tends to reduce one's fear of death. Thus, it seems that the widespread dissemination of the findings of this research would in itself tend to bring comfort to the last days of those who are about to die. But one could do more than this—much more.

If a dying person were open to it, it might be possible to play for him specially prepared audio or video tapes in which near-death survivors describe their own experiences when close to death. In other cases, it should be possible to bring together, directly, dying individuals with those who have almost died; the near-death survivor's experience could serve as a powerful reducer of death anxiety. Indeed, my colleagues and I have already made a start toward doing this work on an informal basis here in Connecticut, with gratifying results.

Of course, I do not mean to imply that such procedures, or elaborations of them, will, in themselves, dissolve all fears of death or necessarily lessen the pain often associated with dying. But they will, I feel sure, help the dying person become better prepared for death and approach it with a heightened awareness of its transcendent possibilities.

Such an approach could easily be adopted in settings where professionals work with the dying, for example, in hospices (community-oriented hospitals for the dying), in general hospitals with units for the terminally ill, and in private homes. It could also be the basis for an entirely new kind of facility that is especially designed for dying individuals—a Center for the Dying Person. I offer my thoughts on this particular topic in Appendix IV.

I have so far discussed applicational ideas that are targeted to those who know that they are soon likely to die. But what about those who *wish* to die by their own hand? Can near-death research help in deterring suicide attempts?

My own belief—which research could easily be undertaken to confirm or refute—is that the findings in such books as Moody's and my own (and, I trust, from other books that are not yet published at this writing) would tend to discourage a person from taking his own life. In my own study, it was not that suicide-related near-death experiences were in themselves unpleasant that would tend to give one pause. Indeed, they were *not* unpleasant, but merely abridged when there was any recall at all. Rather, it was the testimony of *other* near-death survivors, which tended to imply that a *successful* suicide would probably regret his action, that might serve as a deterrent. The message in Moody's books is, of course, much the same.

In fact, it has *already* been shown that exposure to near-death research findings can apparently be helpful in reducing the likelihood of suicide. Psychologist John McDonagh practices what he calls "bibliotherapy" with his suicidally minded patients. He simply has them read Moody's book *Life After Life.* His findings? It works.

Of course, we need more research than this to buttress the point, but it already seems clear that near-death research can be beneficial to those bent on suicide as well as those who will soon die as a result of disease.

Near-Death Survivors

Knowledge about near-death experiences should prove useful to those who find themselves dealing professionally with individuals who have recently survived such an episode. Particularly for physicians (including psychiatrists, of course), nurses, chaplains, and social workers whose work brings them into contact with people who have been close to death, it is highly desirable to have some familiarity with and understanding of these experiences. I am not thinking of such obvious matters as realizing that a patient may be able to hear, while comatose, a conversation taking place among the members of a medical team or that he may even be able to see his own operation taking place—from a position outside his body. These possibilities are evident from our (and others') data and medical personnel should become familiar with them—if only to save themselves from later embarrassment!

What is more consequential here is not simply awareness of these possibilities at the time of a near-death episode, but *how that episode is handled afterward.* Even if one chooses not to regard a core experience as "real," it must be recognized that to most individuals it *is* real. And, more than that, it is a psychologically powerful event with a rich potential, as we have seen, for deep personal transformation. For these reasons alone, it is extremely important for professionals working with individuals who have had this kind of experience to be alert and sensitive to the immediate psychological state of the individual following a close confrontation with death. Although I do not believe that it is necessarily wise to inquire directly as to whether the individual has had any kind of experience (such question *may* be appropriate in some cases, however), the professional should remain open to the possibility that one has occurred and that the patient may wish to talk about it. He may also be confused, afraid, or deeply disappointed (at least at first) upon finding himself still alive. An understanding of the nature and dynamics of near-death experiences is, accordingly, essential if a professional is to be able to relate sensitively to a person who has survived such an incident. In my opinion, a professional ignorant of this kind of experience can sometimes inadvertently prove an obstacle to a patient's attempt to understand and integrate it.

Moody, who is, of course, himself a medical doctor, has recently advocated a similar approach.[4] The implication here for the training of those who work with the dying is fairly straightforward: At a minimum, it involves the dissemination of information about near-death experiences. Along with other near-death researchers, I have been attempting to do precisely this in my talks to professionals in medical settings.

Individuals Concerned with Death

Of course, the vast majority of those who learn about near-death experiences are neither terminally ill nor near-death survivors. They are instead united by a single characteristic: One day they too will die. Everyone, then, has a stake in understanding what it is like to die since no one is exempt from it, however far away it may seem psychologically. Let us therefore ask: What can we—who are not confronting (so far as we know) an imminent death—learn from the study of near-death experiences? Are there lessons here that we can apply to our own lives?

Some lessons are so clear, it seems to me, that hardly any discussion is needed for them beyond merely pointing them out. *If*, for example, we take these experiences to be authentic intimations of what death itself will be like (and, as I pointed out earlier, such a view is *not* strictly warranted by our data, but represents an extrapolation from them), then our view of death *must* be affected by this interpretation. Like near-death survivors themselves, we will probably come to think of death as representing a very beautiful and joyous transitional state. This may make it a good deal easier not only to accept our own deaths, but the death of loved ones, especially those who have died prematurely. One of the profoundly gratifying experiences I have had in the aftermath of this work is to hear people tell me, following one of my talks, that they can now readily accept the death, say, of a child, in the light of these experiences. Such statements are not usually made out of intellectual conviction only, of course; they are usually expressed in a heartfelt way, sometimes accompanied by tears. These moments (and I am not claiming they are frequent episodes) bring home to me just how profound the implications of this work can be for the living.

There are, of course, other applications as well. To the extent that we, too, can live *as if* we have almost died, then the ways of being in the world evinced by our near-death survivors become *our* ways, their perceptions, our perceptions, and their values our own. To live in the shadow of death, as if each day might be our last, can clearly promote a quickening of one's spiritual sensitivity. Pettiness and selfishness recede; expressions of love and compassion are natural to this state. If you actually thought—right now, this minute—that this was really the last time you were going to be able to see your spouse, your mother, your child, this world, how would you act? Near-death survivors have been there; they almost "left" without being able to say good-bye. Since returning, many of them have had occasion to think about "what might have been." And their subsequent lives are a powerful testimony to our common ability to live more deeply, more appreciatively, more lovingly, and more spiritually. In these near-death experiences are lessons in living that apply to all of us. As one near-death survivor commented, "I somehow feel that *everyone* should have this experience one time in their life. Maybe the world would be a happier place."

Well, obviously, not everyone *can* have the experience. But everyone *can* learn from it—if he chooses to. In their book, *The Human Encounter with Death,* Grof and Halifax quote a seventeenth-century monk: "The man who dies before he dies, does not die when he dies." This aphorism speaks not only to death, however; it is a prescription *for* life. If only through the power of imagination, we can all now experience what it is like to die in order truly to live.

These reflections bring me to a final point. As I remarked in the last chapter, near-death experiences are *not* uniquely associated with the moment of apparent death; that is simply one of the more reliable pathways to them. Instead, they seem to point to a higher spiritual world, and confer the possibility of a greater spiritual awareness for those who wish to nourish the seed that they have been given. But one does not have to nearly die in order to feel the beginnings of spiritual insight. There are many paths leading to spiritual awakening and development. The people we have studied in this book all happened to have stumbled onto a common path, which some followed further than others. That is their way. What our way may be is for each of us to discern. But perhaps another lesson we can glean from the study of near-death experiences is to realize that there is indeed a higher spiritual dimension that pervades our lives and that we will discover it for ourselves in the moment of our death. The question is, however: Will we discover it in the moments of our lives?

Appendix I

Interview Schedule

Date(s) of interview______________________________
Name of interviewer______________________________
Name of interviewee______________________________
Condition of the patient at time of interview________________
____
Circumstances of the interview (other persons, noise, interruptions, and so forth)______________________________
____
____

(In introducing yourself to the patient, you should explain the purpose of the interview pretty much as follows. These initial comments should be as standardized as possible across interviewers and hospitals.)

Hello, my name is________________. I'm a [graduate student, professor] at________________. How are you feeling today? [Take whatever time necessary to establish rapport with patient.] I believe________________[name of contact] told you a little about why I wanted to speak with you. Some associates and I at the University of________________ are working on a project concerned with what people experience when they undergo a life-threatening situation, like having a serious illness or accident. I understand that you recently may have experienced such an occurrence. Is that right? [Wait for patient to respond.] Naturally it is extremely helpful to us to be able to speak with people who have had this kind of experience themselves; that's why I'm grateful to you for being willing to talk to me about this. So, in a few minutes I'd like to ask you some questions that I've prepared for this purpose, but first let me mention a few things that may help us.

The first thing I should say is that some people—not necessarily everyone, though—appear to experience some unusual things when they have a serious illness or accident or when they come close to dying. Sometimes these things are a little puzzling and people are somewhat hesitant to talk about them. [Be a little jocular here; try by your manner to put the patient at ease.] Now please don't worry about this in talking with me! I just want you to feel free to tell me *anything* you can remember—whether it makes sense to you or not. O.K.? [Wait for patient to respond.]

Now let me assure you about one further thing. These interviews will be held in strictest confidence. When we analyze our results, any information you may furnish us will never be identified by name. Since we can guarantee that these interviews will be kept anonymous and confidential, you can feel free to tell me whatever you wish without having to worry that others may learn of your private experience.

As you may remember from the informed consent sheet you signed, Mr. [Mrs., Ms.]________________, we are going to tape-record this interview. This is standard practice in these studies and makes it possible to have an absolutely accurate record of what you say without my having to try to write everything down. Naturally, the tape-recorded material will also be available *only* to my associates.

Hopefully we'll be able to complete this interview today, but if you should grow tired, please let me know and we shall complete it another time. After we're finished, I would be happy to answer any [further] questions you may have, but I think it would be best if I spoke with you first.

[Turn tape cassette on at this point—*and make sure to check it for sound level;* an inaudible or poorly audible recording is useless to us.]

INTERVIEW PROPER BEGINS HERE:

Now, Mr. [Mrs., Ms.]________________, I first need to ask you just a few questions about yourself. First of all, may I know your *age,* please? What is your *occupation*? What is the *highest grade* you completed in school? May I know your *religious preference* or affiliation, please, if you have one? [Also make a note of *race, sex*; if apparently foreign, get nationality. All this information should be written down on the prepared form even though it is on tape.] Are you *married*? [If not, find out what marital status is: Widowed? Divorced? Single? Separated?]

Now, according to________________ [name of contact], you recently________________ *[specify condition,* for example, attempted suicide, had a serious accident, illness, experienced cardiac arrest, and so forth]. Can you tell me how this came about? [Let patient narrate this as much as possible in his/her own words, but probe, as necessary, for pertinent details if not otherwise forthcoming: date, location, circumstances, witnesses, and so on. Try to get patient to describe circumstances as specifically as possible.]

Sometimes people report experiencing certain things during an incident like yours. Do you remember being aware of anything while you________________ [specify condition]. Could you describe this for me? [Probe here, if necessary, for any feelings, perceptions, imagery, visions, and so forth. Try to make the patient aware that you understand that some aspects of his/her experience may be difficult or impossible to put into words. If you think it would facilitate matters, give patient a paper and pencil in case he/she would prefer to depict some aspect of his/her experience visually. But again, allow the patient to describe the experience in his/her own words as much as possible.]

Now, I'd like to ask you certain more specific questions about your experience. [For those patients who report no awareness during their episode, say, "Even though you don't recall anything specific from this time, let me just ask you whether any of these things rings a bell with you."]

[Modify this section, as necessary, depending on what a patient has previously said.]

1. Was the kind of experience difficult to put into words? [If yes:] Can you try all the same to tell me why? What was it about the experience that makes it so hard to communicate? Was it like a dream or different from a dream? [Probe]
2. When this episode occurred, *did you think you were dying or close to death? Did you actually think you were dead?* [Important questions to ask!] Did you hear anyone actually say that you were dead? What else do you recall hearing while in this state? [Ask these questions in turn.]
3. What were your feelings and sensations during the episode?
4. Did you hear any noises or unusual sounds during the episode?
5. Did you at any time feel as though you were traveling or moving? What was that experience like? [If appropriate:] Was this experience in any way associated with the noise (sound) you described before?
6. Did you at any time during this experience feel that you were somehow separate from your own physical body? During this time, were you ever aware of *seeing* your physical body? [Ask these questions in turn. Then, if appropriate, ask:] Could you describe this experience for me? How did you feel when you were in this state? Do you recall any thoughts that you had when you were in this state? When you were outside your own physical body, where were you? Did you have another body? [If yes:] Was there any kind of connection between yourself and your physical body? Any kind of link between the two that you could see? Describe it for me. When you were in this state, what were your perceptions of time? of space? of weight? Is there anything you could do while in this state that you could not do in your ordinary physical body? Were you aware of any tastes or odors? How, if at all, were your vision and hearing affected while in this state? Did you experience a sense of loneliness while in this state? How so? [Ask these questions in turn.]
7. During your episode, did you ever encounter other individuals, living or dead? [If affirmative:] Who were they? What happened when you met them? Did they communicate to you? What? How? Why do you think they communicated what they did to you? How did you feel in their presence?
8. Did you at any time experience a light, glow, or illumination? Can you describe this to me? [If affirmative:] Did this "light" communicate anything to you? What? What did you make of this light? How

did you feel? [Or how did it make you feel?] Did you encounter any religious figures such as angels, guardian spirits, Christ, and so forth? Did you encounter any frightening spirits such as demons, witches, or the devil? [Ask questions in turn.]

9. When you were going through this experience, did your life—or scenes from your life—ever appear to you as mental images or memories? [If so:] Can you describe this to me further? What was this experience like? How did it make you feel? Did you feel you learned anything from this experience? If so, what? [Ask questions in turn.]
10. Did you at any time have a sense of approaching some kind of boundary or limit or threshold or point of no return? [If so:] Can you describe this to me? Did you have any particular feelings or thoughts that you can recall as you approached this boundary? [Ask questions in turn.] Do you have any idea what this boundary represented or meant?
11. [If patient has previously stated that he/she *came close to dying*, ask:] When you felt close to dying, how did you feel? Did you want to come back to your body, to life? How did it feel when you did find yourself conscious again in your own body? Do you have any recollection of how you got back into your physical body? Do you have any idea why you didn't die at this time? Did you ever feel judged by some impersonal force? [Ask questions in turn.]
12. This experience of yours has been (very) recent but I wonder if you feel it has changed you in any way. Do you think so or not? If it has changed you, in what way? [If necessary and appropriate, then ask:] Has this experience changed your attitude toward life? How? Has it altered your religious beliefs? If so, how? Compared to how you felt before this experience, are you more or less afraid of death, or the same? [If appropriate:] Are you afraid of death at all? [If patient had attempted suicide, ask:] How has this experience affected your attitude toward suicide? How likely is it that you might try to commit suicide again? [Be tactful.] [Ask these questions in turn.]
13. [If this has not been fully covered in question 12, then ask, if patient has stated that he/she has come close to dying:] As one who has come close to dying, can you tell me, in your own way, what you now understand death to be? What does death now mean to you?
14. Is there anything else you'd like to add here concerning this experience or its effects on you?

Religious Beliefs and Practices

Now, I have just a few more brief questions to ask you and then we'll be done. This time I'd like you to answer these questions from two points of view: How things were *before* this incident occurred and how things were *afterward.* Do you understand? [Make sure patient does.] If you feel that something *remained the same afterward* as it had been before, just say "same," O.K.? [Record responses on the appropriate form.]

1. Before this incident occurred, how religious a person would you say you were: very religious? quite religious? fairly religious? not too religious? not religious at all? [If patient selects last alternative, ask him/her if he/she would call him/herself an atheist or nonbeliever.] How would you classify yourself now? [If patient has previously classified him/herself as a nonbeliever, ask him/her if this has remained the same.]
2. Before, how strongly would you say you believed in God: absolute belief in God? strong belief? fairly strong belief? not too strong belief? no belief at all? How about now?
3. Before, how convinced were you that there was such a thing as life after death: completely convinced? strongly convinced? tended to believe there was? not sure? tended to doubt it? didn't believe it at all? How about now?
4. Before, did you believe in heaven? in hell? How about now? [If patient's views have changed, encourage him/her to say why. We are especially interested in his/her conception of *hell* here, so try to solicit his/her views on that especially.]
5. Before, had you read, thought or heard about the kind of experience you came to have? Do you recall seeing anything about this sort of thing on TV, in books and magazines, and so forth. [Try to find out *specifically* what patient has seen or read.] [If appropriate:] Have you had time or the inclination to look into this matter since your own experience? Have you talked with anyone besides me about the experience? Who? When was this? Do you remember what you talked about? [Ask these questions in turn.]

(This ends the formal portion of the interview.)

Well, Mr. [Mrs., Ms.]_________________, that's all the questions I have. Do you have any you'd like to ask me? [Answer these questions in however much detail the patient seems interested to hear no matter how long it takes—even if you have to make an extra trip back to do so; consider it part of your job.]

[When this is done] Mr. [Mrs., Ms.]___________________, I want to thank you very much for your willingness to grant us this interview. Your comments will be of great help to us in our research and if you're interested, we'd be happy to send you a brief report of our findings when our research is completed. Would you be interested in this? [If patient expresses interest, obtain an address where the report can be sent.]

Now, if for any reason, Mr. [Mrs., Ms.]___________________, you should wish to get in touch with me, this is my name and phone number—or you can write to me at this address. [Give either home address or university address. Have *cards* typed or printed up for distribution.]

I'll gather my things together now. Thank you again for helping us out. [If it applies:] We'll send you a copy of our report when our preliminary work is finished—probably in the late summer of 1978. [If appropriate, wish the patient a speedy recovery or good health—or at least—diminished pain. *Don't leave, however, until you've done all you can, if necessary, to relieve any stress or anxiety the interview may have occasioned.]*

APPENDIX II

Factors Affecting Category Comparability

The three categories of near-death survivors studied in this investigation are not directly comparable to one another for a variety of reasons. The principal differences among them are considered in this appendix.

A total of 208 names of potential interviewees was submitted to us during the course of our project; 156 of them were hospital-based referrals. Of the 52 persons who came to our attention either through nonmedical referrals or self-referrals (including responses to our ads), 48, or almost all, were interviewed. With hospital-referred cases, however, our success rate was only slightly better than one in every three. A complete breakdown of these data, for hospital referred cases only, is presented in Table A (see p. 272).

In the upper part of the table it will be seen that we had our best success (proportionately speaking) with accident victims, our least with suicide attempt victims, and illness cases falling in between. The relatively high rate (24%) of physician refusals is attributable mainly to a judgment that the patient or individual would not be sufficiently recovered from his near-death incident to be able to discuss it coherently; relatively few physicians were flatly uncooperative with the aims of this study. Potential respondent refusals, on the other hand, were motivated by a variety of reasons and excuses. If we restrict ourselves to the individuals who were genuinely available for us to interview (by eliminating those who died or could not be reached), we arrive at the figures displayed in the lower half of Table A. There it will be seen that the percentage of refusal varies widely according to condition of classification. Accident victims, though few in number, were almost always agreeable to an interview, whereas four of every five suicide attempters were either not available to us or refused on their own, as might have been expected. With illness victims, the most plentiful category, it was essentially a fifty-fifty split.

These differences in category availability and category refusal rates led us to seek out other sources to be considered in conjunction with issue of respondent selectivity. Table B (see p. 273) gives the relevant figures.

Table A

Summary of Hospital Referral Data

Condition	*No. referrals*	*Died*	*Physician refusal*	*Respondent refusal*	*No contacts made*	*Interviewed*
Illness	101	16	18	17	14	36
Accident	17	1	1	0	4	11
Suicide attempt	38	0	18	9	4	7
Totals	156	17	37	26	22	54

Refusal Rate Data

Condition	*No. possible*	*Physician refusal*	*Respondent refusal*	*Total refusals*	*% Refusals*
Illness	71	18	17	35	48.7
Accident	12	1	0	1	8.3
Suicide attempt	34	18	9	27	79.4
Totals	117	37	26	63	53.8

Table B

Source of Respondents by Condition

Condition	*Hospital/ Physician*	*Nonmedical*	*Self*	*Advertisement*	*Totals*
Illness	38	8	4	2	52
Accident	12	7	1	6	26
Suicide attempt	9	1	1	13	24
Totals	59	16	6	21	102

Inspection of Table B discloses, as the preceding discussion implied, that the source of referral is confounded with the condition of the respondent. Specifically, most (73%) illness victims were referred by medical sources; accident victims were referred by medical sources less than half the time (46%); while suicide attempters were predominantly obtained from those who replied to our ads (54%).

Taking into account all the data on category availability, source of referral, and refusal rates, it is clear that a very different pattern of selectivity was operative for each of the three conditions of near-death onset represented in our study. Illness victims were (relatively speaking) plentiful, generally referred to us by medical sources, but only available for interviews on a fifty-fifty basis. Accident victims were difficult to locate, were recruited from a number of different sources, but were almost always willing to consent to an interview when contacted. Suicide attempters were also difficult to locate, were recruited mainly by ads, and had a very high refusal rate. The net effect of these differences in selectivity is that the three principal categories of near-death onset are obviously not directly comparable for the purpose of estimating the frequency of the core experience parameter in the population from which they can be assumed to be (nonrandomly) drawn. In this regard, the illness category appears to be the most representative, owing to its size and source features, though its refusal rate is a clearly troublesome matter. One way of minimizing, but not eliminating, the problem of self-selection, is to analyze some of the frequency data according to source of referral and this I will do. This issue will be considered again following the presentation of my findings, but it was necessary to raise it here, in what may seem a premature way, in order to alert the reader to sources of noncomparability and nonrepresentativeness across categories.

Appendix III
Tape Rating Form

Respondent ______________ Rater ______________

Coding symbols and instructions:
Use + + if a characteristic is present *and* strong, vivid, stressed, or otherwise compelling.
Use + if a characteristic is present.
Use ? if a characteristic might have been present.
Use − if a characteristic has been inquired about *and* is either denied or not present.
Make no mark next to a characteristic that is not mentioned.

In the space for comments, write down any memorable quotes verbatim or indicate that there is good, quotable material by writing a large Q in the relevant space. Also use this space to note anything pertinent to your ratings or to the comments of the respondent.

With regard to uncertainty concerning the proper section to note *feelings or sensations,* when in doubt make your entries in Section D, along with any appropriate comments.

CHARACTERISTICS	*RATING*	*COMMENTS*
A. Ineffability of experience		
B. Subjective sense of dying		
C. Subjective sense of being dead		
D. Feeling and sensations at time of near-death experience (use 22.–25. to specify others)		
1. Peacefulness		
2. Calmness		
3. Quiet		
4. Serenity		
5. Lightness		
6. Warmth		
7. Pleasantness		
8. Happiness		
9. Joy, exaltation		

CHARACTERISTICS	*RATING*	*COMMENTS*
10. Painlessness		
11. Relief		
12. No fear		
13. Relaxation		
14. Resignation		
15. Curiosity		
16. Anxiety		
17. Fear		
18. Anger		
19. Dread		
20. Despair		
21. Anguish		
22.		
23.		
24.		
25.		
E. Unusual noise(s); if +, describe		
F. Sense of movement, location		
1. Quality of movement, experience		
a. Walking		
b. Running		
c. Floating		
d. Flying		
e. Movement w/o body		
f. Dreamlike		
g. Echoic		
h.		
i.		
2. Feelings on moving		
a. Peaceful		
b. Exhilarating		
c. Struggling		
d. Fearful		
e. Panicky		
f.		
g.		
3. Sensed features of location		
a. Dark void		

CHARACTERISTICS	*RATING*	*COMMENTS*
b. Tunnel		
c. Path, road		
d. Garden		
e. Valley		
f. Meadow		
g. Fields		
h. City		
i. Illumination of scene		
j. Vivid colors		
k. Music		
l. Human figures		
m. Other beings		
n.		
o.		
p.		
G. Sense of bodily separation		
1. Felt detached from body, but did not see it.		
2. Able to view body		
3. Sense of time		
a. Undistorted		
b. No sense of time		
c. Timelessness		
d.		
4. Sense of space		
a. Undistorted		
b. No sense of space		
c. Infinite, no boundaries		
d.		
5. Feeling bodily weight		
a. Ordinary bodily weight		
b. Light		
c. Weightlessness		
d. No sense of body		
e.		
6. Sense of loneliness		
H. Presence of others		
1. Deceased relative(s); if +, specify		
2. Deceased friend		

CHARACTERISTICS	*RATING*	*COMMENTS*
3. Guide, voice 4. Jesus 5. God, the Lord, a higher power, etc. 6. Angels 7. Evil spirits, devil, etc. 8. Living person(s); if +, specify		
I. Light, illumination 1. Color(s) 2. Hurt eyes?		
J. Life flashbacks 1. Complete 2. Highpoints 3. Other (specify) 4. Sense of sequence		
K. Threshold effect		
L. Feelings upon recovery 1. Not relevant 2. Anger 3. Resentment 4. Disappointment 5. Shock 6. Pain 7. Relief 8. Peace 9. Happiness 10. Gladness 11. Joy 12. 13.		
M. Changes 1. Attitude toward life a. Increased appreciation b. More caring, loving		

CHARACTERISTICS	*RATING*	*COMMENTS*
c. Renewed sense of purpose		
d. Fear, feeling of vulnerability		
e. More interested, curious		
f.		
2. Religious beliefs/attitudes		
a. Stronger		
b. Weaker		
c. Other (specify)		
3. Fear of death		
a. Greater		
b. Lesser		
c. None		
N. Idea of death		
1. Annihilation		
2. Body dies, soul survives		
3. Transitional state		
4. Continuance of life at another level		
5. Merging with universal consciousness		
6. Reincarnation ideas		
7. Peace		
8. Bliss		
9. A beautiful experience		
10. A journey		
11. No idea		
12. Nothing, nothingness		
13.		
14.		

APPENDIX IV

A Proposal for a Center for the Dying Person

I have in mind the establishment of a facility where terminally ill individuals would live while being prepared to die with full awareness of the transcendent potentialities inherent in the process of dying.

Research by Raymond Moody, Elisabeth Kübler-Ross, Karlis Osis, and many lesser-known investigators has clearly established a common pattern of transcendent experiences that appears to be triggered by the onset of death. The effect of these experiences for those who survive such near-death episodes is a virtual elimination of the fear of death, coupled with a feeling of certainty that physical death is followed by a profoundly beautiful transformation in consciousness. Through their experiences such men and women are admirably prepared to face death not only fearlessly but joyously.

It is time to draw on the implications of these experiences in order to assist others to make their life-death transition a fully transcendent one.

Toward this end, I am proposing the creation of a Center for the Dying Person. Its principal aim would be to prepare the terminally ill to die aware of what death really is: a passage into another dimension of life. This kind of preparation would have three components:

1. *The alleviation of pain.* It is hard to focus on anything while experiencing pain. The first task of the center's medical personnel would be to minimize pain. In this respect, our center would function like a hospice.

2. *The working through of fears about death.* To clear the way for an easeful death, various fears would need to be expressed and discharged and all "unfinished business" taken care of. Trained counselors and therapists would work with the patient and his family to achieve this sense of closure.

3. *Preparation for the death experience.* Dying individuals need to know what it is like to die. This information can be provided in a number of ways: (a) by discussing the findings of near-death research; (b) by playing audio and video tapes of persons describing their own near-death experiences; (c) by encouraging direct interaction between dying patients and those who have survived near-death episodes; (d) by the staff sharing their own experiences with other dying individuals; and eventually (e) by showing the dying patient (through journals, audio tapes, photographs, and so forth) how other patients at the center approached and experienced their own death.

Thus, the patient-focused program at the center would consist of *medical, therapeutic,* and *educational* features combined and blended in such a way as to facilitate a pain-free and fear-free transition into life after death.

In addition to its principal task of helping patients to die in the manner just described, the center would be designed to accomplish two other objectives:

The first would be to serve as a *training institute.* Since only a small number of patients could live and die at the Center, it would be necessary to expose professionals concerned with dying people to our procedures. In this way, our approach to death could be used in other facilities, for example, in hospitals, hospices, homes, and so forth. Thus a training program for interested professionals is a necessary adjunct to our primary work with patients at the center.

The second objective would be for the center to function as a *research facility.* Patients would understand that it is necessary to study the process of dying and to witness the moment of death if we are to help others die more easily. In this way, our patients would be "donating their deaths" to medicine just as others bequeath bodily organs. Patients thus become our teachers as they share their experience of dying with us. Accordingly, to the extent a patient's health allows, we would ask him to keep a journal, record his feelings and reactions on tape, and to participate in periodic, informal interviews. Since staff and patients would be coparticipants in the endeavor to contribute to our understanding of dying and death, the research phase of our work should not be marred by a "clinical" orientation on the part of those concerned with this aspect. *Collaborative* research is the keynote here.

The center I envisage would be small, perhaps six to ten beds. Personnel required for the operation of the center would include administrative staff, medical personnel, researchers, and therapists (including those who have had near-death experiences themselves) and religious personnel. It is possible, of course, that a given member of the staff would fall into more than one of these categories.

Eventually, if this idea proves workable, various centers could be constructed, all serving the aim of helping persons to die peacefully and joyfully. In fact, our role would be to create not only a new institution for the dying, but a new variety of midwife—one who assists not in the process of birth, but in the process of rebirth. All of us connected with this undertaking, however, would be participants in a sacred rite of passage, marking the transition from life to Greater Life. In the acting out of our respective parts, we should be always mindful that this is a journey each of us must one day take.

APPENDIX V

The International Association for Near-Death Studies (IANDS)

In order to reach the objectives discussed in the last chapter, an association was recently formed to bring together all those who share an interest in this work. Reproduced below is the association's statement of purpose and a description of its present programs and publications.

Statement of Purpose

The primary purpose of this organization is to encourage and to promote the study of a phenomenon of great contemporary significance and worldwide interest: the near-death experience (NDE). This experience, which has now been reported in many parts of the world and has been documented in thousands of cases, may well serve to enrich our understanding of the nature and scope of human consciousness itself and its relationship to physical death. By exploring the near-death experience—and related phenomena—the association hopes to make a lasting contribution to questions of perennial concern to all humanity.

IANDS was formed to serve the interests of professional and lay persons alike who are concerned with the study of NDEs and with the judicious application of knowledge based on such study in appropriate settings. The principal objectives of IANDS are:

1. To impart knowledge concerning NDEs and their implications.
2. To encourage and support research dealing with NDEs and related phenomena.
3. To further the utilization of NDE research findings in such settings as hospitals, hospices, nursing homes, funeral establishments and in death-education programs.
4. To form local chapters of near-death survivors and others interested in NDEs.
5. To sponsor international symposia, conferences and other programs concerned with NDEs and related phenomena.
6. To maintain a library and archives of material pertaining to NDEs.

All of these goals are currently being implemented by the association. IANDS publishes a quarterly newsletter, *Vital Signs,* for its membership and also publishes semi-annually a scholarly journal, *Anabiosis—The Journal for Near-Death Studies,* for persons interested in the field of near-death studies. IANDS now has three separate categories of membership: (1) The Local Chapters Division, which brings people interested in NDEs together for purposes of study, discussion and support; (2) The Research Division, for persons interested in the scholarly and professional aspects of the field; and (3) The Applications Division, for persons in the helping professions who wish to use the knowledge gained from NDE studies in their own work.

If any reader is interested in joining IANDS or in finding out more about its work, please write for free literature to:

IANDS
Box U-20
University of Connecticut
Storrs, Connecticut 06268

If you prefer, you may call IANDS directly at (203) 486-4170.

Notes

Preface

1. Such research has recently begun to appear. After my own project was underway, the important cross-cultural work of Osis and Haraldsson, *At the Hour of Death,* on deathbed visions was published. In addition, Sabom and Kreutziger's studies of near-death experiences—whose findings are impressively congruent with my own—appeared during this time. These investigations will be cited later in the book.

One

1. I. Stevenson, "Research into the Evidence of Man's Survival After Death," pp. 152–70.
2. R. Noyes, Jr., and R. Kletti, "The Experience of Dying From Falls," pp. 45–52.
3. Noyes, "The Experience of Dying," pp. 174–84; Noyes and Kletti, "Depersonalization in the Face of Life-Threatening Danger: A Description," pp. 19–27; "Depersonalization in the Face of Life-Threatening Danger: An Interpretation," pp. 103–14; "Panoramic Memory," pp. 181–93.
4. I have omitted reference to still other investigators and authors interested in near-death phenomena on the grounds that their work, though sometimes useful, is of questionable relevance, either because it is unsystematic, unreliable, or intended for popular audiences. Included here are books by Crookall, Hampton, Wheeler, Matson, and Tralins, among others. Nevertheless, some of the theoretical speculations presented by some of these authors appear to have possible merit and will be considered at a later point in this book.
5. R. A. Moody, Jr., *Life After Life,* pp. 23–24.
6. I have omitted the postexperience effects Moody includes in his original list.
7. D. H. Rosen, "Suicide Survivors: A Follow-Up Study of Persons Who Survived Jumping from the Golden Gate and San Francisco–Oakland Bay Bridges," pp. 289–94; "Suicide Survivors: Psychotherapeutic Implications of Egocide," pp. 209–15.

Two

1. This report was sent in August 1978.
2. My thanks to Charlene Alling for her contributions.
3. Our two most extreme cases were persons having had a close brush with death forty-five years and fifty-one years ago, respectively.

4. For the sake of readers not familiar with statistical terminology, the phrase "statistically significant" refers to a difference that is unlikely to have occurred by chance. For example, if one reads that a difference is (statistically) significant at the .01 level, written $p < .01$, it means that such a difference would occur less than one time in a hundred by chance. Similarly, if a difference is said to be "nonsignificant," it may be regarded as a chance fluctuation.
5. I have assigned each respondent an identification number so as to make possible for the interested reader the comparison of remarks made by respondents who are multiply quoted. These identification numbers will usually appear at the conclusion of an interview excerpt.
6. I have rearranged some of the quoted remarks for the sake of expositional coherence, but the changes do not alter the substance of this respondent's account.

Three

1. All of the data in this chapter are based on the ratings of the taped interviews. Each tape was independently rated by three judges, including the author, who were familiar with the project. In order for any given characteristic (such as peacefulness) to be coded positively, at least two raters had to agree on its presence. Thus, our criterion is a conservative one in that it probably slightly underestimates the proportion of persons exemplifying any given experimental feature. Data bearing on interrater reliability will be presented later in this book. The tape rating form itself will be found in Appendix III.
2. R. A. Moody, Jr., *Life After Death,* p. 90.
3. It should be noted that these cases are unusual only in the context of my sample. Many such cases have been reported in the extensive literature on out-of-body experiences. (See Crookall, *Out-of-the-Body Experiences;* Green, *Out-of-the-Body Experiences;* Greenhouse, *The Astral Journey;* Monroe, *Journeys Out of the Body;* Tart, in *Psychic Exploration.)*
4. Moody, *Life After Life,* p. 90.
5. Ibid., p. 84.
6. C. Hampton, *The Transition Called Death.*
7. R. Crookall, *Out-of-Body Experience,* p. 23.
8. I have been told by those who profess to have some knowledge of this phenomenon, that in order to see the alleged connecting cord, one must "turn around" while in the hypothetical second body so that one is looking back at one's physical body. Even if this is so, it is still not obvious why, if this cord does exist, more persons did not

report it, since many of my respondents did claim to have a clear view of their physical body.

9. This respondent's account is unusual in that she reports having been aware of whitish-smoky coloration in the "funnel." It is of interest that a classic manual for the dying—*The Tibetan Book of the Dead*—alludes to a smoky white light in connection with the postmortem state. The respondent herself was not familiar with this book.
10. This respondent was, however, familiar with Moody's work (from a *Reader's Digest* excerpt) *before* his near-death episode. Nevertheless, some findings to be presented later in this book indicate that such knowledge did *not* serve to bias or contaminate the accounts from informed respondents.
11. Only one respondent implied that the illumination hurt his eyes. All others denied that this was the case—usually emphatically.
12. A few others described a similar phenomenon—seeing a dazzling and rapidly changing array of beautiful rainbowlike colors—but they are not included in the figure given here.
13. The phenomenology associated with the transition from stage III to stage IV of the near-death experience appears to bear an unmistakable resemblance to certain features of the psychedelically induced "perinatal experience" as described by Grof, in which an individual seems to relive some of the events of his own birth. In these perinatal episodes, there is often a subjectively compelling experience of dying, which is, according to Grof, always followed by a sense of rebirth. The rebirth phase is said to be accompanied by "visions of blinding white or golden light" (*Realms of the Human Unconscious*, p. 139). I will discuss these parallels in Chapter Eleven.
14. There were only three such instances in my sample.
15. However, it is possible in this case that the individual received an injection of nitrous oxide at the time of his tooth extraction. He is not sure and the dentist's records are not available.
16. Two other persons used the same biblical phrase to describe their experience of a "valley."

Four

1. This term was used by a number of my respondents and seems as phenomenologically appropriate as any.
2. I did not systematically ask about the gender associated with a presence who spoke until after a couple of respondents volunteered that "it was a man's voice." Altogether six respondents identified the voice they heard as a "man's voice" or a "male voice." The voice is never recognized as belonging to anyone the respond-

ent knows or has known, though quite a few people identify the presence with God and feel they are communicating directly with Him. In two instances—both related to suicide, incidentally, unlike any of the six cases just mentioned—the respondents reported hearing a woman's voice, but the nature of the communication in these cases seemed to be qualitatively different from and a good deal less specific and vaguer than the six cases involving a distinct sense of a male presence. In the two instances where an unrecognized female voice was reported, then, it is not clear whether it is the same phenomenon as in the six nonsuicide related cases.

3. In a few cases here counted as positive, the respondent did not actually use the term *presence* or *person* or *God* to externalize the source of the communication, but the phenomenological features associated with this event were otherwise in keeping with the description given here.
4. In fact, the experience of the presence and that of encountering deceased loved ones were almost always mutually exclusive—a respondent would encounter either one or the other, *but not both.* The sole exception to this pattern is a woman who felt she "had a conversation with God" but who also claimed to have had a vague sense of deceased others. Her perception of them, however, was very indistinct compared to most of the instances where an encounter with a loved one was claimed.
5. There are some exceptions.
6. A check of her medical records reveals that the arrest was mentioned, but not its duration.
7. In this respect, this respondent was very unusual. As will be discussed later, most persons who recall a core experience are quite clearly unconscious or comatose during the time it takes place. To my knowledge, only one other woman in my sample was conscious at the time of her experience—and she, too, was aware of a light.
8. This case is very similar to that of a woman who was interviewed by some students of mine as part of a course project on near-death experiences. This woman had accidentally nearly suffocated after giving birth and found herself feeling very peaceful and light and "speaking with God." She relates: "I got there and I said, 'Gee, you know, I just couldn't die at this particular point because I had one small child at home and was about to have another one and I just had to take care of this child. And next time, I'd be very happy [laughs] to come, but at this point, it was just impossible for me and that really is the end of it.'" The next thing she knew she had regained consciousness and was talking to her incredulous husband about her experience.

9. Later in this report, in connection with accidental near-deaths, more material will be furnished concerning one of the aspects of the core experience perhaps insufficiently described here—the life review phenomenon.

Five

1. As my own case histories suggest, however, it may be that through the publication of books like Moody's, the publicity given to Kübler-Ross's work, and the films and television documentaries dealing with near-death research, near-death survivors will no longer be as hesitant to share their experiences with others.
2. H. B. Greenhouse, *The Astral Journey,* p. 54.
3. After completing this study, I did informally interview one near-death survivor who said that she was being ferried across the River Styx when she decided to come back. She also claimed her physician later told her she was clinically dead for five minutes.
4. The panoramic life review, which is an aspect of the decisional process, is, of course, imagistic, but the images do not conform to the features enumerated by Moody in connection with the threshold phenomenon.

Six

1. As it happens, the trends in the accident and suicide attempt categories are sufficiently similar that they can be safely combined. The sex ratios for these two categories (that is, illness and accident/suicide attempt) are also very similar: twenty-nine women fall into the illness category, twenty-eight into the combined accident/suicide attempt category; for men, the respective figures are twenty-three and twenty-two. Therefore, it seems justified to conduct a chi-square test for core experiencers only, according to sex and condition.
2. For readers not familiar with statistical analysis, ANOVA is the conventional abbreviation for a statistical procedure called analysis of variance. The results of this procedure disclose whether differences among a set of means are statistically significant.
3. A statistical procedure similar to an analysis of variance in which a possible "contaminating variable" can be statistically controlled for and its influence assessed.
4. R. Noyes, *Panoramic Memory,* pp. 181–93.
5. I need to emphasize that this description is based solely on my limited sample of twenty-four cases. I have heard, *secondhand,* of at least two cases where a tunnel phenomenon was apparently experienced and of one case where a light was alleged to have been

seen, but I have been unable, despite persisting efforts, to interview these people. Rosen has also obtained some intriguing data from a small sample of suicide attempters who survived leaps from either the Golden Gate or the San Francisco–Oakland Bay bridges. His findings suggest that this mode of suicide attempt may lead to certain more positive and transcendent features—if one is lucky enough to survive, that is!

6. K. Osis and E. Haraldsson, *At the Hour of Death,* p. 71.
7. By Dr. Michael Sabom, a cardiologist, who also has done an extensive near-death study; in personal communication.
8. Where this condition was specifically noted in the case of several accident victims, no recall of core experience elements was ever recounted.
9. A. M. Greeley, *Ecstasy: A Way of Knowing,* p. 46.
10. Even this fact is ambiguous, however. If one considers this voice that of a "lower order entity" (see Van Dusen, *The Natural Death in Man),* one may perhaps properly interpret its remarks as goading the individual to commit a self-destructive act. If, on the other hand, one understands this voice to represent a "presence" or a "higher order entity," the remarks acquire a different meaning, namely, "even if you try to kill yourself, you won't succeed and [thus] it will be all right." The rest of the interview gives us no real basis to favor one interpretation over the other nor does it exclude other more conventional explanations.
11. This flatly *disagrees* with Moody's statement in the Afterword of his first book, but I believe the case histories on which his assertion rests were quite few in number.
12. Recent research by Stephen Franklin and me ("Do Suicide Survivors Report Near-Death Experiences?"), has made it clear that in at least some cases of attempted suicide a full core experience *does* occur even when it is associated with drug ingestion. As a result of these new research data, I am now prepared to argue that the suicide-related near-death experience is substantially the *same* as that which is induced by illness or accident.

Seven

1. Sabom and Kreutziger, using a slightly different religiousness index, also failed to find any difference between core experiencers and nonexperiencers in religiousness.
2. A biserial correlation measures the relationship between a dichotomous variable and a continuous one.
3. B. Greyson and I. Stevenson, "Near-Death Experiences: Characteristic Features," p. 10.
4. We failed to ask these questions of 4 of our 102 respondents.

5. This unanticipated difference may not be a fluke. In a study of seventy-eight survivors of near-death episodes, Sabom found that only 12% of his core experiencers had prior knowledge of near-death research whereas 60% of nonexperiencers had such knowledge, a highly significant difference ($p<.01$).
6. It might be thought that perhaps proportionately more core experiencers had their experience before the work of Moody, Kübler-Ross, and others, was well known, thus giving rise to an artifactual rather than a "true" difference. However, analysis shows that this difference *cannot* be attributed to differences between core experiencers and nonexperiencers in incident-interview intervals. The difference between groups is just as marked for those whose near-death incident was recent (within two years of interview) as for those whose incident took place before publicity about near-death experiences was widespread.

Nine

1. The reader may rightly infer from the numbers appearing in this table (and others to appear in this section) that data from a few respondents are missing. In these cases, the relevant question was simply not asked, owing to interviewer error.
2. All these ambiguities could have been avoided, of course, if we had asked a simple pre/post form of the question, as we did with religiousness items. Unfortunately, the correct form of the question only occurred to me when the study was halfway completed. Future researchers, take note!
3. In fact, case 79—the young man who smashed his head on a rock while contemplating suicide—is officially classified as an accident.
4. Unfortunately, the number of cases here is just too small to make much of this finding. Nevertheless, the work by David Rosen and Stanislav Grof and Joan Halifax is consistent with it and with the proposition of the deterrent role of suicide-related transcendental experiences. Accordingly, I will consider it in the interpretative portion of this book.

Ten

1. Moody, *Life After Life,* p. 10.
2. Ibid., p. 93.
3. Greyson and Stevenson; Osis and Haraldsson, *At The Hour of Death,* C. Lundahl, "The Near-Death Experiences of Mormons"; M. B. Sabom, *Recollections of Death: A Medical Investigation;* Sabom and S. A. Kreutziger, "Physicians Evaluate the Near-Death Experience," pp. 1–6; Fred Schoonmaker, article in *Anabiosis,* (July 1979), pp. 1–2.

4. Moody, *Life After Life,* pp. 23–24.
5. Russell Moors. Personal communication; Sabom, *The Near-Death Experience.*
6. G. Ritchie *Return From Tomorrow.*
7. Moody *Life After Life,* p. 23.
8. Though the terms *spirits* and *presence* are used throughout this paragraph, this usage should not be taken to imply that such "entities" necessarily exist in some external sense. These terms are used for narrative convenience and because respondents themselves tended to speak in this way; this usage, however, does not imply any ontological acceptance of such entities as self-existent.
9. It has recently been reported in a newsletter of the Association for the Scientific Study of Near-Death Phenomena (now the International Association for Near-Death Studies—see Appendix V) that a Denver cardiologist, Fred Schoonmaker, has been quietly amassing data on near-death survivors since 1961. Although his research has not yet been published, it appears that better than 60% of his more than 2,300 cases have disclosed to him Moody-type near-death experiences.
10. Moody, *Life After Life,* p. 36.
11. R. Bayless, *The Other Side of Death;* Grof and J. Halifax, *The Human Encounter with Death;* R. Tralins, *Buried Alive.*
12. M. Rawlings, *Beyond Death's Door.*
13. Rawlings. Personal communication.
14. Indeed, one of the "cases" Rawlings cites—that of a Christian minister who had had a hellish near-death experience prior to entering the ministry—was previously made known to me by a correspondent who sent me a brochure written by this minister describing his experience. As might be expected, the minister makes use of this experience in a hortatory way to support a Christian belief system.
15. Rawlings. Personal communication.
16. Rawlings, *Beyond Death's Door,* p. 66.
17. Moody. Personal communication.
18. Sabom. Personal communication.
19. Grof, *Realms of the Human Unconscious;* R.E.L. Masters and J. Houston, *The Varieties of Psychedelic Experience.*
20. Grof and Halifax.
21. Noyes, "The Experience of Dying," p. 174–84.
22. Of course the phenomenon itself—quite apart from its triggers—would have to be explained in any case. This is a question we will address later in this book.
23. The data from the recent study by Stephen Franklin and me (see footnote 12, chapter 6) strongly support the invariance hypothesis.

24. Osis and Haraldsson, p. 173.
25. Moody. Personal communication.
26. Sabom and Kreutziger, pp. 1–6.
27. Ibid.
28. Sabom was skeptical of Moody's findings whereas I was persuaded that they were authentic. Sabom undertook his work to "disprove" Moody, I, to corroborate him.

Eleven

1. S. Freud, *Civilization and Its Discontents.*
2. Bayless; F.W.H. Myers, *Human Personality and Its Survival of Bodily Death;* J. H. Hyslop, *Psychical Research and the Resurrection.*
3. E. Kübler-Ross. Interview on the *Tomorrow Show* (February 14, 1978).
4. Ibid.
5. Moody, *Life After Life,* p. 98.
6. Sabom, *Recollections of Death;* Osis and Haraldsson.
7. Moody, *Life After Life,* p. 119.
8. Nancy Miller. Personal communication.
9. Ibid.
10. Moody, *Life After Life,* p. 110.
11. Sabom and Kreutziger, "Physicians Evaluate the Near-Death Experience," p. 5.
12. This is not to assert, of course, that some drugs can't artificially induce experiences that may be similar or even identical to the core experience. This is, in fact, precisely the thesis of the book by Grof and Halifax, which holds that LSD is one such agent. Although their argument is not without its weaknesses, there is clearly some support for it. I myself have talked to (though not yet interviewed formally) two people who claim to have had deep core experiences as a result of using LSD.
13. This does not mean that the use of, say, narcotics or antidepressants, would always *prevent* such an experience. As with anesthetics, such drugs can sometimes be associated with its occurrence, even if they do not initiate the experience.
14. Moody, *Reflections on Life After Life,* p. 109.
15. Osis and Haraldsson, p. 71.
16. J. C. Lilly, *The Center of the Cyclone;* R. E. Byrd, *Alone.*
17. *Mind/Brain Bulletin,* p. 8.

Twelve

1. T. X. Barber. Address at the Parapsychology Association annual convention, 1978.
2. T. S. Kuhn, *The Structure of Scientific Revolutions.*

3. A. Koestler, *The Roots of Coincidence.*
4. Koestler; L. LeShan, *The Medium, the Mystic and the Physicist;* K. R. Pelletier, *Toward a Science of Consciousness.*
5. Pelletier.
6. This may provide only cold comfort to my more scientifically minded skeptical readers, but I might add here that I came tentatively to embrace the parapsychological interpretation offered here only with reluctance and because I simply could find nothing else that seemed to fit the explanatory requirements.
7. Tart; J. Mitchell, "Out of the Body Vision"; Osis, "Out-of-the-Body Experiences: A Preliminary Survey"; Greenhouse.
8. *Re-Vision;* entire issue.
9. R. Crookall, *The Study and Practice of Astral Projection; The Techniques of Astral Projection; More Astral Projections; The Mechanisms of Astral Projection; Out-of-the-Body Experience; Casebook of Astral Projection; The Supreme Adventure.*
10 C. Green, *Out-of-the-Body Experiences.*
11. Tart.
12. Greenhouse.
13. Osis, "Out-of-the-Body Experiences."
14. Greenhouse.
15. R. A. Monroe, *Journeys Out of the Body;* S. Muldoon, *The Case for Astral Projection;* Muldoon and H. Carrington, *The Projection of the Astral Body;* O. Fox, *Astral Projection;* Yram, *Practical Astral Projection;* Turvey, *The Beginnings of Seership.*
16. Green, pp. 33, 40 41, 72, 73, 75–76, 85, 90, 93, 104.
17. Tart, p. 353.
18. Ibid., pp. 355–56.
19. Kübler-Ross. Article in *The Hartford Courant* (March 30, 1975).
20. Greenhouse, p. 26.
21. Crookall, *Out-of-the-Body Experiences.*
22. Ibid., pp. 161–62. Crookall's italics.
23. Ibid. Crookall's italics and ellipses.
24. T. Moss, *The Probability of the Impossible,* pp. 289–90.
25. Hampton.
26. Ibid.
27. Moody, *Life After Life,* p. 98.
28. Tart, p. 368.
29. G. Krishna, *Kundalini;* R. L. Peck, *American Meditation.*
30. Lilly; Swedenborg; Monroe; I. Bentov, *Stalking the Wild Pendulum.*
31. *Re-Vision:* Bentov, *Stalking the Wild Pendulum;* M. Ferguson, "A New Perspective on Reality," pp. 3–7; Pelletier; F. Capra, *The Tao of Physics.*

32. K. H. Pribram, *Languages of the Brain;* "Problems Concerning the Structure of Consciousness"; Address at the American Psychological Association annual convention, 1978; "What the Fuss is All About," pp. 14–18; Interview in *Psychology Today* (February 1979), pp. 70–84.
33. Ferguson, p. 3.
34. Pribram. Interview in *Psychology Today,* p. 84.
35. Ibid., pp. 83–84. My italics.
36. Bentov. Personal communication.
37. There is one feature of the tunnel experience that may not be conformable to this states-of-consciousness interpretation. Individuals sometimes describe the trip through the tunnel or void as an *ascent.* Likewise, one may have the feeling that the light is coming from *above.* At one level, these may be mind images that symbolically represent the shift from a *lower* to a *higher* state of consciousness. On the other hand, some might wish to argue that these perceptions *actually* reflect the experiences of the double as it traverses bands of space in dimensions to which it alone is sensible. To add a note of paradox to this puzzle, it must be recalled that since we are talking about experiences that *transcend* both space and time, almost any spacelike interpretation is bound to be false or drastically distorted.
38. Moody. Personal communication.
39. See, for example, Greenhouse, pp. 41–42.
40. R. Fremantle and C. Trungpa, eds., *The Tibetan Book of the Dead.*
41. Swedenborg.
42. Bentov, *Stalking the Wild Pendulum.*
43. Perhaps it is also worth noting here that although the voice may appear to be all-knowing, it always seems to speak in a style consistent with the respondent's own speech patterns. This is another feature that suggests that the voice or presence is an aspect of the individual's (higher) self, rather than the "voice of God" Whom we would not expect to be so colloquial!
44. Interestingly, both Grof and Halifax and Keith have interpreted the life review in holographic terms. Bentov also claims that at this level "knowledge comes in a nonlinear way . . . in large chunks, imprinted on the mind in a fraction of a second" (p. 80).
45. Advanced yogis, Zen masters, and other spiritual adepts are sometimes said to be able to forecast the time of their death, often well in advance of the actual date. Perhaps the best-known documented case of this kind in the West is that of the famous eighteenth-century scientist-seer, Emanuel Swedenborg, who told John Wesley in February 1772 that he, Swedenborg, would not be

able to meet him later that year since he was to die on March 29—which he did. Presumably, such information is available by making contact with the higher self *before* the moment of death.

46. Craig Lundahl's work on near-death experiences among Mormons gives some particularly striking examples of this kind.
47. Moody, *Life After Life,* p. 75.
48. Lilly, p. 28.
49. Ibid., pp. 26–27.
50. Pribram. Interview in *Psychology Today,* p. 84.
51. Lilly, p. 27.
52. C. G. Jung, *Memories, Dreams, Reflections,* p. 296.
53. Ibid., pp. 304–5. My italics.
54. J. C. Eccles, *The Understanding of the Brain.*
55. W. Penfield, *The Mystery of the Mind.*
56. This interpretation is obviously consistent with "the doctrine of correspondences" as taught by Swedenborg and similar ideas which can be traced back to Plato and the hermetic tradition. The aspect of that teaching relevant here is that the physical world is merely a reflection of a higher world and that everything in this world has its correspondent *there.* It seems reasonable to suppose that visionary "after-life" experiences (for which Swedenborg was famous during his lifetime) may have contributed the experiential foundation to this doctrine.
57. M. Rawlings, *Beyond Death's Door,* p. 118.
58. Ritchie.
59. Bentov. Personal communication.
60. Moody, *Reflections on Life After Life,* p. 20. Moody's italics.
61. Pribram. Interview in *Psychology Today,* p. 84.
62. A. Einstein, *Living Philosophies,* p. 6.

Thirteen

1. H. Smith, *Forgotten Truth.*
2. W. James, *The Varieties of Religious Experience.*
3. That is one reason why it is so important that medical and religious professionals in particular be knowledgeable concerning these experiences. If they are, they can help the seed to take root just through their understanding rather than inadvertently destroying it through ignorance. My hope is that this book might contribute something toward that end. In any event, we will return to this matter toward the close of this chapter.
4. Moody, "Near-Death Experiences: Some Clinical Considerations."

Bibliography

Barber, T. X. Address at the Parapsychology Association annual convention, St. Louis, Mo., August 1978.

Barrett, W. *Death-Bed Visions.* London: Methuen, 1926.

Bayless, R. *The Other Side of Death.* New Hyde Park, N.Y.: University Books, 1971.

Bentov, I. *Stalking the Wild Pendulum.* New York: E. P. Dutton, 1977.

———. Personal communication, 1979.

Byrd, R. E. *Alone.* New York: Ace Books, 1938.

Capra, F. *The Tao of Physics.* Berkeley: Shambhala, 1975.

Crookall, R. *The Study and Practice of Astral Projection.* London: Aquarian Press, 1961.

———. *The Techniques of Astral Projection.* London: Aquarian Press, 1964.

———. *More Astral Projections.* London: Aquarian Press, 1964.

———. *The Mechanisms of Astral Projection.* Moradabad, India: Darshana International, 1968.

———. *Out-of-the-Body Experiences.* New York: University Books, 1970.

———. *Casebook of Astral Projection.* New Hyde Park, N.Y.: University Books, 1972.

———. *The Supreme Adventure.* Greenwood, S.C.: Attic Press, 1975.

Eccles, J. C. *The Understanding of the Brain.* New York: McGraw-Hill, 1973.

Einstein, A. *Living Philosophies.* New York: Simon and Schuster, 1931.

Ferguson, M. "A New Perspective on Reality." *Re-Vision,* 1 (1978): 3/4, 3–7.

Fox, O. *Astral Projection.* London: Rider and Co., 1939.

Fremantle, R., and Trungpa, C., eds. *The Tibetan Book of the Dead.* Berkeley: Shambhala, 1975.

Freud, S. *Civilization and Its Discontents.* Garden City, N.Y.: Doubleday, 1958.

Greeley, A. M. *Ecstasy: A Way of Knowing.* Englewood Cliffs, N.J.: Prentice-Hall, 1974.

Green, C. *Out-of-the-Body Experiences.* New York: Ballantine, 1968.

Greenhouse, H. B. *The Astral Journey.* New York: Avon, 1974.

Greyson, B., and Stevenson, I. "Near-Death Experiences: Characteristic Features." University of Virginia, unpublished manuscript, 1978.

Grof, S. *Realms of the Human Unconscious.* New York: Viking, 1975.

———, and Halifax, J. *The Human Encounter with Death.* New York: Dutton, 1977.

Gurney, E. et al. *Phantasms of the Living.* London: Trubner and Co., 1886.

Hampton, C. *The Transition Called Death.* Wheaton, Ill.: The Theosophical Publishing House, 1972.

Heim, A. "Notizen ueber den Tod durch Absturz." *Jahrbuch des Schweizer Alpenklub* 27 (1892): 327–337.

Hyslop, J. H. *Psychical Research and the Resurrection.* Boston: Small, Maynard and Co., 1908.

James, W. *The Varieties of Religious Experience.* New York: Mentor, 1958.

Jung, C. G. *Memories, Dreams, Reflections.* New York: Vintage Books, 1961.

Keith, F. "Of Time and Mind: From Paradox to Paradigm." In J. White, ed., *Frontiers of Consciousness.* New York: Harper & Row, 1976.

Koestler, A. *The Roots of Coincidence.* New York: Vintage Books, 1972.

Krishna, G. *Kundalini.* Berkeley: Shambhala, 1971.

Kübler-Ross, E. "Doctor Says Death is 'Pleasant.'" Article in *The Hartford Courant,* March 30, 1975.

———. Interview in *People,* November 24, 1975.

———. Address at the annual conference of the Association for Transpersonal Psychology. Stanford, California, July 1975.

———. Interview in *Psychology Today.* September 1976.

———. Public lecture. Harvard Divinity School, Cambridge, Mass. December 1, 1977.

———. Interview on the *Tomorrow Show.* February 14, 1978.

Kuhn, T. S. *The Structure of Scientific Revolutions.* Chicago: University of Chicago Press, 1962.

LeShan, L. *The Medium, the Mystic and the Physicist.* New York: Viking, 1974.

Lilly, J. C. *The Center of the Cyclone.* New York: Julian Press, 1972.

Lundahl, C. "The Near-Death Experiences of Mormons." Paper read at the American Psychological Association annual convention. New York, September 1979.

Maslow, A. *Toward a Psychology of Being.* New York: Van Nostrand, 1968.

Masters, R.E.L., and Houston, J. *The Varieties of Psychedelic Experience.* New York: Delta, 1966.

Matson, A. *Afterlife.* New York: Tempo Books, 1976.

McDonagh, J. "Bibliotherapy with Suicidal Patients." Paper read at the American Psychological Association. New York, September 1979.

Miller, N. Personal communication, 1979.

Mind/Brain Bulletin. 14 (1979): 8.

Mitchell, E., ed. *Psychic Exploration.* New York: Putnam's, 1974.

Mitchell, J. "Out-of-the-Body Vision." *Psychic.* April 1973.

Monroe, R. A. *Journeys Out of the Body.* New York: Doubleday, 1971.

Moody, R. A., Jr. *Life After Life.* Atlanta: Mockingbird Books, 1975.

———. *Reflections on Life After Life.* Atlanta: Mockingbird Books, 1977.

———. Personal communication, 1979.

———. "Near-Death Experiences: Some Clinical Considerations." Paper read at the American Psychological Association annual convention. New York, September 1979.

Moors, Russell. Personal communication, 1978.

Moss, T. *The Probability of the Impossible.* Los Angeles: J. P. Tarcher, 1974.

Muldoon, S. *The Case for Astral Projection.* Chicago: Aries Press, 1936.

———, and Carrington, H. *The Projection of the Astral Body.* London: Rider and Co., 1929.

Murphy, G., and Ballou, R. O., eds. *William James on Psychical Research.* New York: Viking, 1969.

Myers, F.W.H. *Human Personality and Its Survival of Bodily Death.* London: Longmans, Green, 1903.

Noyes, R., Jr. "The Experience of Dying." *Psychiatry,* 35 (1972): 174–184.

———, and Kletti, R. "The Experience of Dying From Falls." *Omega,* 3 (1972): 45–52

———. "Depersonalization in the Face of Life-Threatening Danger: A Description." *Psychiatry,* 39 (1976): 19–27.

———. "Depersonalization in the Face of Life-Threatening Danger: An Interpretation." *Omega,* 7 (1976): 103–114.

———. "Panoramic Memory." *Omega, 8* (1977): 181–193.

Osis, K. *Deathbed Observations by Physicians and Nurses.* New York: Parapsychological Foundation, 1961.

———. "Out-of-the-Body Experiences: A Preliminary Survey." Paper presented at the Parapsychology Association annual convention, St. Louis, Mo., August 1978.

———, and Haraldsson, E. *At The Hour of Death.* New York: Avon, 1977.

Peck, R. L. *American Meditation.* Windham Center, Conn.: Personal Development Center, 1976.

Pelletier, K. R. *Toward a Science of Consciousness.* New York: Delta, 1979.

Penfield, W. *The Mystery of the Mind.* Princeton, N.J.: Princeton University Press, 1976.

Pribram, K. H. *Languages of the Brain.* Englewood Cliffs, N.J.: Prentice-Hall, 1971.

———. "Problems Concerning the Structure of Consciousness." In C. G. Globus et al., eds. *Consciousness and the Brain.* New York: Plenum, 1976, pp. 297–313.

———. Address at the American Psychological Association annual convention, New York, September 1978.

———. "What the Fuss is All About." *Re-Vision,* 1 (1978): 3/4, 14–18.
———. "Holographic Memory"; interview in *Psychology Today.* 12 (February 1979): 70–84.
Rawlings, M. *Beyond Death's Door.* Nashville: Thomas Nelson, 1978.
———. Personal communication, 1979.
Re-Vision, 1 (1978): 3/4, entire issue.
Ring, K., and Franklin, S. "Do Suicide Survivors Report Near-Death Experiences?" *Omega,* 12 (1981–1982): 191–208.
Ritchie, G. *Return From Tomorrow.* Waco, Texas: Chosen Books, 1978.
Rosen, D. H. "Suicide Survivors: A Follow-Up Study of Persons Who Survived Jumping from the Golden Gate and San Francisco–Oakland Bay Bridges." *Western Journal of Medicine,* 122 (1975): 289–294.
———. "Suicide Survivors: Psychotherapeutic Implications of Egocide." *Suicide and Life-Threatening Behavior.* 6 (1976): 209–215.
Sabom, M. B. Personal communication, 1979.
———. *Recollections of Death: A Medical Investigation.* New York: Harper & Row, 1981.
———, and Kreutziger, S. A. Personal communication, 1977.
———. "Physicians Evaluate the Near-Death Experience." *Theta,* 6 (1978): 1–6.
Schoonmaker, Fred, "Denver Cardiologist Discloses Findings After 18 Years of Near-Death Research," Article in *Anabiosis,* 1 (July 1979): 1–2.
Smith, H. *Forgotten Truth.* New York: Harper & Row, 1976.
Stevenson, I. "Research into the Evidence of Man's Survival After Death." *Journal of Nervous and Mental Disease,* 165 (1977): 152–170.
Swedenborg, E. *Heaven and Its Wonders and Hell.* New York: Citadel, 1965.
Tart, C. T. "Out-of-the-Body Experiences." In Mitchell, E., ed. *Psychic Exploration.* New York: Putnam's, 1974, pp. 349–373.
Tralins, R. *Buried Alive.* North Miami Beach: Argent Books, 1977.
Turvey, V. *The Beginnings of Seership.* New Hyde Park, N.Y.: University Books, 1969.
Van Dusen, W. *The Natural Depth in Man.* New York: Harper & Row, 1972.
Wheeler, D. *Journey to the Other Side.* New York: Tempo Books, 1976.
Yram [pseud.] *Practical Astral Projection.* London: Rider and Co., 1935.

Index